CONVERTIBLE TOP
Restoration and Installation

Fred Mattson

CarTech®

CarTech®

CarTech®, Inc.
838 Lake Street South
Forest Lake, MN 55025
Phone: 651-277-1200 or 800-551-4754
Fax: 651-277-1203
www.cartechbooks.com

Edit by Wes Eisenschenk
Layout by Connie DeFlorin

ISBN 978-1-61325-446-2
Item No. SA438

Library of Congress Cataloging-in-Publication Data
Names: Mattson, Fred, 1960- author.
Title: Convertible top restoration and installation / Fred Mattson.
Description: Forest Lake, MN : CarTech, Inc., [2019]
Identifiers: LCCN 2018055676 | ISBN 9781613254462
Subjects: LCSH: Automobiles, Convertible–Bodies–Maintenance and repair–Handbooks, manuals, etc. | Automobiles, Convertible–Bodies–Conservation and restoration–Handbooks, manuals, etc. | LCGFT: Handbooks and manuals.
Classification: LCC TL255 .M3195 2019 | DDC 629.2/6–dc23
LC record available at https://lccn.loc.gov/2018055676

Written, edited, and designed in the U.S.A.
Printed in China

10 9 8 7 6 5 4 3 2 1

DISTRIBUTION BY:

Europe
PGUK
63 Hatton Garden
London EC1N 8LE, England
Phone: 020 7061 1980 • Fax: 020 7242 3725
www.pguk.co.uk

Australia
Renniks Publications Ltd.
3/37-39 Green Street
Banksmeadow, NSW 2109, Australia
Phone: 2 9695 7055 • Fax: 2 9695 7355
www.renniks.com

Canada
Login Canada
300 Saulteaux Crescent
Winnipeg, MB, R3J 3T2 Canada
Phone: 800 665 1148 • Fax: 800 665 0103
www.lb.ca

CONTENTS

Acknowledgments

Installing a convertible top is not for the faint of heart. Convertible tops are considered the most difficult installation element of auto upholstery. It is all about getting your head wrapped around what it takes to install a convertible top. When you understand the process involved, installing a convertible top is not as difficult as it may seem . . . or is it?

I want to thank Don, Jeff, Joe, Kimmy, Skip, Rick, Sid, Erika and Vic.

And special acknowledgement to the masters that are no longer here, Ed and my old friend Ron. Their dedication to this industry has made the world better one top at a time.

Preface

Each chapter of this book is written with a specific theme that will guide you through the process of how and why a convertible top functions and is installed. Not all procedures are written for the novice, and it may be best to read a project's entire chapter before actually starting on the project.

Reading the book before beginning will help you gain a general perspective on how to disassemble and install a convertible top. Working on a convertible top is challenging, but it is not as difficult as you might think. If you have some knowledge before starting on a project, it will give you a better result than diving into uncharted waters without being prepared.

Take the time to understand what needs to be done and have all the necessary tools and supplies to accomplish the job. Being prepared will ease the fear of what will come next.

Introduction

There are many components to a convertible top. Each individual part of the frame has a specific job, and when they work together, the convertible top will operate flawlessly. Worn or damaged components will need to be identified and repaired before a new top can be fitted.

Before any work on the convertible top begins, a thorough inspection of the project should be done. This evaluation will help determine what will need to be done to restore the convertible top to peak working condition.

A visual inspection of the convertible top frame and the hydraulic system must be performed to determine any abnormalities or obvious broken or worn components that need to be addressed and restored. Start by looking for any tears in the convertible top fabric. This will indicate a potential underlying problem with the convertible top frame. Also look for bulges or distortions in the shape of the convertible top. This may reveal a bent component in the convertible top frame. A lumpy header bow is a strong indicator that there is corrosion on the header bow that will need to be repaired before the new top can be installed.

It is my recommendation that when the convertible top has obvious damage or it is missing parts, it is best to have another person help guide the top so that it will not cause any additional damage as it is being raised or lowered. Once the top frame has been stabilized, a proper repair can be made to correct the defect in the frame.

After the visual inspection, you should then operate the top and listen to it while it is being raised and lowered. Determine if the convertible top is to be operated manually or it is a power-assisted top.

If the top can be operated, unlatch the top from the windshield and lower it into the well compartment. Listen to the convertible top frame as it is being operated. You will notice that manually operated tops may creak when they are raised and lowered. The creaking from the assist springs expanding or contracting are normal sounds to hear. A power top should make a dull whirring sound.

Sharp scratching or grinding sounds are not normal, and you should slow down and try to locate the cause of the noise. This noise is an indication that there may be a bent or broken component of the top frame. You will need to identify the cause of the noise so that a proper repair can be made.

Look for any shinny spots on the frame where parts may be rubbing. Also look at each pivot point and verify that the rivet or fastener has not failed. Compare the left frame rail to the right and make note of any differences. When the left and right frame rails show no irregularities, work can proceed. If variations are present, then repairs will need to be made to the frame so that it can operate correctly.

EVOLUTION OF THE CONVERTIBLE TOP

Everyone knows that there is nothing more romantic than driving along a country road on a moonlit evening with the top down. What most people don't remember is that the automobile started out as a modified horse carriage. These primitive buggies were commonly referred to as an open car because they had no doors, windows, windshield, or roof.

An open carriage meant that the driver and passengers were directly exposed to the elements. And, because most early roads were unpaved, road dirt, rain, and the often-unpleasant scent of nature would envelop the occupants. By wearing heavy slickers, protective goggles, and gloves, the auto enthusiast could endure this modern convenience of driving.

As the automobile evolved with internal combustion and electric engines, passengers also wanted more creature comforts, such as being shielded from the elements. This soon led to the addition of a glass windscreen and, later, a folding top and side curtains. These crude devices limited the amount of road dirt and rain that fell on the occupants, but there was still a desire for more comfort. That eventually led to the development of the fully enclosed cab.

Early American cars, like this 1906 REO, were not much more than a rolling chassis with little comfort other than the sofa taken from Grandma's parlor. Passengers were exposed to the weather and the open road with very little protection.

Early Top Frames

Before the automobile, horse-drawn buggies and wagons were used to transport people and goods from place to place. Having a top on the vehicle kept the sun and rain off of passengers, and having it fold out of the way when it wasn't needed aided in hauling larger parcels.

Early buggy top frames were very crude but functional. The frames were fashioned by a blacksmith out of smaller pieces of forged iron, and then they were assembled to create the articulating side rails. The *side irons* were connected parallel to each other by wooden bows, usually hand hewn from ash or oak. These wood species made the best choice for top bows due to their tight grain and strength.

Because the bows were made from wood, the attachment of the canvas cover material with tacks was almost

The Ford Model T was introduced in 1908. This popular car offered the driver some shielding from inclement weather with a split windscreen and a folding top, but the Model T still left its passengers exposed due to the lack of side windows.

effortless. All a blacksmith had to do was drive the tack into the wooden bow instead of making attachment holes in a metal frame so that the canvas cover could be tacked on.

Taking a cue from the horse-drawn buggies, the convertible top frames were very similar on early model cars. Steel frame components would soon be mass-produced by stamping the pieces from sheets of metal and then bending and welding them together.

Enclosed Cabs

Between 1910 and the early 1920s, many of the cars produced were being enclosed with fitted doors and windows. This made the riding experience a lot more enjoyable by keeping the road dirt and weather out, but some occupants felt boxed in and eventually became claustrophobic because of the nature of the enclosed cab.

It wasn't long before car owners and passengers wanted the option to open up the car by dropping the top to allow for a more-natural airflow through the car. This option of

a folding top was soon adopted as a standard throughout the automotive world.

Folding Tops

Until the mid-1940s, American convertible top frames were constructed with wooden bows and iron rails with articulating hinge components. The simple frames were covered in canvas to allow the folding of the articulated top without damaging the cover material. These early convertibles were also very drafty and noisy, and because they did not

Fitted doors with side windows met the public's demand for a vehicle with an enclosed cabin but resulted in a car that left the occupants with a feeling of being closed in. Drivers began to look for options that would give them a car that would convert to an open car.

Early convertible top frames used wooden bows to support the roofing fabric. The cross bows also tied the side irons together, keeping them parallel with each other. After World War II, car manufacturers began using stamped steel for top bows.

seal well, they also leaked when it would rain.

As factory tooling improved, better-fitting windows and rubber door seals were added to make the riding experience much more comfortable, but it just wasn't the solution motorists were looking for. It wasn't until after World War II, when an abundance of superior materials became available, that the convertible top took on a better shape. With an ample supply of steel and aluminum, convertible top frames began to function and seal much better. The topping materials used to cover the frame also improved, and additional color choices were available.

Modern Innovations

The ultimate convertible top wouldn't be realized until the mid-1950s, when Ford Motor Company introduced the first fully retractable hard top. Solving the problem of leaking and noise, the rigid top would not only fit better but it was able to disappear completely into the trunk of the car, transforming the sedan into a modern open-concept roadster. This engineering marvel was used by Ford on several models until the mid-1960s.

A new concept in convertible tops was realized in 1971. That year, General Motors came up with a sleek convertible top with an unusual operating system for its full-size car line. The top was referred to as a scissor top, mainly because of the way it would fold into itself.

The scissor top sported a low, swept-back profile with a glass rear curtain. The operating system that was used on these cars was also changed from the standard hydraulic pump and cylinders to a cable-driven system operated by electric motors.

The main reason for this dramatic redesign was to get more seating area in the rear of the car and appeal to the growing family of many car owners. Traditionally, the rear seat was narrower on a convertible to accommodate the convertible top frame and fitment of the hydraulic cylinders that moved the top up and down. Changing to a slimmer and more compactable top frame allowed for the fitment of a full-size rear seat. In 1976, the design was dropped with the last of the tops being used by Cadillac.

Convertible Top Components

There are many elements that make up a convertible top. Each part has an important function, and they all work in unison to keep the weather out as well as allow the top to articulate and stow away.

This complex assembly needs to be properly serviced to keep it in peak operating condition. If any part

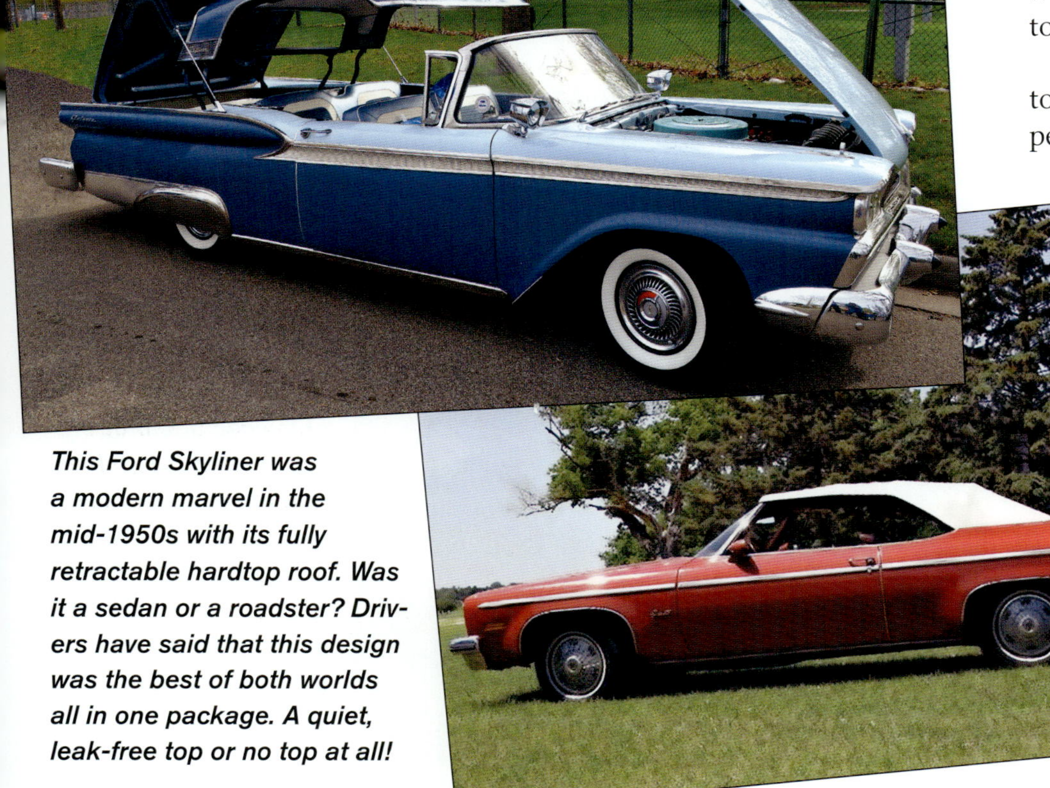

This Ford Skyliner was a modern marvel in the mid-1950s with its fully retractable hardtop roof. Was it a sedan or a roadster? Drivers have said that this design was the best of both worlds all in one package. A quiet, leak-free top or no top at all!

One of the most unique convertible top designs that the General Motors Corporation made was the scissor top. Appearing in 1971 and lasting until 1976, the top design was created to give the car more passenger space by eliminating the traditional hydraulic cylinders that occupied the rear seating area.

---

of the system fails to do its job, it can damage the top. Making repairs on a convertible top can seem overwhelming, but if you understand how each component functions, you will have no trouble putting a top back into perfect working order.

The Frame

A convertible top frame is made up of a complex mix of pieces. Rails, bows, hoses, and fabric are all components that make up the articulating convertible top. These parts all interconnect and serve a specific task. The convertible top frame also defines the shape of the top, giving the car its distinct look and character.

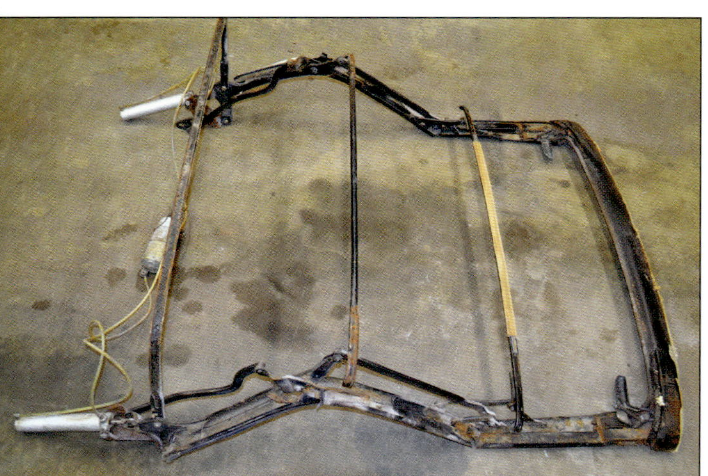

A standard convertible top frame supports the vinyl or canvas topping material and defines the roofline of the car. Each frame is comprised of many simple components that work in unison, allowing the frame to fold and resume its shape without damaging the top material.

Bows

The horizontal pieces that connect to the side rails are called bows. These bows support the bulk of the top material and keep it from falling into the car. Early model convertible top cross bows were typically made of wood. With advancements in modern manufacturing methods, postwar cars had bows made of stamped and formed steel.

The number of cross bows used varied upon the size of the roof and model of the car. Generally, there would be at least two cross bows in addition to the header bow.

Header Bow: One key element of a convertible top frame is the header bow. Header bows have been constructed from wood, steel, aluminum, and even ABS plastic. The header bow is the leading component of the convertible top frame and it serves many functions. Latches mounted on the header bow secure the top frame to the windshield of the car. The convertible top cover material is also fastened to the header bow along with a weather seal that helps keep out the wind and rain.

Cross Bows: Support for the top material comes from the second and third bows. They are usually smaller than the other bows, yet they are equally important parts of the top. The convertible top pads are connected from the header bow and attach to the cross bows, giving the top a smooth outward appearance. They also prevent the top material from wearing out due to rubbing against the bows.

Rear Bow: This is the last horizontal bow on the frame. The top of the rear curtain attaches to the rear bow along with the back ends of the protective top pads. The rear bow also defines the rear roof line and is adorned with a decorative trim that conceals the fasteners across the outside of the top.

To allow for additional passenger room in the cab of the car, the rear bow on a two-piece top frame is also set higher, allowing for the separate rear curtain. This rear bow is designed to support the extra weight of the panel containing the glass or clear vinyl window.

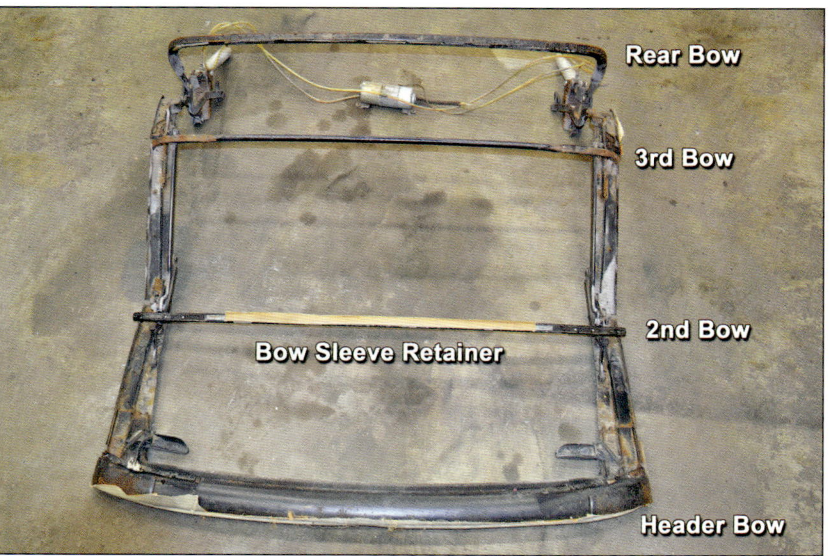

Every convertible top frame has bows that help define the roofline of the car, and they are essential to the support of the convertible topping material and protective pads. While adding to the stability of the entire frame, each bow performs a specific job.

The height of the rear bow is also critical to the function of the folding top. An incorrect height for the rear bow can result in the top not fitting the car properly. It may cause damage to the rear curtain when the top is lowered into the well of the car.

Side Rails

Convertible top side rails are usually comprised of three separate members. Smaller links are attached to the side rails to help them articulate properly. Each side rail runs parallel to the cross bows and forms the outer perimeter of the top frame.

The hydraulic-powered cylinders are attached to the side rails and aid in raising and lowering the top. Also attached to the side rails is the rubber weatherstrip molding. This molding prevents wind and rain from entering the car.

Top Cover

Unlike a sedan or coupe, the convertible has a soft top. A fabric or vinyl covering forms the actual roof over the articulated frame of the passenger car. This material was most likely made by the Haartz Manufacturing Company.

A convertible top cover is specifically tailored to fit the frame of the car so it can fold without tearing. The sewing and seaming process also strengthens the top, allowing it to conform to the shape of the frame.

Two-Piece Top: A standard two-piece top refers to a convertible that has a separate rear curtain. This curtain can have a window made of heavy-gauge clear plastic or a piece of tempered glass. Many of today's

The rear bow is heavier in design so that it can take on the weight of the rear curtain. It also has a wider tack strip embedded to accept multiple rows of staples for the attachment of the top pads, curtain, top material, and wire-on welt.

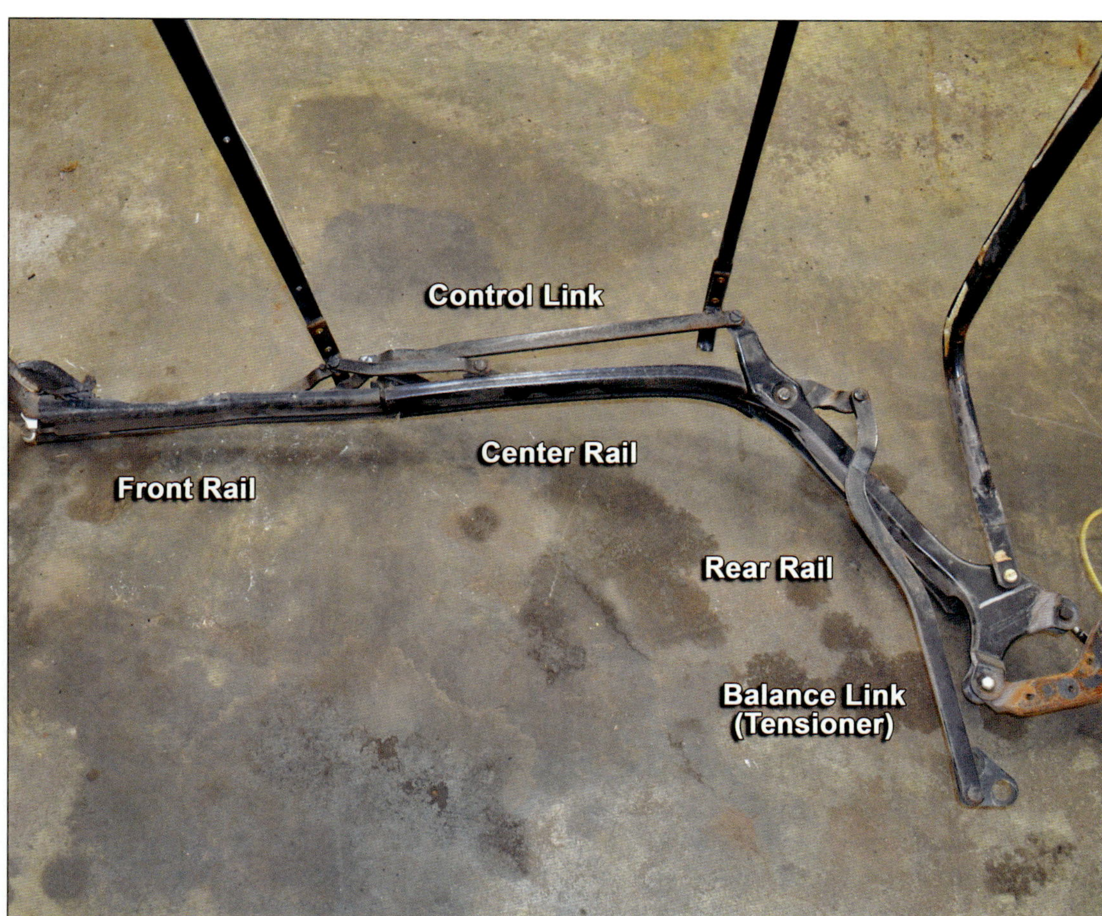

The side rails of the convertible top frame are made up of three main sections. The smaller, flat links help tension the frame and help it return to its correct position when the top is raised and latched. The rubber roof rail seals also attach to the side rails.

This is a premade, ready-to-install convertible top just taken out of the box. The vinyl has box wrinkles and does not look at all appealing. After it is properly installed, the wrinkles will vanish, and it will become the crown jewel of the car.

Most American cars are designed with a two-piece convertible top. The large rear vinyl window of this top is made as a separate component, and it is installed onto the top frame before the outer topping material is applied.

Derived from early European sports cars, this classic Corvette is sporting a one-piece convertible top. The rear window is built into the top and then fitted as a single unit to the top frame. This style of top works well on smaller two-seater cars.

late-model cars are fit with a curtain that is made of glass, and it may also have an electric heating element feature built into them to keep the window defrosted. This allows the car to be driven all year with clear visibility.

Almost all American-made cars were created with a two-piece top. These tops are much easier to fit than a one-piece top and are more cost effective to service if the rear window becomes damaged.

One-Piece Top: A convertible top that has the rear curtain integrated into the top is called a one-piece top. This style of top originated from European sports cars. The one-piece top is generally smaller in size due in part because they are usually found on a two-seater car.

The one-piece top is almost always manually operated because of the limited space that is available in the car. There is just not enough room for the components of a hydraulic system.

Curtains

Windows on a convertible are called curtains and are most commonly found in the rear panel of the convertible top. The term *curtain* actually evolved from the use of a roll-up window covering or curtain that was used to cover the rear and side windows in the car. The curtain was used to shade the occupants of the vehicle, and it also provided some privacy for those who wanted to park and get to know each other better.

The window in the top curtain can vary and change in size and shape with different top styles. The earliest cars had a fixed or folding top with a smaller framed glass window set into two pieces of matching top fabric. This curtain style was referred to as a double-blind curtain. The window frame and size were subject to the owner's personal choice.

In the rear of this Pierce-Arrow is an actual curtain that is rolled up over the beveled-glass window. It was used to block sunlight and create privacy for the occupants of the car. Details like this are no longer used in modern cars.

In addition to a fitted top being added to an open car, side curtains were added to help divert wind and rain from passengers in the car. Side curtains would often roll down from the side rail and fasten to the body of the car. Removable side curtains had an internal wire frame that mounted to the door and could be stored away when they were not in use.

Pads

One of the most overlooked parts to be replaced on a convertible are the pads. Most people do not know what they are or what purpose they serve. This could be why they are not replaced with the new top material. Do not overlook the importance of the pads.

The main function of a convertible top pad is to protect the convertible top material from being damaged by the articulating frame. The pad also helps smooth the appearance of the convertible top along the top of the bows. The convertible top pads are held in place on the top frame with staples and screws.

Top pads help support the top material and keep it from falling into the car. Wide straps were used on buggies and evolved into the soft, wide pads we use today. A convertible top pad is a soft material sandwiched between the convertible top frame and the outer convertible top fabric. The construction of a convertible top pad varies by manufacturer.

Most original top pads were made up of a layer of cotton batting laid over jute webbing and then covered by a color-matched bow drill fabric. The exception is Ford, which used a heavy woven fabric on many of its convertible models. The pad still protected the top from wearing against the frame.

Modern convertible top pads are made from the same material as the top. The fabric is an exact match, making them appear invisible from inside the car. The padding material supplied with a

The convertible top pad is the unsung hero of the convertible top. This simple component separates the top material from the underlying metal frame. It allows the top material to move and flow without being damaged when the top is folded.

An original convertible top pad was constructed of bow drill cloth with a base layer of jute webbing material. The inner padding was made of cotton batting. Modern pads are made from convertible top material with a foam inner liner.

modern pad is made of medium-density foam. The foam compresses just enough to create a smooth appearance and yet allow the correct amount of protection needed for the outer top.

Top pads vary in shape, width, and length, depending on the frame and model of car that is being worked on. Pads are simple to make, or they can be ordered with the top for your car.

Rear Pads

Some car models require an additional set of pads in the rear-quarter section to help give the top a nicer shape. Without the additional pad, the top would develop a gaunt or starved look with the rear-quarter section of the top curving inward. These pads are constructed the same way as the main top pad, and they are attached to the rear tack rail, extending upward, and are secured to the rear bow.

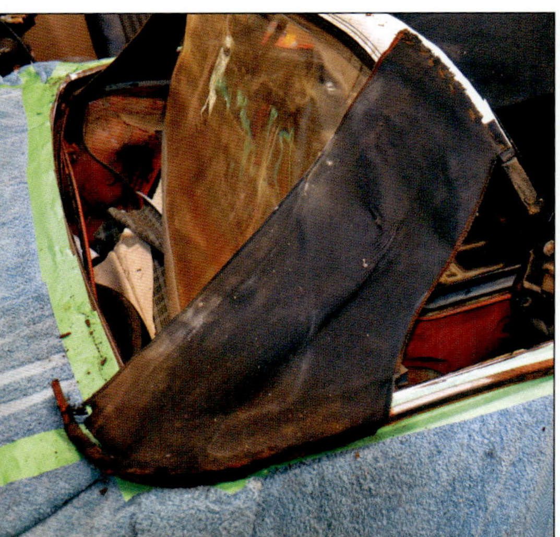

Some car models are equipped with rear pads. These special components help round out the rear sail area of the convertible top to give it a full and rounder appearance. They stretch from the rear bow down to the rear tack rail.

Hydraulic System

Not all convertibles have a hydraulic system. Early convertible top frames were manually raised and lowered. These tops were best operated with two people until the addition of heavy-duty assist springs, which made the task of raising and lowering the top much easier.

As cars evolved and luxury became an important part of the driving experience, power windows, power seats, and power tops were much more desirable and became a necessary option. A typical power system consisted of a motorized pump, high-pressure hoses, and hydraulically driven cylinders to make interior parts move with the touch of a switch. The power top made it possible for just one person to raise and lower the top and never leave the front seat of the car.

Well Liner

The area located behind the rear seat of the car is referred to as the well. When the convertible top is lowered and folds into the down position, it is stowed in the well. The well liner is actually the material that protects the top from the hard surrounding surfaces of the well area.

After World War II, when car bodies and the convertible top styles changed, the convertible top began to lower into a space behind the rear seat. This area was also open

This is a typical hydraulic pump found behind the rear seat of a convertible. The simple components that make the top go up and down on a modern convertible include a hydro-electric pump, high-pressure lines, and lift cylinders.

When the convertible top is lowered, it is stowed behind the rear seat in the well area of the car. The durable cloth material of the modern well liner separates the space between the cab of the car and the trunk.

to the trunk area of the car. The modern-style well liner now refers to the sewn material that separates the trunk from the cab area.

Rain Gutter

A vital component to the preservation of the body on a convertible car is the rain gutter. The convertible top is designed to be water resistant, and since rain is a part of the driving experience, watershed and seepage is inevitable.

In an attempt to prevent the inner structure of the car from rusting, channels or *gutters* were added into the beltline well area of the convertible. They help redirect any water that is not shed by the convertible top to an opening in front of the rear wheel well. It then exits the body through a weep hole underneath the car.

The gutter system can consist of a metal or a plastic channel that is welded or screwed to the upper inside of the well area. The gutter should be checked periodically for debris and cracks. Any problems found should be repaired as necessary so that the system will continue to perform as it was designed.

Weatherstrip

To keep the wind and weather out of the car, rubber seals are attached to the side rails of the frame. These rubber seals make contact with the glass to help keep the cabin of the car weathertight. The problem with all convertible tops is that the frames are hinged, and they will leak air and water at any connecting joint. It is because the top is not rigid that the best weather seal that you can hope for will be about 85 to 90 percent.

Not all rubber weatherstrip roof rail sets are good. Some fit better than others, and the quality of the rubber varies greatly among manufacturers. The better-quality weatherstrip that you can buy is soft and pliable. The rubber will compress and allow the frame to latch without difficulty and yet be rigid enough to hold its shape and spring back to seal against the side glass. As the rubber ages, it will begin to get harder and develop cracks. This condition will also cause leaks and make the top more difficult to latch.

Some of the higher-end classic cars have weather seals that are covered in a matching bow drill cloth. Even though they worked the same as the plain rubber weather seals, the bow drill cloth did not have a function other than to give the car a finished and tailored look of luxury along the length of the outer frame rail.

Keeping the car dry on the inside is accomplished with high-quality rubber weatherstripping. This is a basic roof rail weatherstrip kit. It contains the side rail pieces along with a form-fit header seal. It is always wise to install a new roof rail set with your new top.

The rain gutter is found inside the well area of your car. Its main purpose is to divert water out of the car and prevent the cab from flooding during a rainstorm. Rain gutters can vary in design and material, but they are all designed to do the same job.

Sometimes the rubber weather seal is covered in a fabric that matches the interior lining of the convertible top. This treatment of wrapping the rubber in bowdrill cloth is strictly a cosmetic detail used on higher-end cars.

Tools

I have good news for those who want to learn how to install a convertible top. You do not need any special tools to get professional results while working on your convertible top and frame. However, it may be helpful to know that there are several specialty tools available to make the task of replacing a convertible top much easier.

It only takes a moment to cause serious damage to your car or yourself if a tool is improperly used. This is why I strongly recommend that you observe all safety practices when using any tool while restoring your project.

Specialty Tools

Some specialty tools make the installation and servicing of a convertible top go much smoother. These tools can be obtained from most online suppliers, or you can get them at a professional upholstery supply house.

Staple Puller

The tool you will be using most is a tack or staple puller. Staple removers are available in many different styles. The most efficient staple-removal

Basic tools from a well-equipped toolbox are all you need to replace a convertible top. You will need a standard socket set, ratchet, and assorted screwdrivers, along with a few simple upholstery tools (a pair of scissors, tack hammer, and a tape measure) can get the job done.

Removing the old top material and pads from the frame can be a challenge. One of the best upholstery tools that I have ever used is the Berry's Staple Remover. The unique shape of the tool fits comfortably in the hand and allows you to lift the most difficult of staples with ease.

tool that I have found is the Berry's Staple Remover. The Berry's is made in Lubbock, Texas, and it is a workhorse. The simple design is comfortable to use for extended periods of time and it works great at lifting the most stubborn tacks and staples. It costs less than $20, and it is well worth the investment.

Other tack and staple lifters are also available and do a fine job. All of these tools are sharp and can hurt you if you slip, so always use caution, pay attention, and wear safety glasses when working with staple removers.

Stapler

Every well-equipped shop should have at least one staple gun. I have several and they all are different. The reason is that each can be task specific, and yet they can be used for general assembly as well. Staplers can use a variety of staple sizes, and staple widths will vary depending on the manufacturer and model.

Manual or spring-loaded staplers are great if you do not have a power source, such as electricity or air (pneumatic). Manual staplers can be a lifesaver if you are in the field or your power stapler goes down. They will allow you to get the job done, but with a lot more effort. The cost of a manual stapler can range from $12 to $45 based on features.

Electric staplers are always useful. The biggest drawback is the physical size of the tool itself. They can be heavy and awkward at times, limiting access to staple placement. Both mechanical and electric staplers can also be limited on the amount of driving force a staple needs to penetrate the substrate to achieve a good bond. Commercial-grade electric staplers can run up to $240. Household versions are not recommended because of their light-duty cycle and will most likely fail and burn out due to the amount of use put on them.

Ultimately the stapler of choice for a trim shop would be a pneumatic or air stapler. These devices can drive a staple into just about anything by adjusting the amount of air pressure behind them. The one drawback to the pneumatic stapler is that it will require a source of air pressure. Some shops—believe it or not—do not have an air compressor, and that is just one tool that I could not live without. Air staplers are very affordable and can be purchased from $50 to $140. The big cost is in an air compressor that has enough power to make the tool work.

Steamer

Another tool that is of great use is a steamer. The steamer is used to help with shaping and relieving small wrinkles in the convertible top material. A steamer will not work miracles, but when used correctly, small imperfections can be removed without hurting the top material. I use a Jiffy Steamer model J-4000 professional steamer.

This steamer can be ordered with the interchangeable-head feature. The upgraded unit allows the user to change from a flat iron to a pipe wand in seconds. This makes the

A heavy-duty mechanical staple gun is needed to attach convertible top material to the frame. Electric staple guns make the task less laborious, and those who can afford an air compressor may choose to use a pneumatic stapler. Any of the three options are suitable for service.

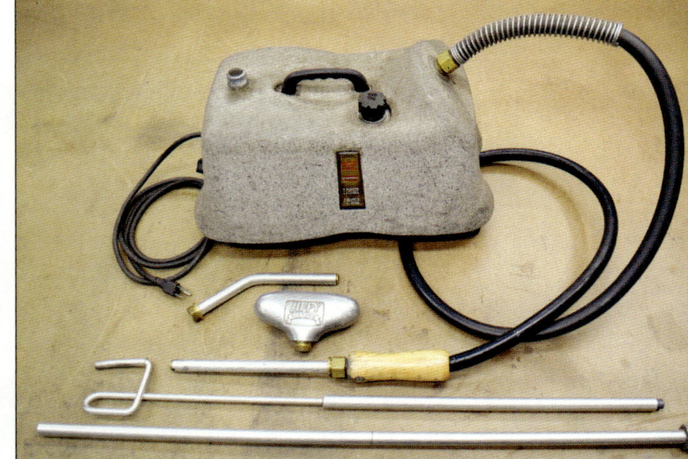

Without a doubt, a steamer is a nice tool to have when finishing a convertible top installation. This model, J-4000 from Jiffy Steamer, has interchangeable hose ends that are more than capable of getting into those tight places to relax away small imperfections in the top fabric.

tool more useful, and the versatility of replacing the steamer head allows me to work faster and efficiently. A professional-model steamer will cost about $350, depending on the model and accessories you order.

Heat Gun

One very powerful tool to have is a heat gun. This tool allows you to soften materials so they will assume the shape you want them to. They are most useful when working on heavy vinyl rear curtains and for setting rubber tack strips into channels. Extreme care must be taken when using a heat gun. Always remember to keep the heat gun in motion so that you do not scorch, melt, or burn your project when you are working on it.

There are some things to consider when choosing a heat gun. The first is heat settings. You need to know how hot the temperature will be at the nozzle end of the tool, and if the heat gun has a replaceable element. Another thing to look for is a cool-down or fan-only feature. This will help extend the life of the heat-

ing element. You also want a heat gun with a built-in tool rest that will allow you to set the tool down without it harming the surface you are setting it on.

Not all heat guns are equal in performance, and you should not make your decision on cost alone. Prices of heat guns range from $15 to more than $250, depending on the features of the tool.

Master Appliance: I have used a Master Appliance Model HG-501A for many years. The interchangeable heating element of this model has a temperature range from 500 to 750°F. This temperature range works great for all my interior projects. I also like the tool rest on this model because it is large enough to prevent the tool from tipping over and it is adjustable, allowing for the discharge to be positioned for static applications.

Milwaukee Tool: This type of heat gun is great for heat shrinking and other smaller projects. The Milwaukee Model 1220 is a two-speed heat gun with two preset temperature settings of 750 and 1,000°F. This type of

heat gun does not have a cool-down feature to prolong the life of the non-replaceable heating element. During use, the tool can be set on its end to keep the hot discharge from causing unwanted damage.

Fluid-Matic

If you do a lot of convertible top work, the tool to have is the Fluid-Matic. This tool will allow you to service a hydraulic system with little effort. The best part about using a Fluid-Matic is there is very little hydraulic oil spillage while performing a system service. This gallon jug and pump have a unique hose setup that will allow you to fill and bleed a

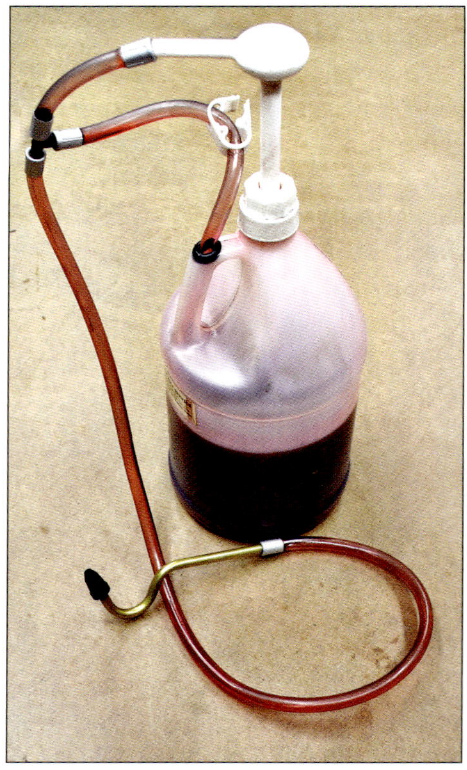

Convertible Service makes the Fluid-Matic pump, which allows you to service the hydraulic system with almost no effort. This simple device can save you time by filling the pump reservoir to the correct level without spilling fluid while it bleeds the system for perfect operation.

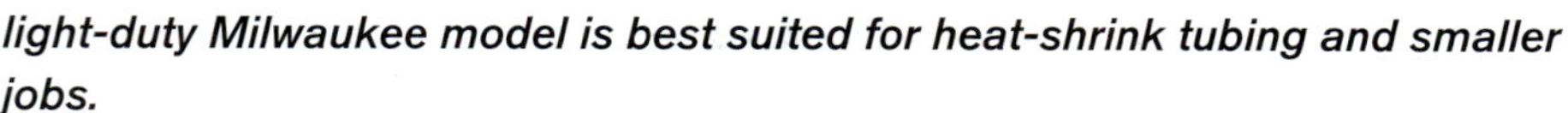

Removing wrinkles from heavy, clear vinyl curtains is best done with a high-output heat gun, such as this model from the Master Appliance Corporation. It has all the features needed to service your projects. The light-duty Milwaukee model is best suited for heat-shrink tubing and smaller jobs.

convertible's hydraulic system without the mess of trying to fill and bleed a pump from a quart bottle of oil. The Fluid-Matic was developed by Paul Terry, and it is available from Convertible Service in California for less than $45.

1/4-inch Drive Ratchet

A big problem with convertible top replacement is the repeated removal and tightening of the rear tack rail body bolts. Often, you will find that the bolts have been over-torqued, and the holes in the body have become too large, resulting in the bolt no longer being able to hold the tack rail tight to the car.

To prevent this, I recommend the use of a fine-tooth 1/4-inch drive ratchet. The fine-tooth ratchet (84 teeth) allows you to advance the body bolt without the usual backlash of a standard (75-tooth) ratchet handle. The smaller size of the ratchet also helps prevent over-torquing merely because of the physical size of the tool.

To prevent busting your knuckles when using the smaller ratchet, I also recommend adding a 14-inch extension to the ratchet handle. You will be able to work inside the car, which makes it less strenuous on your arms than reaching and working deep inside the well area.

Protecting the finish while you replace the top requires draping the car. Various materials can be used as a protective drape. A soft terry cloth bath towel, a flannel sleeping bag, or a quilted moving blanket can all be used as a drape to protect the car's finish while working on the top.

Car Drape

Before work begins on the car, a drape should cover the trunk and rear fenders to prevent any accidental scratches or damage to the car's finish. I purchased some heavy bath towels and sewed two together to make the drapes for my business.

Bath towels are relatively inexpensive and yet they provide a soft barrier to work on. Other materials that are commonly used for a drape are moving blankets, old sleeping bags, and painters' drop cloths. If you use an old sleeping bag, remove the zipper before you lay it over the car to prevent harming the paint.

Snap Setter

One of the best tools that I have ever invested in is the HooVer Products Pres-N-Snap setter. This tool has interchangeable dies used to install snap fasteners and grommets in materials. Most hand appliances will crush or dent the cap of a snap when it is installed, but this tool works perfectly every time without causing damage to the snap or the material.

It only takes a few seconds to load a fastener into the snap tool, and then a quick squeeze secures the fastener into the material where you want it. If you are making a convertible top boot cover for your car or a tonneau cover for your truck, you will like using this tool.

Use a smaller ratchet to tighten and remove the tack rail bolts to help prevent over-torquing and stripping out the sheet metal in the body of the car. Adding an extension between the socket and ratchet allows easier access to the tack rail bolts, preventing fatigue during the installation of a new top.

This is a must-have tool for achieving professional results when setting snaps in a convertible top or boot cover. The precision of this tool has saved me a lot of time and effort by getting the job done quickly without damaging the fasteners during installation.

Rivet Tools

There are many different brands and styles of rivet tools, and you may already own one. A simple pop-rivet tool is very handy to have. Most have interchangeable tips to work with different sizes of rivets. These small features allow you to use the tool on multiple projects without buying more tools.

Manual Rivet Tool

I like the swivel-head feature of the Stanley Professional model. By rotating the head of the tool, you can access areas that may not be reachable with a rigid rivet tool.

Hydraulic Rivet Tool

The Huck HK-150A is one little powerhouse of a tool. Not only will this hand-operated rivet tool install all sizes of rivets, it will also install threaded rivnuts into sheet metal with little to no effort. It comes in quite handy when repairing a stripped-out tack rail retainer hole in the body of a car. The straightforward design allows you to get the fastener in place without pinching

Having a standard rivet tool is always a good bet when you're starting out and need to get a job done quickly. The advanced features included with this hydraulic tool give you more power and options when you need to get into the tough places on a project.

your knuckles on the inner beltline of the car body. The ease of setting a heavy-steel 1/4-20 rivnut is made possible by the hydraulic action produced just by squeezing the handles on the tool.

Although the tool is a little bit on the expensive side, it greatly reduces the amount of effort needed to set a fastener, allowing you to continue working without straining your hands.

SUPPLIERS OF CONVERTIBLE TOP PARTS

There are many places that sell replacement parts for your convertible, and obtaining the correct parts for your project is not easy. What you need to know is where to get the parts and what to ask for. Having a reliable resource for parts and knowledgeable help is vital to completing a project.

I spent many years working with some of these vendors and have come to trust that their goods and services are the best of the best. These suppliers and manufacturers are more than helpful when it comes to getting what you need for your convertible top project. They all are reputable dealers and are very good at what they do. Please take the time to do the research on your project by at least knowing the make, model, and year of what you are working on.

The Haartz Corporation

Where would the convertible top industry be without the Haartz Corporation? They are the innovators of coated fabrics for automotive and non-automotive markets. Its main headquarters is located in Acton, Massachusetts, and the company has offices and facilities in several countries.

Haartz has been making convertible top material for more than a century. Most people are familiar with its Pinpoint vinyl and Stayfast cloth-topping materials, but it also makes all the other designer weaves that adorn Audi, Jaguar, Porsche, Rolls-Royce, and others. When it comes time to purchase a new top for your convertible, insist that it

Every project needs parts. Where you get the parts makes all the difference in the final result of your project. There are many vendors to work with, and developing relationships with them will ensure great results.

This convertible top material was made by the Haartz Cor-poration. The black and white Pinpoint vinyl topping are standard colors found on many cars. The more-luxurious Stayfast tan and black topping material give a car the look and feel of distinction. Haartz has many additional colors and patterns available.

Inside the office and warehouse space of Hydro-E-Lectric are all the parts necessary to repair your convertible top. In addition to the parts, it also offers complete convertible top installation and hydraulic pump rebuilding service for your convertible.

is made of genuine Haartz topping material.

Hydro-E-Lectric

If your project car is in need of new hydraulic cylinders, Hydro-E-Lectric is the source for all the parts you may need. The company began due to a failed window cylinder on Paul Wies-man's 1953 Oldsmobile Holiday. As the story was told, Paul noticed that the rear window of his prized 1953 Oldsmobile Holiday was down and there was a puddle of fluid under the car. Paul went looking for some assis-tance from his neighbor, a mechanic. He was told that the cylinder was a sealed unit that could not be repaired by the neighbor, but a machinist friend may be able to help.

Impressed by the process and complexity of the repair, Paul realized that there was a need for this type of service, and in 1976, he started a brand-new business. Shortly, Paul expanded his product line to include replacement hydraulic cylinders for convertible tops as well as window cylinders.

The business kept growing and continued to expand with other much-needed and requested resto-ration supplies. Hydro-E-Lectric is now known as *America's Convertible Headquarters* and is operating in Punta Gorda, Florida, as a third-generation business under the care of Paul's daughter Erika and her son.

As with any business, innovation and service is the only way to main-tain a standing in the restoration community. With some parts becom-ing harder to find, Hydro-E-Lectric offers restoration and repairs of your original hydraulic pumps as well as convertible top and interior restorations.

Electron Top

Fred Strauss Jr. was a great auto trimmer, and he handcrafted some of the finest convertible tops for his cus-

The finest-made con-vertible tops come from Electron Top in Richmond Hill, New York. The pride and craftsmanship that goes into making an Electron Top is second to none for this family-owned-and-operated busi-ness that has served the convertible top industry since 1960.

tomers. After purchasing heat-sealing equipment to make his convertible tops, other vendors in the industry requested that Electron Top start to distribute the tops for sale. Fred realized that there was a need for a high-quality top, and after years of dedication to the trade and giving the customer a great product at a fair price, he had made Electron Top the leader in the industry. Automation and precision craftsmanship helped make it the company it is today.

Now, Electron Top is a third-generation manufacturer of some of the finest convertible tops ever made. The people at Electron Top are friendly, knowledgeable, and most helpful if you run into problems or have an issue with installation.

I have been purchasing my tops from Electron Top through my local distributor, Pyramid Trim Products, in Saint Paul, Minnesota. One service that I am most grateful for is that I am able to get a ready-made top with custom features. I request to have cable sleeves put into all of my tops and, of course, my signature lower valance on the vinyl curtains. Thank you, Electron Top, for making my work stand out and look great!

Metro Moulded Parts

It is often difficult to find rubber roof rail sets that are pliable enough to actually allow the top to latch without difficulty. Metro Moulded Parts Inc. has always had the highest-quality rubber parts for my customers. The consistency of the rubber and accuracy of the molding assures a good fit and long wear.

Metro Moulded Parts is located in Minneapolis, Minnesota, and has a wide dealer base throughout the country. This family-owned

The highest-quality rubber roof rail sets, along with so many other hard-to-find seals and parts, can be acquired at Metro Moulded. If you also need door, trunk, and other rubber seals to restore a complete car, you can save more money when you buy a Master Kit.

company started business as car enthusiasts, and the tradition continues with the best reproduction rubber classic car parts available anywhere.

Al Knoch Interiors

When it comes to Corvette tops and interior components, there is no questioning that Al Knoch has

Hands down the best Corvette reproduction tops available are produced by Al Knoch Interiors of Canutillo, Texas. All Al Knoch top kits come complete with the top, pads, and everything else that is needed for the installation of your new top.

the most authentic and best-fitting pieces that you can get. Everything that it produces is made in America and built to the highest standards to meet the needs of restorers everywhere.

Because the fitment and installation of Corvette soft goods requires a little extra effort and knowledge, it is good to know that there is a company that specializes in this one area. Al Knoch does not sell shirts and hats and is not distracted by trying to sell you everything else for your car. Al Knoch concentrates on making the best Corvette reproduction seat covers and convertible tops than can be obtained.

The best part of working with Al Knoch Interiors is that if you ever have a problem with any of the company's fine products, you can call and customer service will work with you to resolve any issue. The company stands behind the products that it makes.

Kee Auto Top

From its headquarters in North Carolina, Kee Auto Top has been producing vinyl tops and convertible tops and providing support since 1964. This is not just another family-owned business; it cares about the products that it produces.

Kee Auto Top products fit well and are made from high-quality materials. Many models are available for foreign and American convertibles. If you need a vinyl top for your car, Kee can help with that too. The company has a large selection of colors and patterns that will match your original top.

Kee is a retail source that you should also consider because its employees are easy to work with. They want to help you to get the products you need for your project.

TopsOnline.com

If you need a full-service auto trim supply company then look to TopsOnline.com for everything a trimmer can ask for. The company is based in Southern California and has

More than 30 years in industry sales and service is what makes TopsOnline.com and Vic's Upholstery Supply the one-stop store for all of your convertible top and auto upholstery needs.

Kee Auto Top offers a large selection of colors and patterns for foreign and American autos from 1940 to current models. It is a good source for convertible and vinyl tops that are made at the family-owned factory in Charlotte, North Carolina.

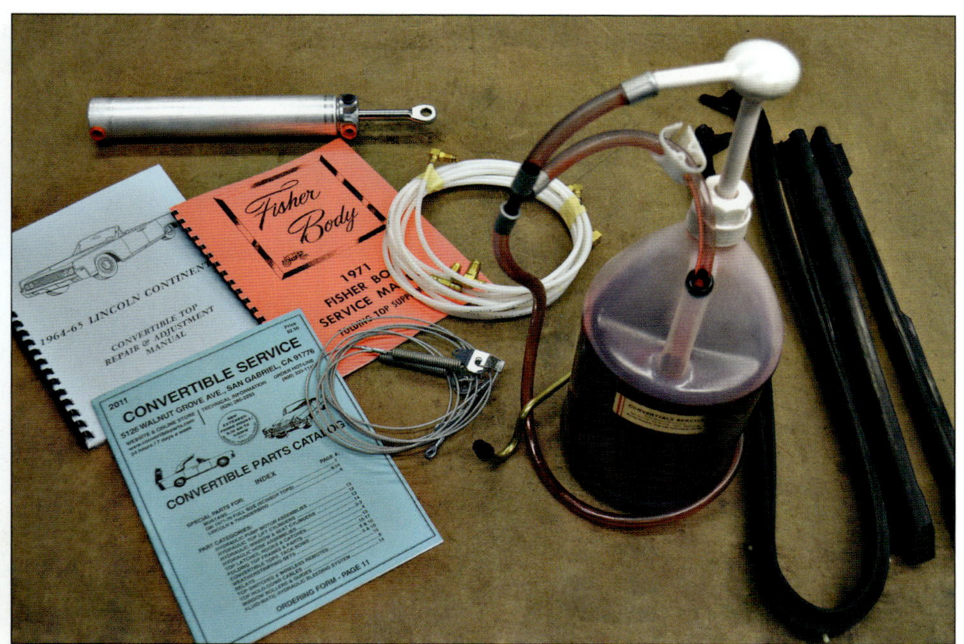

Not just convertible top parts, but the right convertible top parts and absolutely the best troubleshooting and diagnostic advice in the convertible top industry is from Convertible Service. Years of hands-on technical service has given Paul and his team at Convertible Service the knowledge to help you resolve your top problems.

been in the auto trim business since 1987. TopsOnline.com is a distributor for Robbins Auto Top and EZ ON Auto Tops products, but it also sells interior kits and carpet sets as well as auto trim supplies and upholstery tools. Vic and his staff can answer your questions, and they are ready and willing to help get you the correct parts that you need for your project.

Convertible Service

Repairing a damaged convertible top frame is difficult, but when you have a resource like this, you can't go wrong. For more than 35 years, Convertible Service has been repairing and providing replacement parts for convertible tops.

Convertible Service has a repair and manufacturing facility that is located in San Gabriel, California, and it is open to help get your convertible back into working order. All the parts that it carries are correct for the car you are working on, and its employees know how to install them too.

In addition to the great service and help that you will get from Jan, Ron, and Glen, there is an additional benefit of many years of hands-on repair experience from master tech Paul Terry. In my opinion, the best product Convertible Service sells is the Fluid-Matic Convertible System Filling & Bleeding Tool. This device has saved me countless hours and many messes. This is the one convertible top tool that makes my job a whole lot easier.

Online Searches

I have spent a lifetime working on these cars and have compiled many books, catalogs, and service manuals to help me understand and properly repair these classic cars to their original glory. With the ever-changing information available on the internet, there is always a good chance you will be able to find what you are looking for.

However, let me caution you about buying from unknown parts sources: eBay is NOT a store; it is an online auction website. The products you find on eBay may be what you want, but you better make sure they are the correct parts for your project. Most of the time, the parts you see for sale end up there because someone bought them and they were wrong, and when you buy them they are still wrong.

Don't waste your money. Call and talk to the seller, vendor, or owner of the part. Get all of the information that you can before giving them your hard-earned cash. Find out if the part has a warranty and if it can be returned if it turns out to be an incorrect or defective part.

OPEN CARS

Nothing screams *hot rod* more than the open roadster. The most-recognized open car ever produced was the Ford Model T. This car changed the way Americans traveled and felt about the automobile. The Model T took on many forms during its long production run. The most notable was the bucket-style body with a folding top. But in the blink of an eye, the 1930s roadsters stole the hearts of veterans returning home from war and turned these everyday cars into the hot rods we love today.

Modifying a car to suit the personality of the driver was limitless. High-performance engines, elaborate paint, and big tires would transform the basic car into a street rod that would turn heads and set track records all across America. One big drawback to the open design of the Duce was the top—or lack thereof. Some drivers were content to drive without a top, and many others wanted a top that was less bulky and easier to operate.

Bolt-On Accessories

Because of the popularity of the bucket design, the original steel bodies were getting harder to acquire,

Imagine yourself behind the wheel of this all-American hot rod with dual carburetors on top of a flathead V-8 with open headers, ready to make the wide whitewall tires smoke as it tears down the open road. Hang on tight; this is going to be one exciting ride!

The plain fiberglass body of this roadster allows almost any accessory to be added, giving it the unique look and features that are desired. Imagination is the key element used to design and build a machine that meets the personal needs of the owner.

Many hours of customization go into the building of such an iconic car. This dream has it all: a big V-8 engine, soft top, super-wide racing tires, and a custom flame paint job. This T-bucket is the ultimate example of the American roadster.

and alternative materials (such as aluminum and fiberglass) were now being produced to keep up with the demand from car enthusiasts. These aftermarket bodies were offered without any of the factory mounting hardware for fenders, tops, and windshields, making them the perfect blank canvas to be accessorized to the owner's specifications.

Just the thought of drilling into the new fiberglass body to attach the acquired parts presented other challenges for the car owner. Fenders and running boards were not always desired, but having a windshield and a folding top appealed to many enthusiasts. Choosing the right combination for one's prized ride was not always easy to do.

The Windshield

Commonplace to most of the bucket roadsters was the standard frame windscreen. This simple design was made up of a metal frame and a single piece of glass. A similar version of this windshield also featured a tilting frame for the glass.

One of the sexiest windshields ever produced for the Deuce was the DuVall windshield frame. The raked-back glass and swooping base anchors made this a real eye catcher, and you either loved the design or hated it. It is my personal favorite.

The BopTop

If you had access to original hardware, you could buy a premade top or have one custom tailored to fit your car. Many top frames were either neglected and fell into severe disrepair, or they were removed and discarded by a previous owner who saw no value in having a top.

As the 1932 roadster grew in popularity by hot rod owners, the desire to put the top up became an accessory that many felt was a useful option for the unexpected rainfall or just to get the blazing sun off the back of one's neck.

Drilling into a fiberglass body could mean chipped paint or a cracked gel coat. And neither was a desired option for someone who loved to show off his or her car. To avoid drilling into the body, an alternative was needed.

In 2000, a new concept soft-top design was created by Sid Chavers. He understood that the practical side of owning a roadster was to have the option for a top. His revolutionary design did not require any additional holes or hardware to be added to the body of the car, and this eliminated the risk of damaging a flawless paint job.

The unique top design was called the BopTop. It was a fully collapsible

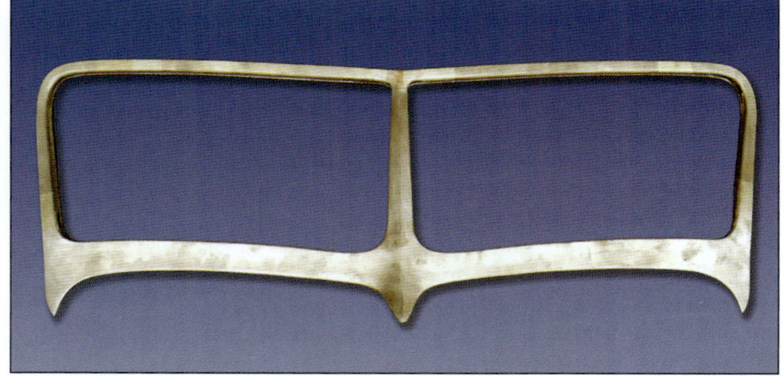

Probably one of the most ornate windshields ever developed for the 1932 roadster was this swept-back design created by George DuVall Jr. In the early days of customization, creative minds would combine ideas from many sources to develop classic designs.

This roadster has been fitted with the classic BopTop developed by Sid Chavers. Adding the classic look of the roadster soft top to a modern hot rod without modifying the body or disturbing the paint has always been a challenge, and this removable top is the solution.

Begin installation of the BopTop with the fitting of the wood header bow. Each bow is custom crafted from seven layers of oak and then contoured to fit the windshield of the car. Standard mounting hardware holds the header bow securely to the windshield.

Sid Chavers works on the fit of a BopTop frame. The body of the car has been covered to protect the painted surface while the new top is being worked on. Getting the top frame to fit perfectly is simple, and it can be done with basic tools.

When the BopTop is not in use, it can be disassembled and stored in the trunk of the car. Each BopTop comes with its own storage bag to protect the top and keep it safe when it is not on the car. The BopTop is easy to put

together and it can be reassembled in just a few minutes.

frame design that could be stored in the trunk of the car when not in use and installed within minutes if you needed protection from the weather. Anchoring the top frame required the standard anchors that were already on the car. Sid also created special B-pillar anchors that can also be added to a car that does not have

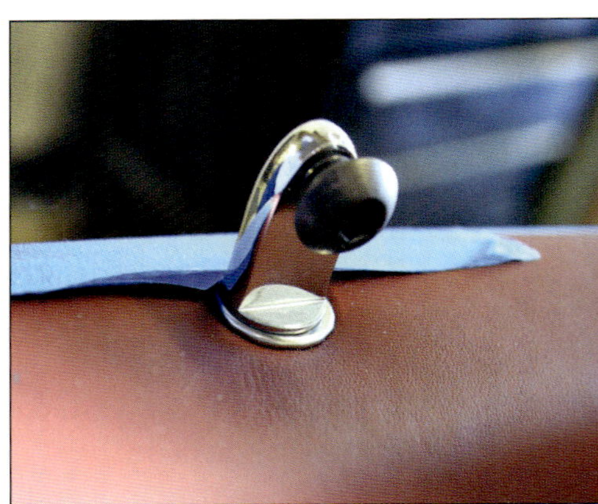

Standard brackets are used to mount the BopTop to the car. Sid Chavers Company offers these custom mounting brackets that can be removed when the top is not in use to leave a flush and smooth appearance to the roadster.

Sid Chavers Company offers these custom-made mounting brackets. Many times, the aftermarket bodies do not include this necessary hardware. Sid gives you a choice of the standard mount or a custom mount that can be disassembled into a flush mount.

Most rear-curtain, mail-slot windows have a fixed piece of glass inside of a metal frame. The frame is then set into the double-blind curtain of a convertible top. This unique Cool Slot™ design by Sid Chavers allows the window to be opened for addition airflow through the car without dropping the curtain.

them. The BopTop frame is designed so that it does not touch the painted body of the car and does not require any additional snaps or fasteners to secure the top to the car.

Sid also offers many options to customize the BopTop. He designed the HotSlot™ rear window that actually can be installed in the rear curtain without causing the top material to pucker once it has been assembled and installed. Sid later created the Cool Slot™ rear window that opens to allow air to flow through the car.

There is a removable rear curtain option for the BopTop as well. This design appeals to old-school enthusiasts who like the traditional two-piece top design.

Carson Tops

What a beautiful 1937 Ford sporting an extremely fine example of the Carson top. The custom top has all the vintage details you would expect to find on a classic like this, plus the contrasting tan color of the Haartz Stayfast canvas complements the superb paint on the body.

Another style of top that was popular in the late 1930s through the mid-1960s was the Carson top. These were custom-built tops that could either be removed or permanently built on the car. The sleek and smooth design originated in California by Glen Houser in 1935.

Glen worked at the Carson Top Shop for Amos Carson, the owner of the shop. Glen created the smooth, padded tops by modifying the roofline of a stock convertible that would transform the car into a rolling work of art. The basic look of the top took on a *chopped* or lowered look with a rounded sweeping profile.

The tops were constructed by adding a framework of metal banding to the original header bow of the convertible top. The metal pieces were then shaped and welded together to make the top rigid. Adding to the custom styling, new side rails were created to fit the side door glass of the car, eliminating the rear quarter window.

After the general structure of the top frame was completed, the frame was then padded with cotton, and a new headliner was added to the inside of the frame. Finishing of the outside of the new top was done by covering the structure with Haartz top material to form a smooth and unique roofline.

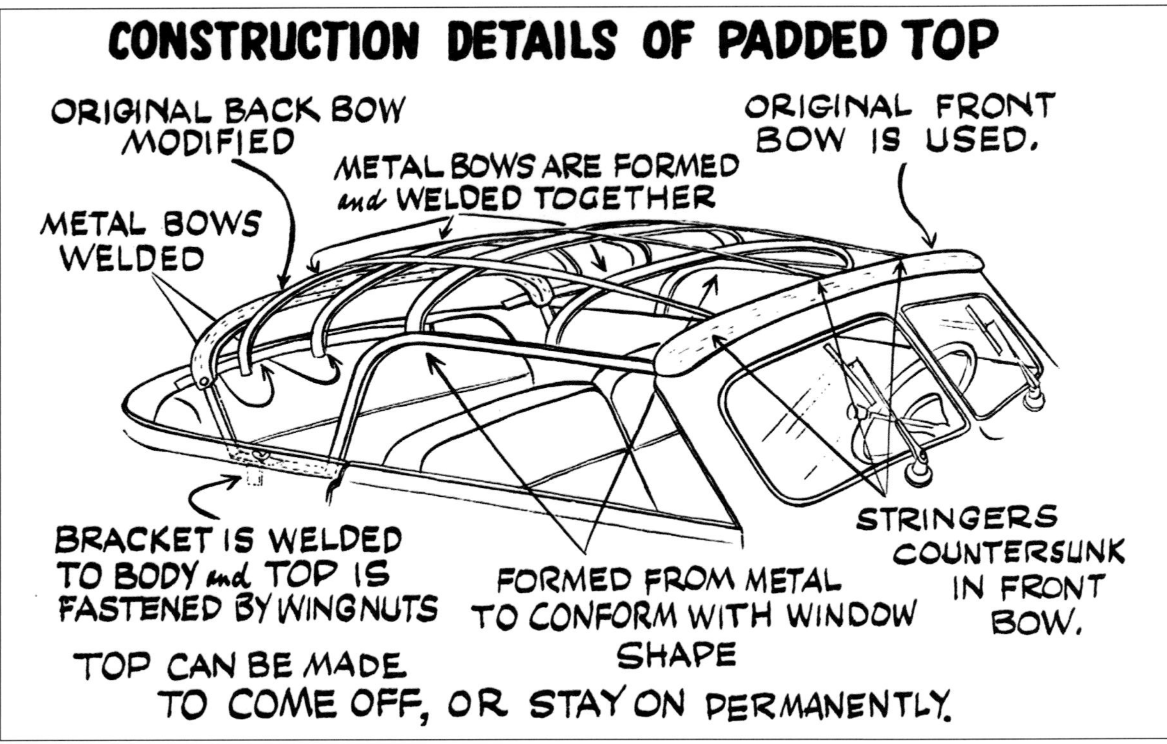

This drawing from Dan Post's Blue Book of Customization *shows the beginning process of how the Carson top frame was constructed. The top used elements from the original frame, while it was styled to fit the car.*

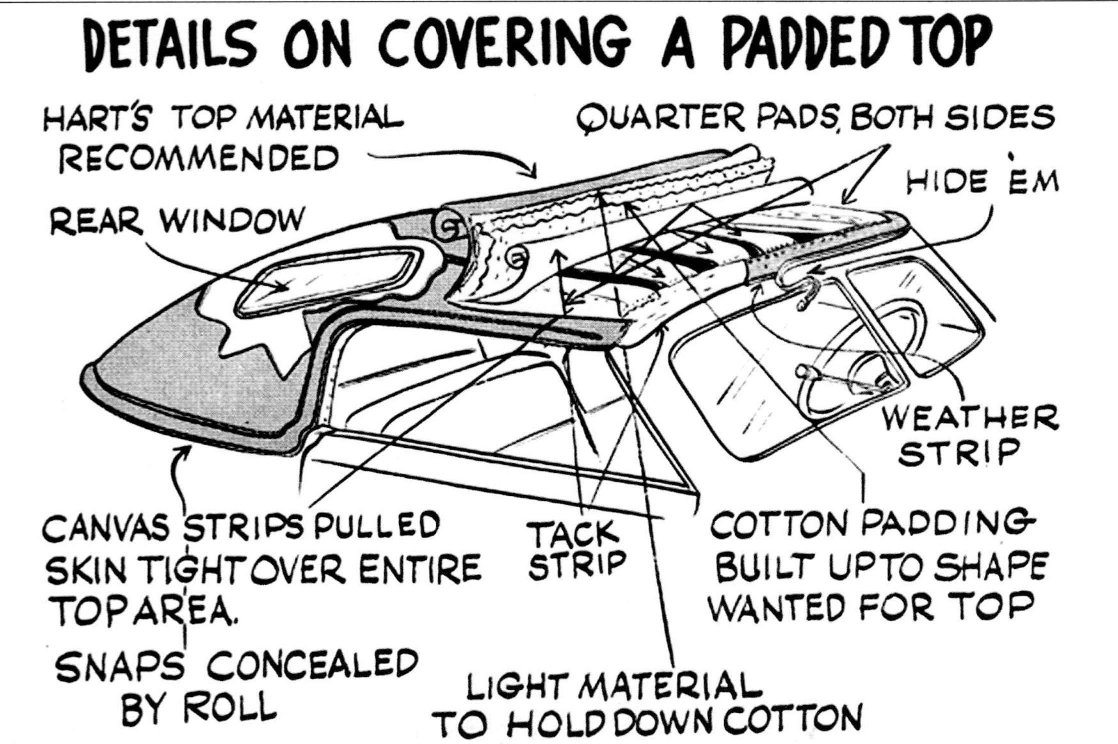

The detail in the upholstering of the Carson top is shown quite well in this illustration from Dan Post's Blue Book of Customization. *Note the detail that was taken to finish the top so that it would look like it could have been a factory option.*

THE CORVETTE

The inception of the Chevrolet Corvette came from the brilliant mind of Harley J. Earl. Earl was the chief designer for General Motors from 1927 until he retired in 1959. In 1951 at Watkins Glen, Earl first saw and fell in love with the Jaguar XK120. The two-seat European-designed open roadster impressed Earl enough that he had to develop an absolutely unique American sports car that the world had never seen or imagined before.

In June 1953, the first Corvettes rolled off the assembly line. Once the Corvette was introduced to the public, it evolved into the first true and ultimate American sports car. Unique to the Corvette was the wraparound windshield and its fiberglass body. The one-piece Euro-design drop top gave the new American sports car a fresh look that had not been used on any other model car up until that time.

What Makes a One-Piece Top?

One of the unique features of the Corvette is its Euro-influenced one-piece articulating top. The one-piece top refers to the built-in rear curtain. This one-piece design required that the top was made to fit the frame with little error. Although the frames on the first model years were very crude in design, the top provided some protection from the elements as well as a stylish dome cover for the occupants of the car.

Another feature of the original Corvette was that it had no side windows. This bodystyle was considered an open roadster. The bodies were fitted with removable side curtains that attached to the doors of the car to help repel the weather. An all-metal articulated frame consisted of a header bow, inward-folding side rails, two top bows, and the rear-deck bow.

This 1954 Corvette is truly an American sports car. One feature of the C1 Corvette was the Euro-designed top. This simple frame was not very durable and quite awkward to operate. It was best to have some help when you wanted to raise or lower the top.

You can clearly see the influence this 1951 Jaguar model XK120 had on the design of the early Corvette. The carriage top with the small roof bows gave a unique appearance that made it stand out against all other cars that came before it.

Without roll-up windows, the first Corvettes relied on side curtains to seal the car. Although they are crude, the side curtains provided some protection from the wind and rain. Thumb screws and guide pins were used to hold the side curtains in place.

Variations

The following explains the top removal and installation process of the C1 (1953 to 1962), C2 (1963 to 1967), and C3 (1968 to 1975) Corvettes. There are many similarities to these different models and a lot of variations that I will point out. Each and every Corvette that I have worked on is a unique experience and most rewarding to complete.

See what happens when you put fresh paint and a new top on an old 1964 C2 Corvette? The car takes on a whole new appearance. This car came in with a bare convertible top frame that needed a lot of adjustment and parts to make it operate correctly.

Because of the many frame issues associated with this 1959 Corvette, the top was kept in the lowered position, and the material had shrunk and was damaged because it has not been able to fold properly. The frame will soon be stripped and then repaired.

Years of neglect and abusive practices have taken a toll on this beautiful 1972 C3 Corvette Stingray. The broken rear window is a result of too many automated car washes that left a lot of soap residue on the top, resulting in a prematurely failed rear window.

Top Removal

Most often the owner of a Corvette would keep the top lowered because he or she enjoyed the openness of the car. I would tend to believe they kept the top stored because the car was small, and there really was no headroom for the passengers. For whatever reason that the top was not kept in the up position, you can bet that the top material had shrunk and eventually would not be able to be latched to the windshield. It is this reason that many top frames became damaged due to the tugging and pulling, trying to get them latched to the windshield of the car.

Removing the Old Top

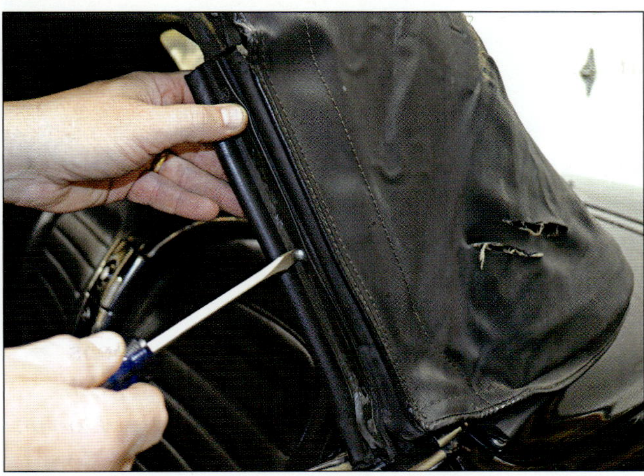

1 *One of the first items to be removed from the old top is the worn-out rubber weatherstripping that is attached to the side frame rails of the car. Use a screwdriver to remove the small screws and T-nuts that hold the weather seal in place.*

2 *Having the top lowered a little helps with accessibility to the trim screws during the removal of the rubber weatherstrip. Replace this old rubber with a new set after the new convertible top has been installed on the car.*

3 *Use a screwdriver to free the small trim screw that is holding the stainless steel, wire-on welt tip to the rear bow of the convertible top. The shiny, metal trim pieces cover up the cut end of the decorative wire-on welt cord.*

4 *Use wire-on welt along the top of the rear bow to conceal the staples used to hold the top material to the bow. The special decorative cord also keeps the weather off of the staples, which are prone to rusting if they were left exposed.*

5 *A lot of staples need to be removed from the rear tack bow. This is the place that all of the convertible top components come together and are attached. The next row of staples to be removed holds the convertible top decking material in place.*

6 *Many errors were made by the last installer of the C1 convertible top. Staples were used to hold the rubber header bow weather seal in place instead of the metal retainer and screws. After the header bow is reconditioned, use the correct hardware.*

7 *Small sheet metal screws were used to attach new tack strip material to the underside of the header bow. Discard all of this incorrect material and install the correct original-type tack strip and weatherstrip hardware into the beveled tack strip channel.*

8 *With the top partially retracted to expose the underside of the header bow, use a staple puller to remove the old, worn-out, foam-core front weather seal. A new weather seal is included in the convertible top kit from Al Knoch Interiors.*

9 *After pulling the staples, pull back the top material to reveal the condition of the header bow tack strip. There are no surprises here, just the typical rust and rot that we always see. The header bow will be restored and put back into service.*

10 *Remove staples from the anchor point at the top of the rear strap. A lot of tension is put on these straps as they help to contour the top and give support to the rear window. Discard the old straps and replace them with new materials.*

11 *Before the rear deck bow can be removed from the C1, remove this small, rubber deck seal. Two small screws hold it in place on the rear deck bow. The condition of this seal makes it no longer serviceable, and a new rubber filler seal will be installed with the new top.*

Replacing the top begins by first draping the car to protect it from any accidental damage that may occur. Be careful when using masking tape on the painted surface of a Corvette. The C1 Corvettes are most likely painted with lacquer, and the finish is very delicate. Use a good grade of painter's tape if you tape your draping to the body of the car. Also remember that you will be opening the decklid of the car from time to time during the installation of the convertible top on all models; do not seal the drape over the edges of the decklid so that it will not open.

Unlatch the top from the windshield and then the decklid. Remove all the rubber weatherstripping from the outer edges of the frame. This will allow access to the side flaps that are glued to the side rails of the top frame to be lifted off.

Unscrew the chrome tips from the wire-on welting with a #1 Phillips screwdriver. Use a staple puller to remove the tacks and staples holding the wire-on to the rear bow of the top frame. Continue to pull the additional staples that are under the wire-on holding the top material across the rear bow.

To remove the top material from the header, it will need to be unlatched, and the top needs to be retracted about halfway down to expose the underside of the header bow.

There is a variation on how the materials are attached on the C1 models. Several screws hold a metal retainer strip across the rubber weatherstrip seal that must be removed to reveal the tack strip that the top decking material is attached to.

C2 and C3 models have a front-sewn, 1/2-inch, rubber-core weather seal stapled across the lead-ing edge of the header bow. This is removed by lifting the staples that hold it to the header bow. Under the weather seal are staples that secure the top material to the header bow. There is also a second rubber weather seal that attached to the header bow with small trim screws and plastic T-fasteners that will also need to be removed.

With the staples removed from the header bow tack strip, the top material can now be peeled back from the header bow. Before removing the rest of the top material, loosen the tops of the rear straps from the rear bow by pulling the staples that secure them to the rear bow.

On the C1, the small, rubber deck weather seal must be unscrewed from the leading end of the rear deck bow tack rail.

Bow Measurement

Before the rear deck bow is removed from the car and the balance of the top material removed, take a critical measurement. Without this measurement, your new top will not fit the car properly, and you will have a very difficult time trying to make it fit.

Measure the distance between the vertical side rail and the front edge on the rear deck bow, and write the measurement down on the instruction sheet that came with your convertible top kit. This measurement will need to be referenced when you are ready to fit the

Take a measurement from the edge of the vertical side rail to the leading end of the rear bow before the rear bow of the C3 is removed. To get the proper fit, this distance must be observed, otherwise the new top material will not fit correctly.

Each Corvette top installation can vary a little, and getting the deck bow measurement correct is vital to the top material fitting the top frame. Transferring the correct measurement to the new C2 top material will make all the difference in the final appearance of the installed top.

The rear deck bow measurement on a C1 is taken from the face of the vertical side rail to the center point of the deck bow pivot bolt. This distance must be observed when installing the new top; it ensures that the top will fit the top frame without any extra wrinkles.

Side tension cables were a welcome addition to the C3 Corvettes to help with the buffeting issue when they were driven at higher speeds. The front of the tension cable is secured to the side rail of the frame with a small sheet metal screw.

Removal of the side tension cable requires that the rivet anchoring the rear of the cable to the frame be drilled out. A 3/16-inch drill bit makes quick work of eliminating the rivet to release the cable from the top frame.

With the convertible top material pulled back, the rear deck bow attaching pivot bolt can be easily accessed for removal. Simple hand tools, such as a wrench and screwdriver, are used to remove the locking acorn nut that secures the pivot bolt to the top frame.

new top to the rear deck bow. The measurement can vary from side to side and on each model of Corvette, so do not assume that it will be the same every time.

An added feature on the C3 was the side tension cables to help keep the convertible top from buffeting while driven at higher speeds. The cable is connected to the forward sec-tion of the side rail near the header bow. The cable is held in place with a rivet or small sheet metal screw. Relieve the tension on the cable by lifting the header bow about a foot off the windshield, and then remove the fastener.

The rear of the cable is fastened to the top of the vertical section on the side rail with a pop rivet. The rivet is removed by drilling it out with a 3/16-inch high-speed drill bit. Use care when drilling. You do not want to enlarge the hole in the side rail. Once the cable has been discon-nected from the frame, the rear deck bow can then be removed.

After the bow distance has been measured and recorded, the rear deck bow can be removed from the

This rear deck bow requires the use of a large Phillips screwdriver to remove the machine screws that secure the pivot bracket to the rear deck bow. The screws are accessed from the inside, near the front of the rear deck bow.

While working on the bench, the hold-in cord and rear rubber weather seal have already been removed from the rear deck bow. Release the top material by prying out the small, beaded flap from inside the channel in the rear deck bow.

is attached to the rear deck bow by staples. Remove the staples with a staple puller to free the material from the rear bow. On a 1961 and 1962 C1, the top material and rear rubber weather seal was held in by a nylon cord that was pressed into a channel in the bow. Pull the hold-in cord out to release the top material.

The hold-in cord was also used on the C2 and C3 models. Use a small screwdriver to pry the nylon hold-in cord from the retaining channel to release the rubber weather seal and top material from the rear deck bow. Set the old top aside for reference later if needed.

Top Pad Removal

Underneath the convertible top is a set of protective pads that hold the correct position of the cross bows and keep the top material from becoming damaged from the hard, steel top frame.

Removal of the top pads requires that the cover tape over the staples along the front of the pad and the

car. On the C1, use a wrench and a screwdriver to remove the pivot bolt that goes through the bow and pivot point on the convertible top frame. Once the bolt is removed, reinsert the bolt through the bow, and replace the washer and acorn nut to keep the bushing in place and prevent the accidental loss of the attaching hardware.

On the C2 and C3, there are two Phillips-head machine screws that hold the rear deck bow to a pivoting bracket on the inside of the leading end of the bow. Use a #3 Phillips screwdriver to remove the machine screws to release the bow from the pivot bracket.

Place the old top and rear deck bow on the workbench. The C1 top

Removing the Top Pad

1 *Now that the convertible top material has been removed from the top frame, we can see that years of wear have taken their toll on the protective top pads. Remove and replace the old pads with a new pair to protect the new convertible top.*

2 *At the front of the top pads, remove the body tape to access the staples that secure the pads to the header bow. Protective tape was placed over the staples to prevent them from damaging the inside of the top material.*

Removing the Top Pad *Continued*

3 *More staples are removed from the rear bow. The back end of the top's protective pad is removed so that the top frame can be inspected and serviced. A new set of convertible top pads will soon be installed on the newly reconditioned top frame.*

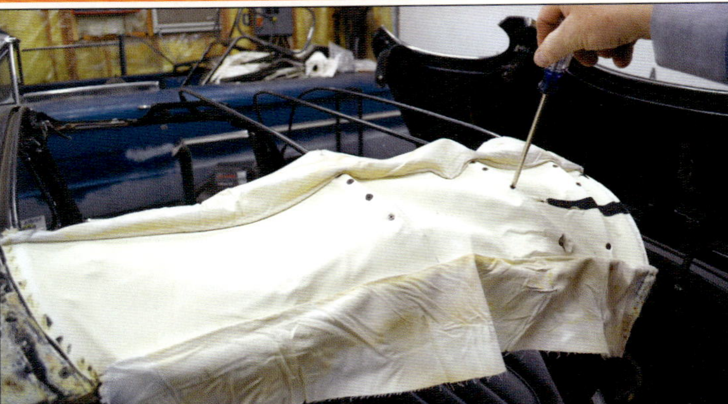

4 *Inside the convertible top pads are many small machine screws that hold the protective pad to the cross bows of the convertible top frame. The screws are also necessary to maintain the position of the cross bows that give shape and support to the convertible top material.*

staples at the rear of the pad material be pulled to allow the material inside the pad to be removed. After the staples have been lifted, the pads can be opened to reveal the padding. Remove and discard the old padding material.

You should now be able to see the small screws and washers that hold the pad in place on the cross bows of the frame. Remove the screws with a Phillips screwdriver. Be careful that you do not break them off while removing the screws from the bow. If they break or have been replaced by some other method, do not panic. Please refer to the *Broken Screws* section in chapter 10 of this book.

Inspecting the Frame

With the pads removed, we can now evaluate the condition of the top frame. The first thing to look for is any obvious problem with the frame, such as missing bolts or broken rivets. These will need to be replaced before the frame can be serviced. Other issues often found are

stress cracks or failed welds in the top frame. When one component fails, it most likely has an adverse effect on the top frame, causing other parts to compensate and they too will develop problems that must be corrected.

The most common issue associated with a Corvette frame is a rusty header bow. Typically, the retaining tabs for the underlying tack strip are broken or too weak to retain the new tack strip, and this condition must be repaired before continuing. Also

check for broken screws in the cross bows and repair them.

Once the frame is serviceable, begin to fold the top frame up and down, and listen for any grinding noises or binding of the frame. This would indicate a bent component that will need to be corrected before proceeding. Sometimes all the frame needs is a good cleaning and some light lubrication to get it to fold correctly again. After the top has been proven to fold properly, proceed with the reinstallation of the top.

This vital pivot bolt is missing, and it is the major cause of the convertible top frame not operating correctly. Replace the missing bolt with the correct shoulder bolt and then fix the other damage caused by folding the top without the bolt.

Broken welds were found on the left side rail due to the missing pivot bolt. Repair this before a new convertible top and pads can be fitted to the top frame. If this damage is not fixed, the new top will surely become damaged.

A lot of grinding has been done to remove the old welds that had failed on the top frame. It was necessary to go to the trouble of getting the metal back to a condition so that the top frame can be reassembled to the way it came from the factory.

A lot of care went into draping the car with a welding blanket to protect the car and prevent any unforeseen problems during the welding process. The new welds have made the convertible top frame strong and have restored its function to like-new condition.

More top frame problems were found and needed to be corrected. The header bow was welded to the side rail of the frame, and it was no longer able to be adjusted. By removing the welds and incorrect mounting hardware and then installing the correct hardware, the joint was made adjustable again.

Header Bow Tack Strip

Inspect the header bow for rust and damage and make the necessary repairs before proceeding with the new top installation. On the underside of the header bow is a long tack strip that holds the top material and front weather seal to the header bow. This tacking material should be replaced to ensure that the new top

Before the header bow can be removed and serviced, the retainer screws were removed from the header trim panel on the C3. This will allow us to properly recondition the panel and then weld in new retainer tabs for the header bow tack strip.

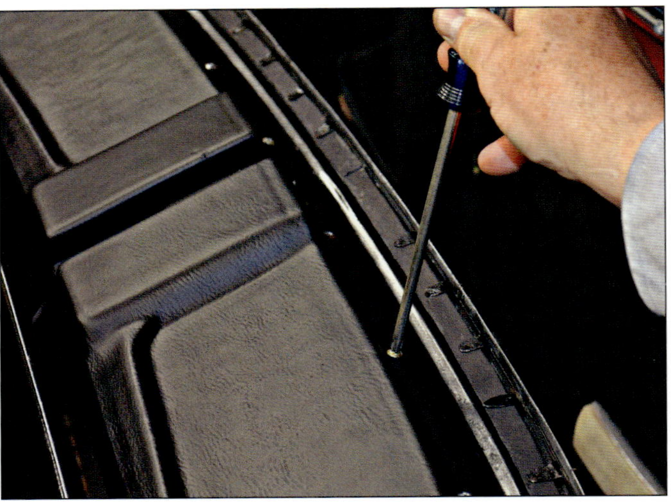

will be secured tightly to the bow. On the top side of the header bow are two smaller tack strips. These are used to secure the front end of the pads. Please refer to the header bow restoration section of this book on how to replace and repair the tack strip and header bow.

Top Frame Adjustment

With the reconditioned header bow back on the car, the convertible top frame can be adjusted so that the window gaps and frame operation are correct. These adjustments must be done before the new top and pads are fitted.

Begin by attaching the rubber side rail weatherstrip sections to the convertible top frame. This will help serve as a reference point for the correct positioning of the top frame as the door glass meets the rubber weather seal. Roll the door glass all the way up to get the proper adjustment for the top frame.

It may also be necessary to adjust the door glass to make the top frame fit better. This requires removal of the door panels to gain access to the inner-door window regulator. If you are not familiar with the procedure on how to adjust the door glass, it may be helpful to consult the Corvette service manual. While the door panel is removed, it is a good time to inspect the internal regulator and replace or repair any worn or damaged components before reinstalling the door panels.

I find it the easiest to work on one side of the top frame at a time. Loosen the retaining nuts at the rear attachment point of the frame and also the header bow fasteners so that the top frame can be moved into proper alignment. Vertical adjustments are made by moving the frame up or down into the correct position over the top of the door glass.

The rear vertical frame adjustment is made by loosening the header fasteners on the side rail and moving the frame forward or backward

eliminate the gap in the side rail and also have the proper spacing around the door glass.

Make adjustments to the C1 top frame by loosening the outer locking nuts and moving the frame either up or down to get the window gap corrected. After adjusting the tension on the inner balance link, the gap in the side rail will be straight.

The top frame has been properly aligned to meet the perimeter of the door glass. Bring the rear edge of the top frame into adjustment by loosening the header attachment hardware and moving the frame into the correct position before tightening all the hardware to lock the adjustments in place.

Adjustments to the rear vertical rail are made on the C3 by loosening these two header screws on the underside of the side rail. The spacing of the vertical rail can be moved by extending or retracting the top frame rail with the header bow adjustment.

To get the proper frame gap around the door glass, the rubber weatherstrip is installed on the convertible top frame. When the door is closed with the window up, the glass should have an even margin across the top and rear edge of the door glass.

Use a ratchet to tighten the mounting points of the top frame on the C2 Corvette after the frame has been brought into adjustment. Perform the same procedure on only one side at a time to align the frame with the door glass.

Here you can see that the rear vertical and horizontal frame rails are in perfect adjustment with the door glass. The convertible top frame can now be tightened down to retain the position of the properly adjusted frame. With the top adjusted, the new top can now be installed.

to fit the rear edge of the door glass. Once you are satisfied with the way the frame is positioned, tighten up all of the fasteners to lock the frame in place.

Raise and lower the frame several times and make any other adjustments that are necessary for a proper fit. After you have the top frame adjusted to fit the glass as well as it can, you can now remove the rubber weatherstrip moldings from the frame rails before cleaning and painting the convertible top frame.

Clean and Paint

After the top frame has been inspected and all adjustments and corrections have been made, the convertible top frame can be thoroughly cleaned and then painted. This is the only time that this can be done, and it gives your car a like-new appearance.

Wipe down every section of the convertible top frame to remove dirt and grime. After covering the car with a poly drape, a fresh coat of satin black enamel will make the top frame look like new again.

Clean the convertible frame with a small chip brush and Formula

After the new paint has cured, it is time to recondition and install all the chrome hardware that was removed. Adjustments to the guide pins and latching hardware may be necessary so that the header bow aligns properly with the windshield.

409 cleaner to remove any dirt and light grease that has built up. Stubborn areas may need special solvents and cleaners to remove old glue and grime. Be careful to not get any of the solvents on the interior or paint of the car.

When you have the frame clean, rinse it with clean water to remove

any residue and wipe the frame down to dry it.

It is very important to drape the car with at least a 1 mil polyethylene sheeting and mask off everything that you do not want to get overspray on. After the new paint on the top frame has dried, refit the top latches and other trim pieces before installing the top pads.

Top Latches

You may need to adjust the header bow latches and guide pins after adjusting the top frame. Having the proper tension on the latches will make locking the top frame in place easier and cause less strain on the latch.

Safety issues and leaks can occur if worn and cracked nylon guide pin bushings are not replaced. The bushings are a low-cost item, and they will help your top and decklid close without damaging the painted surfaces or chrome on the guide pins.

Each and every section of the convertible top frame is wiped down to remove the years of dirt and grime that has accumulated on it.

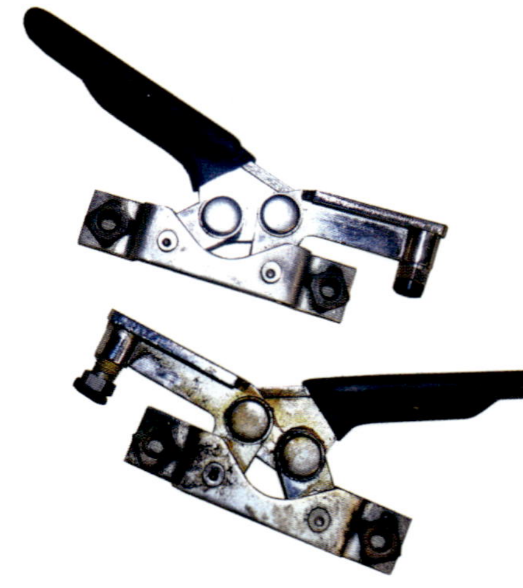

Sometimes all you need to do is give your chrome pieces a little attention to get them in top condition. These top latches needed to be cleaned and new rubber tips added to make them function like new. After they are cleaned, they can be reinstalled.

Over time, the rubber tip of the latch will mushroom out and fail from the stress caused by being latched. A worn tip on an adjuster bolt can scratch the surface of the windshield trim and is not safe to use. New adjustment tips are readily available from Corvette Pacifica.

It is advised that you replace the damaged or missing guide pin bushings with new bushings to prevent the windshield corner moldings from getting torn. The small nylon bushings are easy to replace and cost a lot less than new corner moldings.

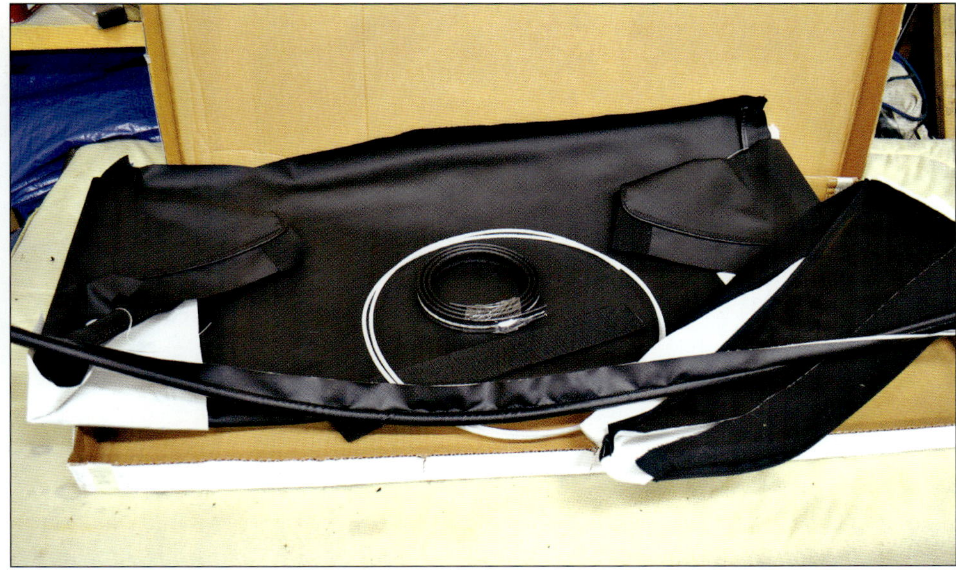

You will find everything you need to replace the top on a Corvette inside the box of an Al Knoch Interiors convertible top kit. Each top has been made from the finest materials available anywhere, and it has been designed to exact specifications to fit your car.

Fitting a New Top

When it comes down to what top kit to buy, I always choose Al Knoch Interiors convertible tops and seat covers for my Corvette projects. These are the best products you can obtain for your Corvette, and you can be assured that the quality and authenticity is always correct. The Al Knoch top kits are shipped complete with the top, pads, and trim accessories needed to complete the installation.

Additional parts can be acquired by contacting Corvette Pacifica in California. It has all the correct weatherstripping and hardware that you may need to bring your Corvette back to perfect operating condition.

A small mallet is used to help set the rear deck bushings into place. These nylon bushings are often missing or broken and aid with proper rear deck alignment. They also help keep the decklid from rattling while driving.

Top Pads

Installing new top pads on a frame could not be simpler. Al Knoch convertible top pads are marked on the inside of the pad decking where the cross bows line up. The kit comes with a chart showing the exact measurements of the bow placement so you can double-check the fitment, but if you just line up the marks to the cross bows, you will have great results every time.

Begin the pad installation by laying the pad over the top frame and opening the flaps to expose the inside of the decking material. Here you will see some drawn lines that indicate the bow alignment. The pads are precut to size and ready to install. Staple the front outside corner of the pad to the top header bow tack strip, and then pull the pad taut and staple the inner rear corner of the pad to the rear tacking bow just before the indent in the bow. The indent compensates for the thickness of the pad material.

New protective pads are must-have items for every new convertible top installation. It all starts with the forward end of the pad getting stapled to the header bow tack strip. This pad has been premarked for its placement on the top frame.

Al Knoch Interiors has precisely marked the bow positions on the inside of the pad material to make the pad placement much simpler. Pull on the pad to help it contour to the cross bows for a wrinkle-free fit as it is stapled in place.

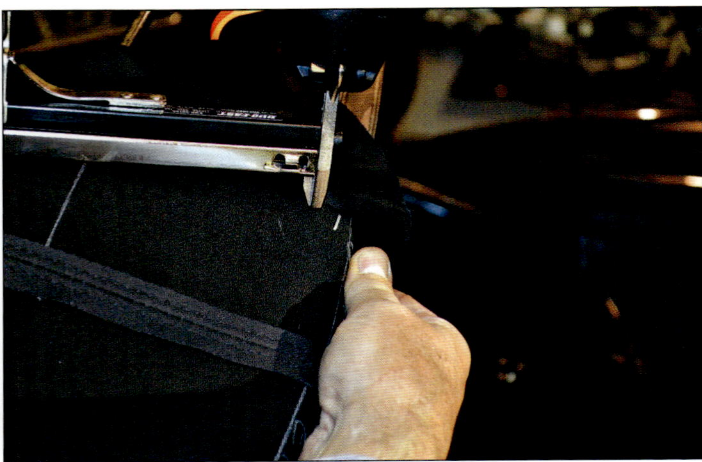

Place a staple on the inside of the pad to hold it in place as it is positioned along the rear bow of the convertible top frame. After the pad has been stretched into position, add more staples to keep the pad from shifting.

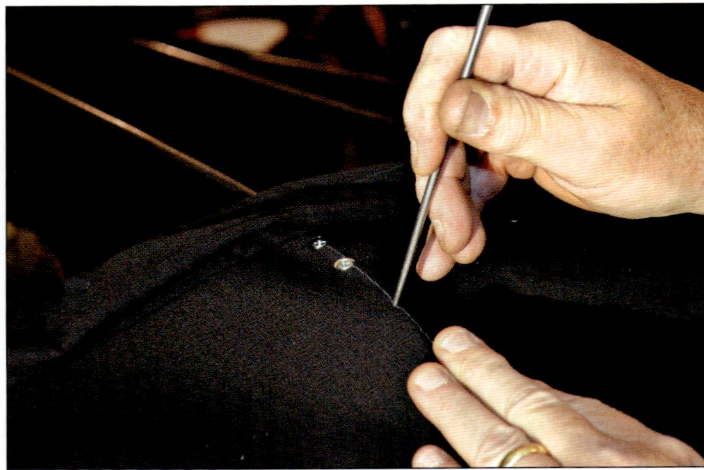

An upholsterer's regulator is used to prepunch a screw hole in the base material of the pad. The hole makes it possible to insert the small machine screw through the pad material. A tapered washer is also used to hold the pad to the bow.

Some pads use both staples and machine screws to hold the material in the correct position on the cross bow of the convertible top frame. The fasteners all must lie flat after they are applied to minimize any bumps in the surface of the pad.

Pull the pad down across the rear bow and staple the lower corner; then, move to the front inner corner and secure it to the tack strip. By attaching the corners of the pad in a cross pattern, you will get a tighter fit, making the pad conform to the curvature of the top frame. Once the corners are set, additional staples can be added to the inside ends of the pad.

With the flaps on the pad open, staple the deck material of the pad to the bows with tack strips. On the bows that require screws, align the inside edge of the pad with the indent on the bow and center the alignment mark inside the pad with the cross bow. Before the small screw and washer can be set in place, use an awl or upholsterer's regulator to pierce a hole through the pad decking, and then insert the screw. Snug the screw down until it locks the pad material to the bow. Pull on the rear bow to make sure that the pad will lie smooth and then continue adding screws until they are all in place.

Insert the new burlap webbing and foam padding by fitting it into the open pad. Staple the materials in place along the front and rear of the pad. The top flaps can then be folded over the padding to seal it in place, and stapling across the ends finishes off the pad. The flaps are also glued down to keep them from pillowing when the car is driven.

Trim the ends of the pad flush with a utility knife to remove the excess material and padding. Apply a layer of Gorilla Tape at the front

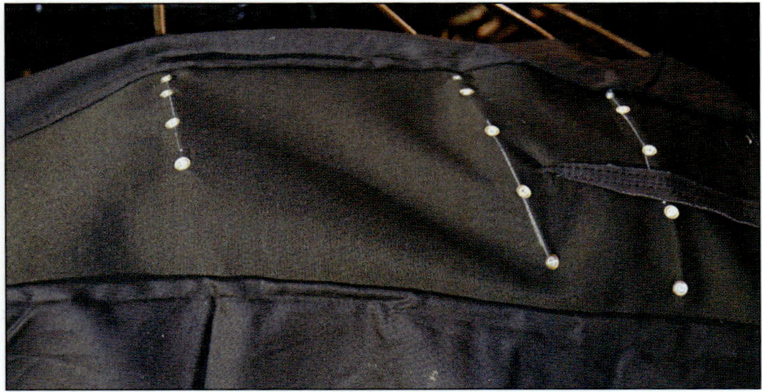

The C1 Corvette uses a total of 28 small machine screws and washers to secure the protective pad material to the cross bows. Each cross bow has a specific place and spacing to offer the correct amount of support for the convertible top.

Modern convertible top pads use a foam filler to soften the convertible top frame. The pad has flaps that are folded over the top of the foam padding to keep it in place. Each end of the pad is stapled closed, locking the foam padding inside.

Contact cement is brushed along both of the facing edges of the flaps to seal in the foam padding. Gluing the pads closed also helps to keep the pad from ballooning up if air gets under the top while the car is being driven at highway speeds.

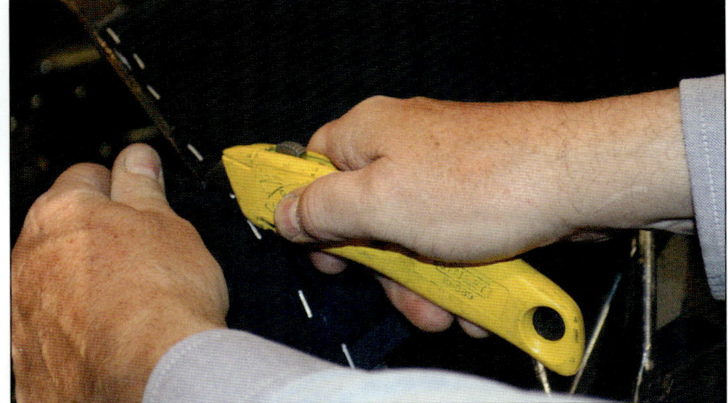

A sharp utility knife is used to trim the excess material from the ends of the convertible top pad. There would be too much bulk on the inside of the car if the pad was not trimmed. Trimming leaves the pad with a cleaner appearance.

of the pad to cover the staples. The tape protects the top material from rubbing on the surface of the staples. Before the new top material can be applied to the rear deck bow, move to the workbench with the top material and rear deck bow so that some preparations can to be made.

Rear Straps

To give the top a full appearance, the Corvette uses a pair of additional straps in the rear of the top frame. These straps are either stapled in place or held onto the rear deck bow by a small metal retainer plate and machine screws.

The straps on the C1 Corvette are stapled to the inside of the rear deck bow and wrap under the bow and then up over the outside of the bow before they are attached to the rear bow with staples. The placement of the rear straps is determined by a small notch in the rear deck bow. In the case of a reproduction rear deck bow, the straps are fitted 2⅛ inches from the center of the outer latch screw hole on each side of the rear deck bow. Measure from the inside of the bow and mark the tack strip material where the inside edge of the strap will be attached.

Attaching the straps on a C2 and C3 rear deck bow is a little different. The strap is attached to the outside of the rear deck bow with two small machine screws that hold a metal retainer plate across the lower end of the strap. Prep the strap to accept the retaining hardware by holding the retainer plate in place on the end of the strap, and then mark the placement of the screw holes with a china marker.

Remove the retainer plate and use a rotary punch to make the through holes in the straps for the anchor screws. Attach the strap to the outside of the rear deck bow by placing the strap in position on the rear bow, and then set the retainer plate on top of the strap with the cleat end up and facing toward the strap. Insert the screws into the bow through the retainer and strap, and tighten them down with a Phillips screwdriver.

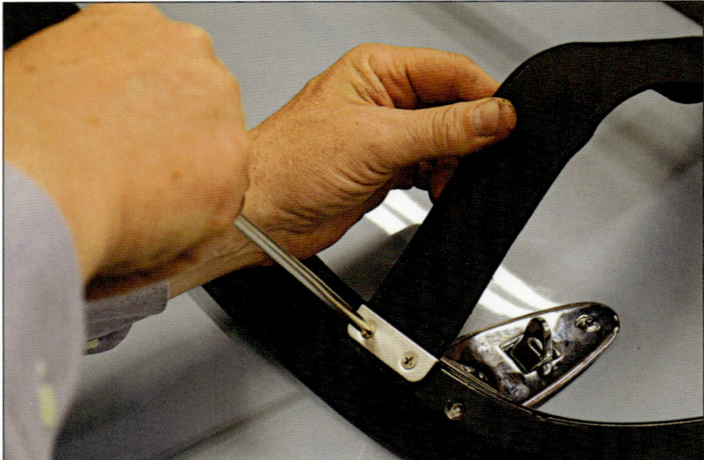

The rear strap is fastened at the bottom edge of the rear deck bow with a small metal plate and two machine screws. This strap will extend upward and attach to the rear bow, concealing the seam in the top material and giving support to the rear window.

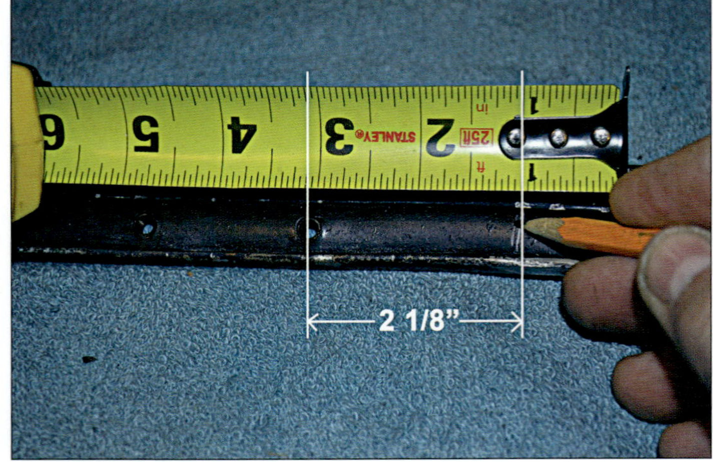

Mark the reproduction C1 rear deck bow for the correct positioning of the rear strap. An original deck bow would have a small indentation in it that indicated the position for the rear strap. Careful measuring and marking is needed, otherwise the strap will show in the rear window of the top.

Aligning the rear strap to the outside of the measured mark will ensure the proper placement of the rear strap. Use staples to secure the strap to the rear deck bow. A lot of pressure will be placed on the strap once the new top is fitted.

Preparing the rear strap on a C3 requires prepunching screw holes in the base of the rear strap. Use a china marker to indicate the position of the screw holes on the strap material so that a rotary punch can be used to make them.

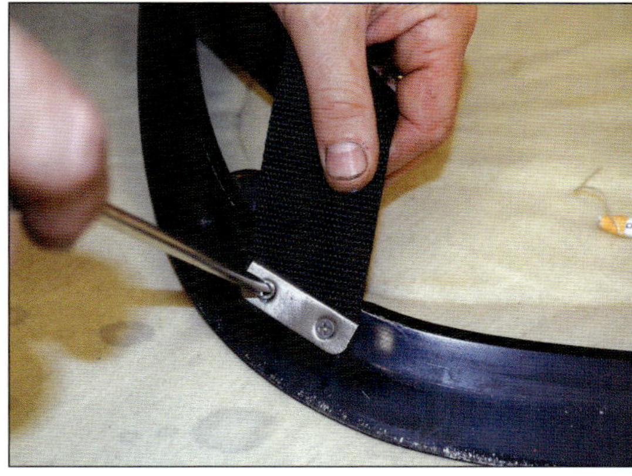

A small metal cleat is used to lock the rear strap to the rear deck bow of the C3. The rear strap material is sandwiched between the rear deck bow and the locking plate while small machine screws are fed through the plate and tightened.

Prep the Top

Now that the straps are in place on the rear deck bow, the top material can be marked for proper alignment on the rear deck bow. The one-piece top has no adjustment, and this measurement is a key step for the proper fitment of the top. If you do not follow this process correctly, the top will not fit the rear deck bow at all.

You must refer back to the measurement taken when the rear deck bow was removed from the car. This measurement will need to be marked on the inside of the top material for proper installation of the top. The object here is to have the vertical seam of the new top line up with the vertical side rail of the convertible top frame. If the seam is too long or too short, the top will not fit cor-rectly, so it has to be exact.

To mark the top, lay the side panel of the top on the workbench, measure from the side flap seam inward the distance of our measurement, and mark on the top material with a pencil. This is where you will line up the rear deck bow and begin attaching the material.

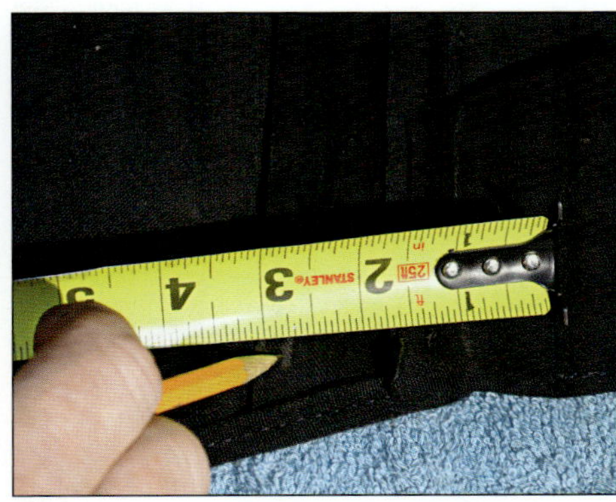

Lay the one-piece top for the C1 Corvette out flat on the workbench to transfer the measurement for the rear deck bow position. Make a mark on the inside lower flap of the top material, referencing off the binding seam of the convertible top.

Before the top can be installed onto the rear deck bow of the C2, the bow position must be measured from the seam of the vertical flap to the inside of the lower top attachment strip. There are no other adjustments to the top, so this must be exact.

Make a precise mark on the inside of the C3 convertible top to serve as a reference point for where the end of the rear deck bow will be placed. Begin installation of the top at this point to assure that the vertical seam will line up properly with the vertical side rail.

Attach the Top

Along the lower inside rear edge of the convertible top is a short flap that is on top of a thin rubber liner that emerges from the sewn-on edge binding. The rear deck bow is placed between the flap and the rubber liner with the rubber liner on the inside next to the top material.

At the front of the flap on the C1 top, cut through the flap material up to the binding behind the vertical seam without cutting the thread. This allows the top material to lay correctly on the rear deck bow. Align the pencil mark you made on the inside of the top with the center of the deck bow bolt, and then position the top material over the bottom edge of the rear bow so that the flap seam is just on top of the bottom edge of the bow.

The material has to be positioned this way, otherwise it will not lay right when there is tension on the top. Staple the flap onto the rear deck bow to keep it in place. Now check that everything is lined up correctly, add a few more staples along the deck bow to secure about 5 inches of the flap material, and then repeat this process on the other end of the deck bow.

After the ends of the top have been properly secured in position, the rest of the top flap material can be worked over the deck bow and stapled in place. Continue to observe

Make a cut in the attachment flap on the C1 top so that the top material will lie correctly against the bottom edge of the rear deck bow. Care is taken to not cut any of the existing stitches in the convertible top material.

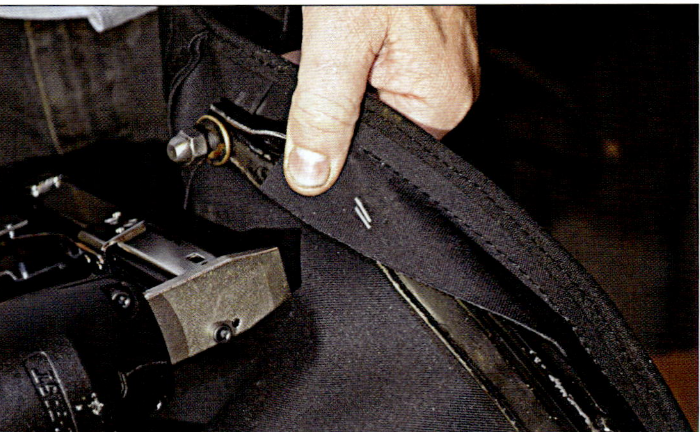

After a lot of manipulation, the convertible top is temporarily stapled to the rear deck bow to verify that the top material is in the absolute correct location before proceeding any further. After the positioning is verified, the top can be permanently attached.

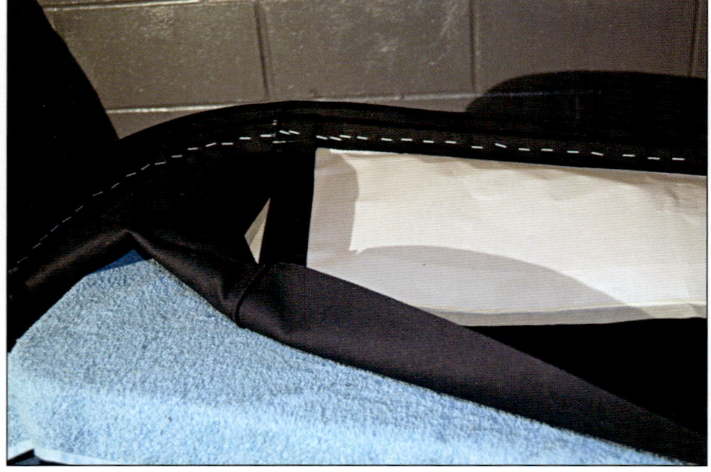

The process of keeping the top material positioned on the rear deck bow while it was stapled in place turned out well. This is one operation that cannot be rushed. After the top is stretched, imperfections show up along the outside of the top as a wavy mess.

Access to the rear latch mounting holes is revealed by cutting away the attachment flap material. The top edge of the flap material is also trimmed even with the top edge of the rear deck bow to allow the installation of the rear rubber weather seal.

After the rear rubber weather seal is fitted onto the rear deck bow, the rear deck latches can be attached. Use new machine screws to mount the latches to the rear deck bow. The latches will be under a lot of pressure, and the screws must be secured tight.

After the reference point on the top material has been lined up with the end of the rear deck bow, use a flat-head screwdriver to work the bead on the hold-in flap of the convertible top into a little channel that is machined into the rear deck bow of the later-model Corvettes.

Push the nylon lock-in cord into place with a large flat-head screwdriver to hold the rear rubber weather seal in the channel of the rear deck bow. As the cord is worked into the open channel, the weather seal locks the top material in place.

alignment of the material on the bow so that it lies smoothly and evenly across the length of the deck bow with the rubber liner on the outside against the top material. Do not worry about centering the top material, as it is already self-centered from attaching the ends first. If you started attaching the top material in the center and worked your way outward, the outer seams would not line up correctly with the vertical part of the frame.

Trim the flap material flush with the upper edge of the rear deck bow and notch out the material to reveal latch-mounting T-nuts in the bow. Fit the rear weather seal to the deck bow, and then install the latch brackets in position on the top side of the rubber seal. There will be a lot of force put on the rear latches, so be sure the screws are secured firmly to the bow to prevent the bolts from bending when they are latched.

1961–1975 Models

Attaching the top to the rear deck bow on 1961 to 1975 models is a little different. There are no staples used at all. The flap on the inside of the top has a welt or bead sewn to the flap that is tucked into a small channel inside the rear deck bow. Begin by aligning the mark you made on the inside of the top to the forward edge of the deck bow. I like to give just a touch more material on these models, so make sure the mark is fully visible on the outer edge of the bow.

Use a large flathead screwdriver to push the bead into the channel on the underside of the deck bow by working the screwdriver against the bead as it is pushed it into the channel. To lock the bead in place, you will need to set the rear rubber weather seal in position over the channel, push the nylon lock-in cord into the channel in the rubber weather seal, and then push the weather seal and lock in cord into the channel on the rear deck bow. Work about 6 inches of the lock-in cord into the channel, and then repeat the process on the other end of the deck bow.

With both ends secured, the top material flap can be worked over the edge of the deck bow. The top will self-center itself, so the small bead can be worked into the small channel on the deck bow. Work from one end of the deck bow, and continue locking in the top with the weather seal and lock-in cord. When you get about 3 inches from the other locked-in section, you will notice that there is extra weatherstrip material that has bunched up. Pull the lock-in cord from the weather seal and remove the first 6 inches from the channel. Continue installing the lock-in cord until you reach the end of the deck bow. The excess rubber weather seal can now be carefully trimmed flush with the end of the rear deck bow.

Attach the Deck Bow

After you have the top material attached to the rear deck bow, the assembly can be reattached to the top frame. Remove the acorn nut, washer, and bolt from the C1 deck

Each end of the rear deck bow is reattached to the top frame pivot point with a shoulder pivot bolt and an acorn nut. A washer and the acorn lock nut are placed on the inside of the frame and tightened with a wrench and flat-head screwdriver.

Two machine screws are used to attach the rear pivot bracket of the C2 and C3 to the rear deck bow. The screws are tightened with a #3 Phillips screwdriver from the inside of the car. After the rear bow is attached, the rear bow deck lock can be adjusted.

While the top frame is unlatched, pull the rear strap on the C3 tighter and position it in the center of the top seam before it is secured to the rear bow. Adjustments can easily be made to the rear strap before it is permanently anchored and then trimmed.

bow, and reposition the top assembly into the well of the car. Align the end of the rear deck bow to the mounting point on the top frame and insert the pivot bolt. Install the washer and acorn nut on the pivot bolt, and tighten the hardware with a wrench and screwdriver.

The C2 and C3 rear deck bow mounts to the pivot bracket with two oval-head machine screws. A #3 Phillips screwdriver is used to tighten the screws to the inside of the deck bow.

Rear Strap Fitment

The rear straps on the Corvette run up the inside of the top along the outer edge of the rear window. The top of the strap is positioned on the rear bow so that the seam in the top is centered on the strap, concealing it from view on the inside of the car. With the top frame unlatched from the windshield, some tension is put on the strap, and it is secured to the rear bow with staples.

After the straps on both sides are secured, the deck can be lowered and the top latched to the deck. Pull the top frame forward, and check the strap tension and fit of the top at the vertical side rails.

Make any adjustment necessary to ensure that the top is aligned correctly and is wrinkle free. Unlatch the top from the windshield and rear deck and trim any excess strap material from the front edge of the rear bow.

When the end of the rear strap is flush and centered to conceal the seam along the rear of the top, it can be anchored to the rear bow with staples. The C1 rear strap also helps give shape to the top and adds support to the rear window.

Rear Bow Detail

While the top frame is still unlatched, the top of the rear window can be attached to the rear bow. Gently pull upward on the top material at the top center of the rear window, and tack it into place at the center of the rear bow.

Pull the top material slightly upward and outward at the seam on the rear window, and tack it in place at the inside corner seam along the rear bow. Now latch the top to the deck and then the windshield to check the tension on the rear window. The top material should be snug and lie smoothly across the rear bow. Unlatch the top and make adjustments until there are no wrinkles in the rear window. You may want to use a little heat to help soften the rear window and relax away any wrinkles that may have formed. After you are satisfied with the appearance of the window, finish stapling across the top of the bow to hold the window in position.

Trim the excess material that hangs over the front edge of the rear bow. Be careful that you do not cut into the pad material while trimming. Latch the top to the decklid and then the windshield to give the top and rear window a good stretch. Work the sail panel material upward and forward to remove any wrinkles in the top material, and staple the top material to the rear bow from the seam outward about 4 inches.

Top Decking

Square up the top decking by pulling on the decking from front to rear to verify that there is enough material to fold over the header bow. Then, place a staple at the center of the rear bow to hold the top material in place.

At this stage, you will notice that there is extra material and some bunching at the rear outer corners of the top as the material curves over the rear bow. This is a normal occurrence. To relieve the top material, cut the top decking material along the front edge of the rear bow down to the last staple so that the top material can lie smoothly over the top of the rear bow.

Do not overcut the material. If you do, you will end up with a hole in the corner of the top. The top decking must overlap itself at the curve in the rear bow to create a seal at the bow.

Use your fingers to pull the decking over the rear bow, and staple the material to the bow so that it lies smooth and is wrinkle free up to the seam in the top. Pull the top material

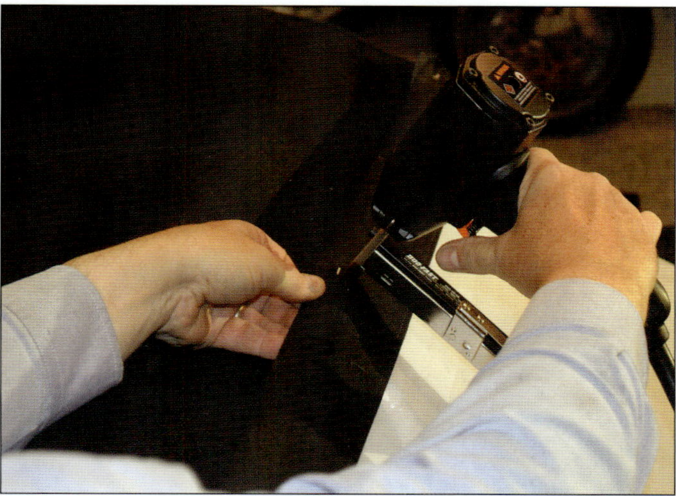

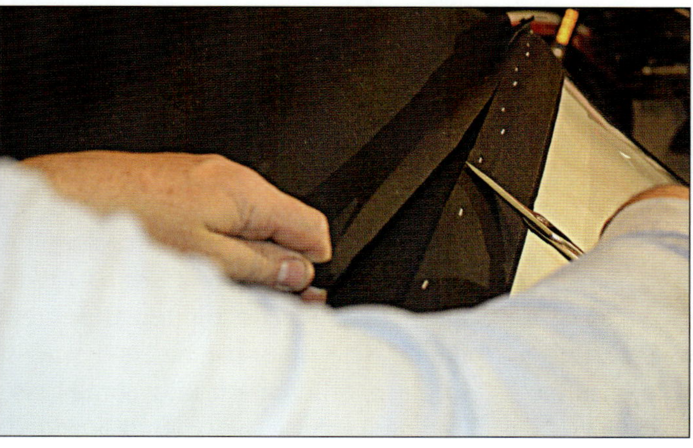

A single staple at the top center of the rear window helps give a good reference point on the adjustment of the rear window. Unlatch the top frame to give the top a lot more movement, and draw the rear window tighter to remove unwanted wrinkles.

Trimming the excess rear window material from the inside edge of the rear bow not only makes the inside of the car look nicer along the rear bow, it also relieves a lot of extra bulk from along the rear bow top decking.

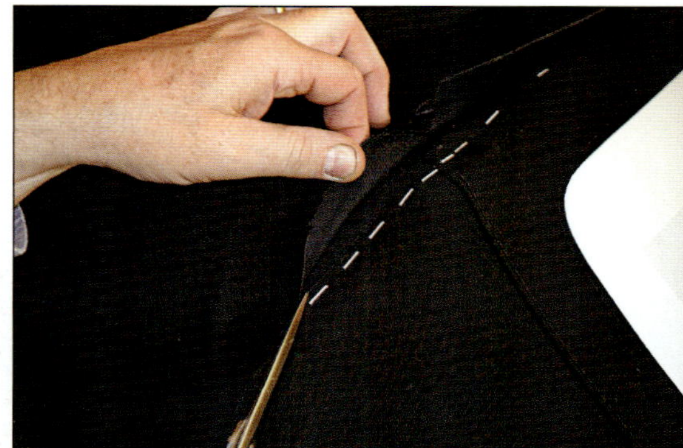

Cutting the top material closely along the forward edge of the rear bow helps relax the pucker in the top decking material. The cut in the material should only go as far as the last staple without causing a gap in the top material.

Pulling the top material forward at the seam will cause it to lie smooth. Now the top material can be stapled to the rear bow without any folds or wrinkles. This can be done to both ends before securing the center of the decking.

To make sure that the staples end up in a straight line along the center of the rear bow, your fingers should be placed along the inner and outer edge of the bow. This way, you can feel the position of the bow and staple in the center.

forward, recheck that the top decking is going to be wrinkle free, and continue adding staples across the rear bow until the rear portion of the top decking is completely attached to the rear bow.

Wire-On Welt

To cover the staples and protect them from the weather, apply a decorative piece of wire-on welt to hide the seam along the rear bow. A good gauge for the wire-on placement is at the end of the underling pad. This will make the wire-on finish about 6 inches past the seam on the C1 Corvette and about 4¾ inches on the C2 and C3.

Measure down from the seam in the top to the desired distance and make a small reference mark to indicate the end point of the wire-on welt. Position the end of the wire-on welt with the small bead facing the rear of the car just above the mark, and staple it to the center of the rear bow.

Move to the other side of the car, pull on the wire-on to straighten it, and add a staple to hold it in place. Trim the wire-on so that it finishes just like the other side. The wire-on should be applied so that it conceals the staple line along the rear bow and hides the overlap seam. Continue to staple the wire-on to the rear bow, fold the top of the wire-on over the staples, and tap the wire-on down with a mallet to seal the staples inside.

Fit the decorative tip over the raw, cut end of the wire-on so that the screw hole is just over the wire-on material, and use a small awl or upholsterer's regulator to make a pilot hole for the small screw. Use a #1 Phillips screwdriver to tighten the screw down. The tip must be held snugly in place, otherwise it may come loose and damage the top when it is folded.

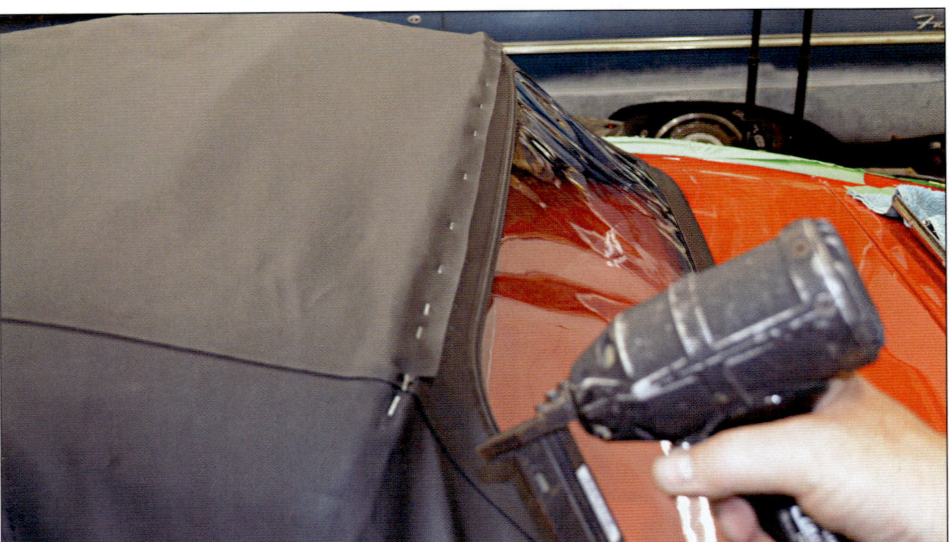

Staples are used to secure the rear decking to the rear bow of the car. Staples are placed every few inches from the center point on the rear bow to ensure that the top material will lie flat and smooth along the top of the rear bow.

Installing the Wire-On Welt

1 *Use the deck seam in the convertible top as a reference point to measure from to set the end point for the wire-on welt. By measuring down equal distances from both seams, symmetry can be reached for the end point on the rear bow.*

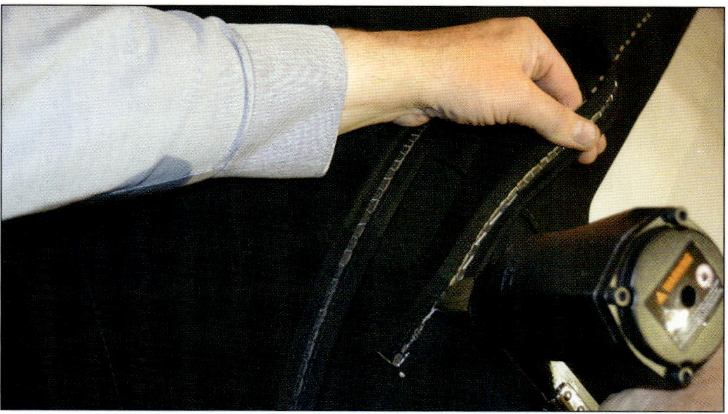

2 *Fasten the wire-on welt just above the finishing point that was marked on the top material. After a few inches have been secured, stretch the wire-on welt to straighten it out, and then anchor it in place on the other end.*

3 *Use a plastic mallet to flatten the wire-on welt after it has been stapled into place. By its design, the wire-on welt will stay flattened because of the internal zig-zag wire that runs throughout the material. Once flattened, it will seal the attaching staples.*

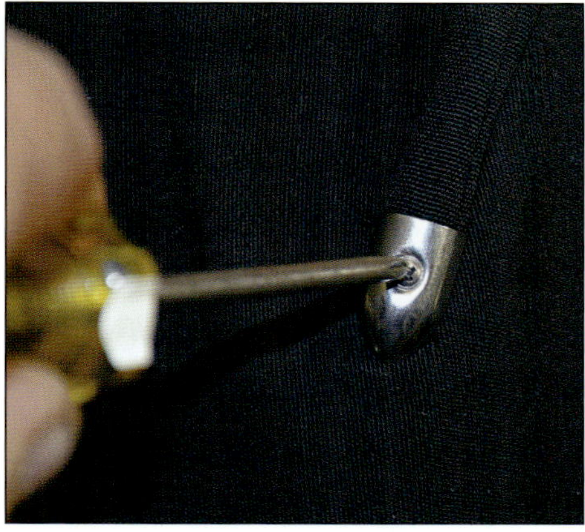

4 *Use a screwdriver to tighten the small screw used to hold the wire-on tip in place on the rear bow. The wire-on tip conceals the raw end of the wire-on welt and gives the new top a little splash of bling.*

5 *The finished wire-on welt has concealed all of the staples along the rear bow and keeps them from direct contact with the elements. As a finishing touch, the chrome dresses up the convertible top with a simple touch of elegance.*

Side Tension Cables

Side tension cables were added to the 1968 to 1975 convertible tops to help hold the tops tighter to the side of the top frame. The idea was to help with the buffeting issue caused by driving the car at highway speeds.

A string has been tied to the end of the tension cable to help draw it through the cable sleeve that has been sewn into the inside edge of the convertible top. The tension cable will keep the top material from buffeting as the car is driven at highway speeds.

Rivets and screws are often used to secure the side tension cables to the convertible top frame. Anchoring the side tension cable to the convertible frame allows the cable to keep the top from ballooning up as the car is driven at highway speeds.

The tension cable runs along the inside of a special sleeve sewn into the outer edge of the top over the door glass. A string is supplied to draw the cable through the sleeve. To install the tension cable, fold the top material back to expose the cable sleeve. Tie the string to the front end of the cable and pull it through the sleeve until it emerges.

The tension cable is attached to the rear side rail with a 3/16-inch pop rivet. Unlatch the top and retract it about halfway down to give enough slack so that the front of the tension cable can be secured. The spring end of the cable is attached to the front side rail near the header bow with a small sheet metal screw or a 3/16-inch pop rivet. Raise the top up and latch it to check the fit and function of the side cable.

Top to Header Bow

To get a good fit on the top decking, the top frame should be latched so the top material can be pulled as far forward as it can. With the top material pulled over the leading edge of the header bow, use a piece of chalk or a pencil to make a reference line on the material the full length of the header bow. Now unlatch the

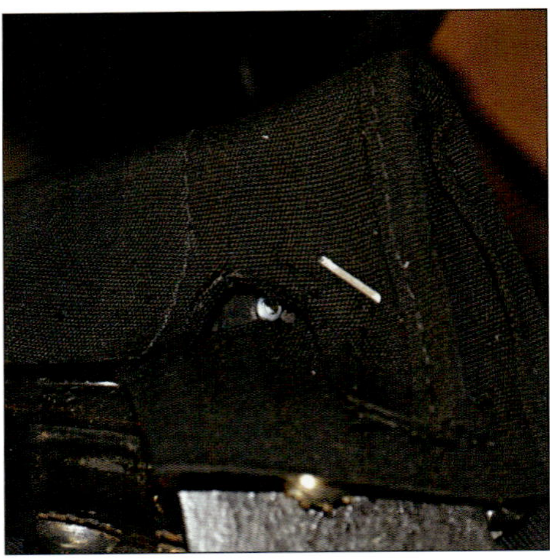

Use a temporary staple on the underside of the header bow to retain the top material in place after it is positioned on the corner of the header bow. After the top material is checked for fit and tensioning, add more staples to secure the material.

top and lower the frame so that the top material can be wrapped over the header bow about 1/4 inch past the reference line you made.

Line up the corner of the top and front flap with the edge of the header bow. Pull the flap under and the top material over so that the reference line is about 1/4 inch past the leading edge of the header, and put a staple into the header bow tack strip to hold the corner of the top in place.

Make a chalk line across the leading edge of the header bow onto the top material as a visual reference for the tensioning and positioning of the top decking. Being able to see how much to move the fabric makes adjustments much simpler.

Now, do the same to the other corner. Pull the top material across the header to make the side flap seam line up with the outer edge of the header.

Latch the top frame and check the tension on the top material. You want the top material to be tight but not overtight. Unlatch the top and make any adjustments necessary to get a proper tension on the top material. If you are satisfied with the way the top decking is stretched, unlatch the top and staple the material to the underside of the header bow tack strip. Latch the top and recheck that the fit and tension are correct. Make any adjustments necessary before moving on.

Front Weather Seal

Unlatch the top and lower it enough to expose the underside of the header bow tack strip. On the C1, remove the material covering the T-nuts in the tack strip. To expose the T-nuts, carefully lift the top material to locate the T-nut, and then make a U-shaped cut around the T-nut. The U shape will not cause the top material to tear out when there is tension on it.

Fit the rubber weather seal to the underside of the header bow and begin installing the weatherstrip retainer screws through the metal retainer strip into the T-nut in the header bow tack strip. Work from the center outward, and be careful about cross threading the retainer screws. If you jam one up, the top material will need to be removed along with the tack strip to repair the T-nut, so be careful. Do not tighten the retainer screws all the way down until you have them all in place. The T-nuts can move from side to side, and a little movement will help get the thick rubber seal set in place much easier. After you have the retainer screws in place, they can all be tightened.

Installing the weather seals on the C2 and C3 is a little different. The inner rubber weather seal is attached to the outer ends of the header by small trim screws. The main body of the seal is attached to the underside of the header bow with small plastic T-fasteners. The T-fasteners are just pushed into the retainer holes in the header bow.

There is also a sewn weather seal that runs along the leading edge of the header bow. This 1/2-inch foam-core seal is blind stapled to the underside of the header bow.

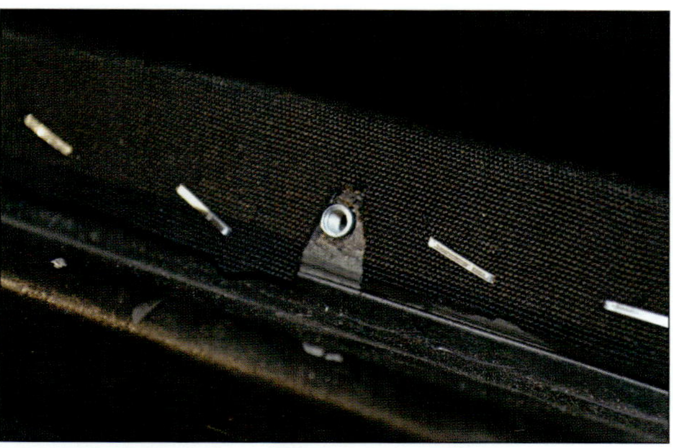

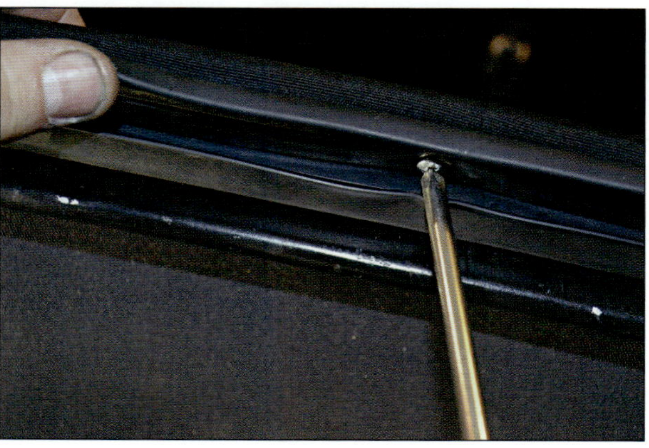

Hidden on the underside of the header bow is a secondary rubber weather seal that is designed to keep out most of the wind and rain as the car is driven down the road. The seal also acts as a cushion when the convertible top frame is clamped to the windshield.

Fastened along the front of the header bow is a soft rubber core seal that will act as the first line of defense to repel wind and rain from the occupants of the car. The weather seal also eliminates the small gap created as a result of the top frame and windshield meeting.

Rear Weatherstrip

One of the last things to be completed on the top installation is the rear flap and rubber weather seal. There is a small rubber filler seal that is attached to the rear bow on the C1 Corvette and connects to the lower end of the rear vertical rail on the top frame. Two small screws secure the seal to the rear deck bow before the rear flap is glued to the vertical side rail.

After the flap has been positioned on the side rail, a small sheet metal screw is added to the flange on the front of the small deck bow seal. The other hole in the flange is secured by the bottom rubber weather seal

This small, rubber filler piece helps keep noise and dust out of the convertible when the top is in the raised position. Small machine screws are used to hold the filler piece in place on the rear deck bow while the flange on the front will be attached to the top frame.

Apply contact cement to the inside of the rear vertical side flap on the convertible top and to the surface of the vertical side rail of the top frame. The sail panel of the convertible top will completely smooth out once the flap is pulled tight and set in place.

Attaching the new rubber weatherstrip seals to the side rail of the convertible frame is the last thing that is required to finish the installation of the new convertible top. Small screws hold the metal retainer in place, keeping the seal in the correct position.

Nothing beats the classic styling of the 1964 Corvette. The distinctive rib down the center of the back panel really sets this beauty off along with the new vinyl convertible top. Look out Route 66, this 'Vette is ready for the road!

screw. Attach the rubber weather seal to the side rail along with the metal seal retainer, insert the machine screws into their appropriate places, and secure the screw through the side rail frame with a T-nut.

There is also a small rubber seal that attaches to the rear deck bow on the C3. This seal is held in place by a small machine screw on the end of the deck bow. After the seal is secured, the vertical flap can be glued in place, and the last piece of rubber weatherstripping can be installed.

The filler seal on the C2 attaches to the bottom of the vertical rail and fills the gap at the rear corner of the door. It may be easier to install this seal with the top partially retracted and with the door open. The seal attaches with a machine screw and is retained by a washer and nut on the inside bottom of the vertical side rail.

The Finished Top

Latch the top frame and inspect the top for any imperfections. A little steam can remove almost any box wrinkle and help relax the top material to make it fit and look better. The convertible top will need to be in the latched and up position for at least two weeks so that the top material can conform to its new shape.

With the top frame fully restored back to like-new condition, the 1959 Corvette will once again turn heads as it cruises through town. The stylish new Stayfast convertible top from Al Knoch Interiors gives this baby a lot of class and some real attitude.

Now that all of the repairs have been done and the new top has been fitted, the owner can enjoy her 1972 Corvette Stingray for many years to come without the worry of getting wet when it rains. With the top up or down this is one sweet ride.

RETRACTABLE TOPS

The concept of a retractable hard top was originated in the mid-1930s. While several major carmakers developed their own versions of a retractable top, it wasn't until the mid-1950s that Ford took the concept of the retractable hard top to a practical level with the Ford Fairlane Skyliner. Lincoln followed by incorporating the retractable top design into its Continental models.

The same frame and design was also adapted to the Ford Thunderbird and then discontinued by the mid-1960s.

It may be a bit overwhelming to get a close-up look at all the wires, relays, hoses, and switches that work together to make the top go down and then come back up again on a Lincoln or Thunderbird. To make this happen on the soft-top models, Ford used more than 600 feet of wire,

11 relays, 12 or more switches, 3 solenoids, and 4 small reversible electric motors.

Lowering the Top

Turn the key to the *on* position, press down on the top switch, and a lot of magical things are going to happen. First, the ignition interlock must engage. This relay is

The marvel of a hard top that will completely disappear into the trunk of the car was fully imagined and put into production in 1957 by the Ford Motor Company. The Fairlane Skyliner has an articulated roof that will fold away, turning the car into a roadster.

This sporty 1962 Ford Thunderbird has a folding soft top that will fold and store neatly into the trunk of the car. The same type of hardware and electronics used on previous retractable top cars has been adapted to work on this model to make the top move.

You can see that the trunk is quite large on this Skyliner. The small box in the middle of the trunk is actually the storage area and does not leave much room for personal items or luggage. When fully retracted, the top will fill the trunk, allowing the lid to close.

in upon itself to store, the hydraulic cylinders used to retract the top are connected to the base of the rear deck panel instead of the side rails of the top frame.

Troubleshooting

The hydroelectric mechanism is generally quite reliable on the retractable, but do not be discouraged by problems that may be encountered with the operation of the convertible top. The sequence of events to lower and raise the top is progressive, and if you encounter an issue, it should

found behind the right kick panel. The interlock triggers the relay that engages the lock motor on the trunk lid. This small motor drives two cables that are connected to the screw drives that unlock the trunk lid from the body.

After the lid is released, a switch triggers a relay that energizes the hydraulic-pump motor and an electric solenoid switch that allows hydraulic fluid from the pump to be directed to the trunk lid lift cylinders. The lift cylinders raise the trunk lid to a fully erect position, triggering two switches that allow the smaller transitional lid to rise until it hits a switch to activate the relay, telling the convertible top to unlatch from the windshield.

When the top latches retract, they make a relay fire to power the two hydraulic top lift solenoids, allowing the pump to engage and pressurize the top lift cylinders. The convertible top can now begin to lower into the trunk. The top frame actually turns back under itself as it retracts into the trunk. When the top is fully lowered, a switch is triggered, activating another relay that causes the hydraulic pump to reverse

and retract the trunk lid. The trunk lid locking motor also powers up, and when the trunk lid reaches its lowered position, the decklid locks into place, completing the top-down procedure.

Retractable Soft Top

In addition to the retractable hard top, a soft-top version was also an available option. Servicing and replacing the topping material is similar to a traditional two-piece top, but there are some unique differences that need to be addressed.

The top frame is designed to articulate and fold into the trunk of the car. Because the top frame turns

This is a physical example of what to look for when the system has failed. The terminal connector that is molded into the plug has corroded away and no longer makes contact with the post on the relay. The solution is to replace the plug.

The top has been lowered, and it is now stored safely away in the trunk of this 1963 Ford Thunderbird. This five-passenger roadster has a rear seat that is large enough for up to three passengers, which not only makes it fun but also a great family car.

This junction point can be found in the trunk of the 1964 Lincoln Continental. There have been some previous repairs made to the system, and a few more troublesome issues will also be addressed to get this Lincoln back into proper working order.

Troubleshooting is much easier when you can refer to the service manual for your car. There are many schematic drawings and diagrams that will help you diagnose a specific trouble area without having to test every circuit.

not take too much effort to figure out what needs to be addressed to correct the problem.

It is helpful to obtain a copy of the factory service manual for your model year. In the service manual, you will get all the system diagrams and schematics necessary to help get your top back into working condition.

Electronic components, such as relays and switches, are available through Convertible Service. If you get in over your head, give Curtis a call at 60s Lincoln Repair.

Old Top Removal

After you've run the top through its cycle, corrected any issues, and worked out all of the bugs of the convertible top mechanism, it is time to drape the car and begin the task of removing the old top material.

There are two pieces of wire-on welt that conceal staples. One is along the top of the rear bow and another follows the beltline around the lower rear deck bow of the top. Start by removing the wire-on tips and screws found at the ends of the wire-on welt.

A #1 Phillips screwdriver will remove the small screws from the welt tip. Remove the welt by lifting it from the car with a staple puller. New chrome tips, screws, and wire-on welt are included with the new convertible top kit, so the old tips and wire-on welt can be discarded.

Rubber Roof Rail Seals

The next items to be removed are the rubber roof rail seals. The seals are attached to the frame with T-bolts and special sealed nuts. To access the fastener hardware, the top will need to be lowered halfway to allow a socket wrench to be slipped over the weatherstrip nut on the inside of the frame rail.

Unless you are replacing all of the rubber, only the front and rear sections need to be removed; the center section will not interfere with the new top installation.

Before removing the old convertible top material, an inspection should be performed to determine what problems need to be addressed.

This 1964 Lincoln just came in for a new top. After it was inspected, problems were found with the trunk hydraulics and the header latch.

Removing the Old Top

1 *Work begins at the rear of the car by removing the decorative wire-on tips. A small Phillips screwdriver is used to unscrew these pieces from the top. The replacement convertible top kit includes new chrome tips and screws, so the old ones can be discarded.*

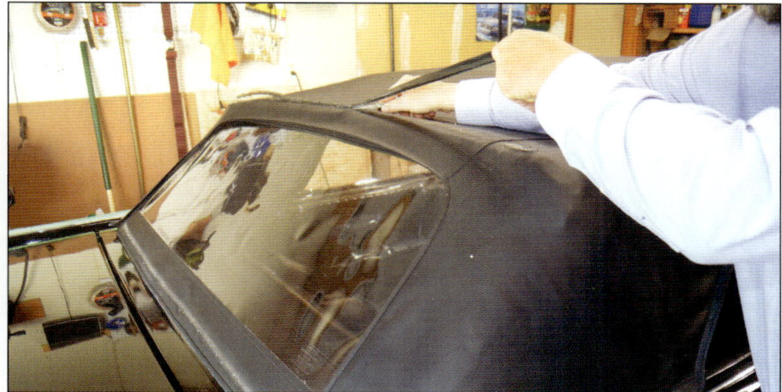

2 *Lift the staples with a staple puller to remove the decorative molding that is stapled across the rear bow of the car. A new piece of wire-on welt is supplied with your new convertible top, so there is no need to save this old material.*

3 *Use a socket and ratchet to remove the weatherstrip retainers from the back side of the convertible top frame side rail. After the fasteners have been removed, the rubber weatherstrip can be set aside. It will be reused with the new top.*

4 *Before the old convertible top material can be removed from the header bow, the rubber weather seal and retainer must be unscrewed from the under side of the header bow. Several small machine screws are removed to release the weather seal.*

5 *The front edge of the convertible top has a decorative stainless steel trim that conceals the staples holding the top material to the header bow. The trim molding is carefully pulled forward to release it from the edge of the convertible top.*

6 *All of the retaining staples have been removed from across the front edge of the header bow, and the top decking is peeled back to reveal the leading ends of the protective top pads and the anchor point of the side retention cord.*

Removing the Old Top *Continued*

7 *The side retention cord that is still inside the cable sleeve that runs along the inside edge of the convertible top is shown. The elastic cord will be reused with the new top to help keep the top from buffeting and bunching when folded.*

8 *Small Phillips-head screws are removed to access the bow sleeve retainers that are still attached to the cross bows of the Lincoln. Reuse the bow sleeve retainers with the new convertible top to anchor the top material to the frame of the car.*

Rubber Header Weather Seal

With the top still lowered halfway, the rubber header weather seal can also be removed. There are 13 small machine screws that hold a retainer strip onto the underside of the header bow, keeping the seal in place. Remove the screws with a #2 Phillips screwdriver. Then label the retainer and rubber seal and set them aside; they will need to be reinstalled later.

Stainless Steel Trim

Along the front of the header bow is a piece of stainless steel trim that conceals the staples holding the top decking material to the header bow. This trim needs to be removed to access the staples for removal. The trim piece was secured to the header by the weatherstrip retainer and screws. Since they have already been removed, the stainless trim can carefully be removed. Work the molding forward by pulling and lifting up and down without damaging the trim. After the trim molding is free from the car, set it aside to be reinstalled later.

Top Material Staples

Under the stainless trim there may be staples along the leading edge of the header bow that hold the top material in place. The top could be glued in place as well. Use a staple puller to remove the staples and then peel back the top material from along the front edge of the header bow. Once the material has been released, it will expose the front of the protective top pads and side retention cord anchor point.

Side Retaining Cords

While the top is still partially retracted, the side retaining cords can be removed. Use a #2 Phillips screwdriver to remove the front and rear retainer screws. Save the screws, remove the elastic cord from the cable sleeve in the top, and set the cord aside with the screws. These items will need to be reused on the new top.

Metal Retainer Screws

From the inside of the car, you will notice four screws in the second and third bows. These Phillips-head screws hold a small metal retainer that is inside the fabric bow sleeve to the bow. Remove the small screws and remove the retainer from the sleeve and set them aside. The top can then be raised up and locked into place.

Top Frame Staples

The top material is still connected to the top frame by a row of staples that were concealed by the wire-on along the top of the rear bow and the lower deck bow. Remove these staples to release the top material from the frame. At this point, there should be nothing else holding the top material to the frame. The old cover can now be removed and discarded.

Rear Curtain

With the old top material removed, you should now be able to see the remaining staples along the top of the rear bow. They retain the curtain in place. Use a staple puller to remove these staples to release the curtain from the rear bow. After the old rear curtain has been removed, it will be replaced with a new curtain. The old rear curtain can now be properly disposed of.

The old rear curtain of this Lincoln is still attached to the rear bow. Removal of the rear curtain requires that the staples across the rear bow are removed with a stapler puller. Once the rear curtain is free from the car, it is no longer needed and will be discarded.

It may be necessary to cut the lower layer of the pad to release it from the wire harness that may be running through it.

With the pads removed, inspect the *A* and *B* wire harnesses for cracks and damage. If the wires are hard and brittle and show signs of age, they should be replaced. The cost of replacing the harnesses now is minimal compared to the top failing to operate properly and needing to go back in and replace the wires later.

Repair Damage

While the convertible top frame is exposed, a thorough inspection can be made of all the moving parts. Replacing bushings, cleaning, painting, and oiling the frame can be completed with relative ease.

Most likely, the tack rails will need to be rebuilt by replacing the old, worn material with fresh, new tack strips. Refer to the section on tack strip repair for guidance.

Pads

The final components to be removed from the convertible top frame are the pads. Note that the Lincoln also has rear quarter pads. Concealed inside each pad is a wire harness that runs to the header bow from the rear deck bow. Care must be taken when removing the pads on a retractable top so that you do not damage the wire harness.

Carefully open the material on the top of the pad to reveal the padding material. The original padding used in the Lincoln was cotton batting layered over jute webbing. Under the cotton is the wire harness that controls the top latching mechanism. Carefully remove the cotton without pulling on the wire harness. Remove the remaining staples that hold the pad and webbing in place.

These are the original pads that were put on the car back in 1964. They should have been replaced with new pads when the last top was installed. After the old materials are removed, new modern top pads will be properly installed to protect the new top from the frame.

Inside this original top pad is a layer of cotton batting that has been applied over some jute webbing. The pads will be replaced with the modern equivalent, and they will perform better and last much longer than the original materials did.

Looking at this rear bow tack strip, I can tell that someone has been watching too many YouTube videos. Many people advise use of a heavy-duty V-belt as new tack strip material, but it is not the proper material to rebuild a rear bow tack strip.

Someone has replaced the original tack strip with a modern plastic tack strip. As you can see, the tacking material does not lie flat or smooth, and this will not make our new convertible top look good. The tack rails will be properly repaired for our new top.

Along the outer corners of the rear tack bow are notches that have been created to allow for the safekeeping of the header lock mechanism wire harness. After replacing the old tack strip material, sculpt the new material carefully to accommodate the wire harness.

New tack strip material has been set into the old retaining strips along the rear deck bow of the convertible top. The new tacking material will be able to hold a staple and secure the new top material to the car for many years without failing.

Adjusting the Frame

With the top operation in order, the frame may need to be adjusted to fit the profile of the side glass. The frame on the Lincoln is different from a traditional convertible. The tensioning, height, and forward adjustments are made on the frame by loosening the bolts and making the necessary adjustments to bring the frame back into the correct position. Before making any adjustments

Adjustments to the Lincoln convertible top frame are made by repositioning the settings at the rear tension bars. Vertical and horizontal adjustments can be made to the frame so that the top frame will fit the side glass of the car better.

to the frame, the rubber weather seals need to be refitted to the side rails of the top frame to get a proper adjustment.

Installing the Top

There are a lot of differences in the installation sequence for the Lincoln top compared to a conventional convertible top. Normally, the pads are fit to the frame and the rear bow height is set. Because there is a wire harness that runs through the pads, the rear quarter pads are set before the main pads, thus establishing the rear bow height.

To avoid stapling errors during the fitment of the new top and pads, I like to have a reference guide indicating the positions of mounting hardware on the rear deck bow tack rail. When a staple hits the fastener, it will surely break, and that can cause a hole, damaging the material.

Avoiding this mishap can be done by simply applying a strip of painter's tape along the perimeter of the rear deck bow and making a reference mark on the tape to indicate the position of the fastener.

Another reference guide that can help while stapling the top to the tack rails can be made from a scrap of

Fashion a simple stapling guide from a small piece of tag board to help reference the placement of staples along the rear edge of the convertible top. A guide like this is most helpful so that unnecessary staples are not added.

tag board. Before fitting the top and pads, place the tag board with the bottom edge on the deck and leaning along the rear deck bow tack rail. Mark the metal edges of the tack strip retainer, and then mark the centerline of the tack strip. Using this guide will help avoid missing the tack rail while stapling.

Rear Curtain

Begin by establishing the center point on the rear bow. Position the center point of the rear curtain with the center point of the rear bow and place a temporary staple in the rear bow tack strip. Use slight tension to pull the top edge of the curtain to the outside, and temporarily tack it to the rear bow. Do the same for the other side of the top edge of the curtain.

Staple the center point of the lower skirt of the curtain to the rear deck bow tack rail. Pull and stretch the curtain to the outside and tack it to the rear deck rail. Temporarily tack each side to the lower rear bow tack rail. Now check the rear bow height and make the necessary adjustments along the top of the rear bow.

Unlatch the frame from the windshield, and lower the top just enough to release the tension on the rear bow. Work out any wrinkles

I find it helpful to place a strip of painter's tape along the rear deck bow and mark the fastener point locations. This reference guide helps when fastening the new top material and pads to the tack rail, noting that a staple obstacle is present.

Use a temporary staple in the top center of the rear curtain to help get the alignment right. Add more staples as the bow height and wrinkles are adjusted in the curtain material. Work the curtain from side to side until it is perfect.

Use only a few staples during the fitting of the rear curtain. This makes it much easier to remove the staples when an adjustment is necessary to reposition the curtain or help stretch the curtain to relieve any excess wrinkles in the plastic window.

Final adjustments have been made to the lower section of the rear curtain as it is stapled to the rear deck tack rail. After fitting the top material, a decorative piece of wire-on welt will cover the row of staples, protecting them from the weather.

from the center point to the outside of the curtain, placing staples evenly across the top of the rear bow.

Staple across the lower skirt of the curtain from the center outward, making sure that there are no wrinkles left in the curtain. Latch the top frame and recheck the bow height. Make any additional adjustments to the curtain so that the curtain will look as smooth as glass.

Pads

Before a new convertible top can be fit to the frame, the new protective top pads must be installed. The protective top pads are actually installed in the reverse order of a standard top: the rear pads will be installed before the main top pads.

The wire harness must be carefully positioned inside the pad so that it will not be damaged by a

Installing the New Pads

1 *As it is shown, the Lincoln has a full set of protective pads that run the entire length of the convertible top frame. The pads soften the top from the hard metal frame, and they also conceal a wire harness that provides power to the header bow lock mechanism.*

2 *In an effort to allow the wire harness to flow effortlessly into the rear deck bow, cut a small oval slot into the lower end of the rear quarter pad. Carefully secure the pad with staples to the lower rear deck bow tack strip and upper rear bow.*

3 *Use care when placing the wire harness inside the main convertible top pad as it is secured to the rear bow and header bow. Protecting the frame is the first job of the pads all while hiding and smoothing the control harness wires.*

Installing the New Pads *Continued*

4 Cut a small piece of material from the convertible top pad and staple it over the header control wire harness to help keep it in position within the pad. The wire harness still has some ability to move while it is safely restricted.

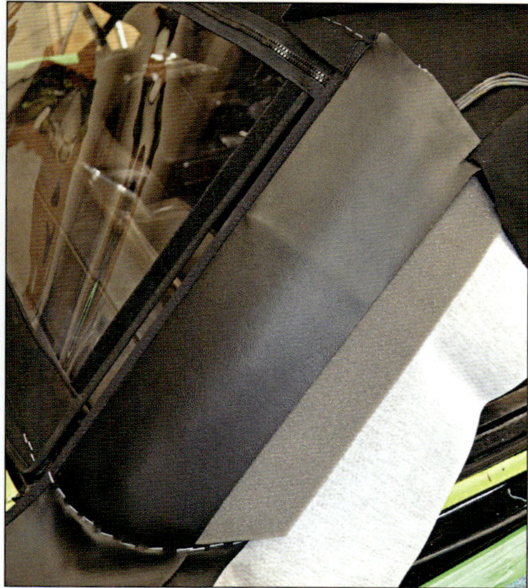

5 Use a piece of foam to fill the rear quarter pad. The foam not only helps with the shape and contour of the convertible top but also it protects the wire harness and keeps it from causing unsightly bulges in the surface of the convertible top material.

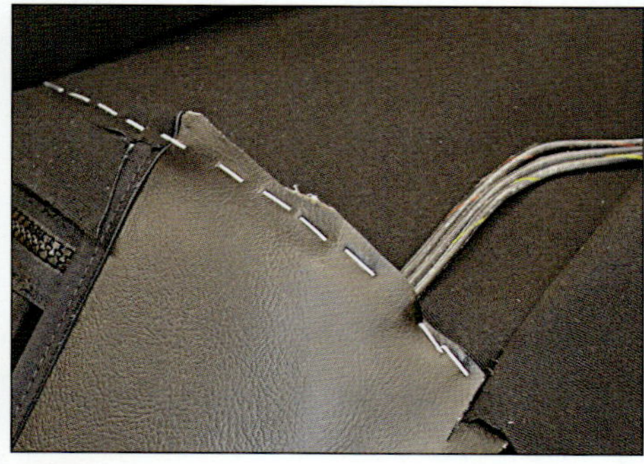

6 Secure the top of the rear quarter pad to the rear bow with staples, and you will see that the staples stop at the edges of the harness to allow the wires to pass into the main pad. Care must be taken to avoid stapling into the wire harness.

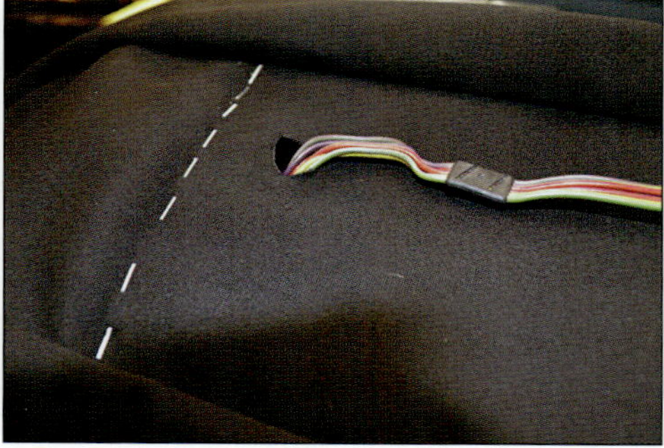

7 Cut a small hole into the front of the base material of the pad to allow the wire harness to pass through without causing a visual lump when the new top material is installed. The harness was unplugged from the header and then passed through the hole.

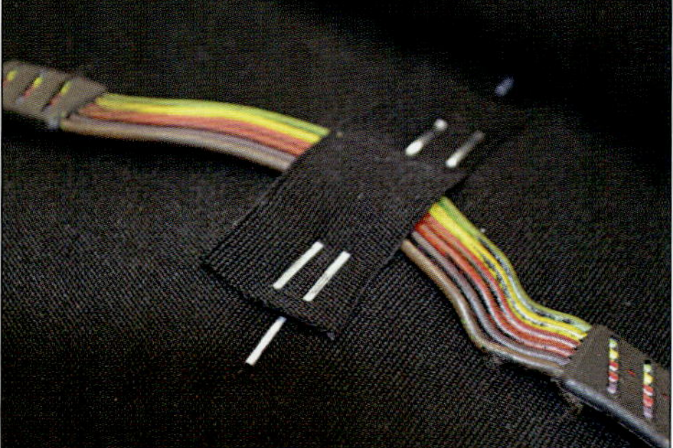

8 Before the pad filler is added, secure a small piece of convertible top material over the wire harness to help keep the wires centered inside of the pad. Preventing the wires from possible damage is vital to keeping the top in working order.

9 Finish the rear quarter pad by smoothing the top flaps and gluing them down to seal the padding inside. You can see that there are a few staples missing along the top of the outside pad flap. This is where the wire harness runs inside the pad.

staple. To encapsulate the wire harness, position the rear quarter pad under the harness so that the flaps will close over it. Place a staple at the outer edges at the rear bow. The pad is then stretched to the lower rear deck rail, and a small slit is made up from the base of the pad to form an almond-shaped hole that allows the pad to lie smoothly around the wire harness as the wires run inside the deck bow.

Staple the underside of the pad to the tack rails, keeping the pad material wrinkle free. Pull the quarter pad tight, staple the under liner along the edge of the rear bow, and trim the under liner flush with the edge of the rear bow. Do not staple or cut the wire harness.

With the quarter pad in place, the main pad will need to be fitted with the wire harness inside. Lay the main pad out across the frame, staple the inside edge of the pad at the relief point on the rear bow, and smooth the pad material under the wire harness and along the bow before stapling the outside corner to the rear bow. With the rear of the main pad secured, smooth out the main pad and staple the corners to the header bow.

The harness should be secured inside the pads to keep it from binding when the top is folded. Begin at the rear bow and position the wire harness into the small cutout made for the harness. Cut a small piece of material from the pad flap to be approximately 2½x3/4-inches wide. Staple it over the harness to keep it in the channel.

Place the new foam pad material inside the quarter pad, and trim the foam to fit the length of the pad. Fold the inside flap over the foam padding and carefully place staples along the

bottom edge of the quarter pad into the lower rear deck tack rail. This will hold the foam liner in place.

Close the top of the rear pad by stapling the inner flap of the pad across the top of the rear bow. Staple up to the wires on both sides, but do not staple into the wire harness. Now, trim the pad flap flush with the leading edge of the rear bow. The outer flap of the rear quarter pad will be finished later.

A small hole will need to be cut into the under liner at the front of the pad to allow the wire harness to pass through to the header locking mechanism. Some people cut a slit into the pad for the harness, but I feel that it makes for a better-fitting pad not to cut more than necessary. Unplug the front harness connectors, and then pass them through the hole in the pad. Reconnect the harness plugs, and then finish securing the underside of the pads to the convertible top frame.

Secure the harness on the other cross bows, keeping the wires centered inside the pad. Insert the foam pad material into the pad and adjust

it so that it fits from edge to edge. Seal the flaps by gluing them closed with contact cement.

Finish off the rear quarter pad by smoothing the outer flap over the top of the main pad and stapling along the rear bow. Feel for the depression in the bow and avoid stapling the wire harness. Glue the quarter flaps closed with contact cement.

Top Fitment

Lay the new convertible top out over the frame and check the fit across the bows and from front to back. If there is a problem with the size or alignment of the top, this step will let you know what to adjust to allow the top to fit better. Flaws in the top will definitely show up at this stage, and if you put staples in the new top, the manufacturer will not take it back.

It is important to note the position of the bow sleeves on the inside of the top and verify that they line up with the cross bows. If they do not line up with the cross bows, the top will not be able to be anchored to the car.

The new convertible top is being dry fit to the frame. This helps determine if any additional adjustments are needed to make the new material fit the car better. Contact the top manufacturer if you have any problems with the fit.

Fitting the Top

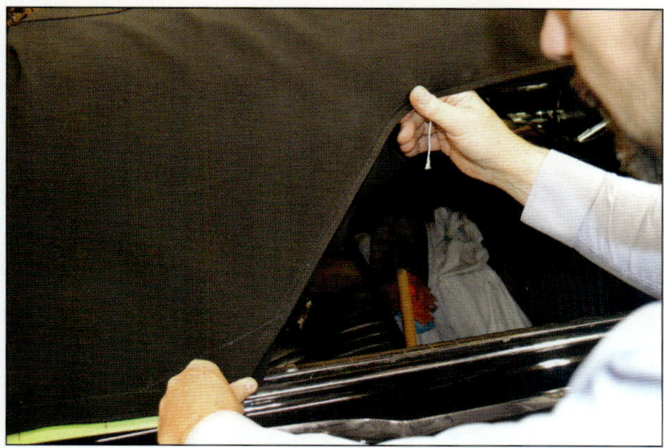

1 Before any stapling can be done, align the bound edge of the convertible top with the vertical portion of the side rail. This puts the top into the correct position and ensures that all the other seams and attaching points line up correctly.

2 Place a temporary staple at the rear bow seam to help the alignment of the convertible top material. Stretch the top material across the rear bow so that the sail area of the convertible top will line up correctly with the vertical frame rail.

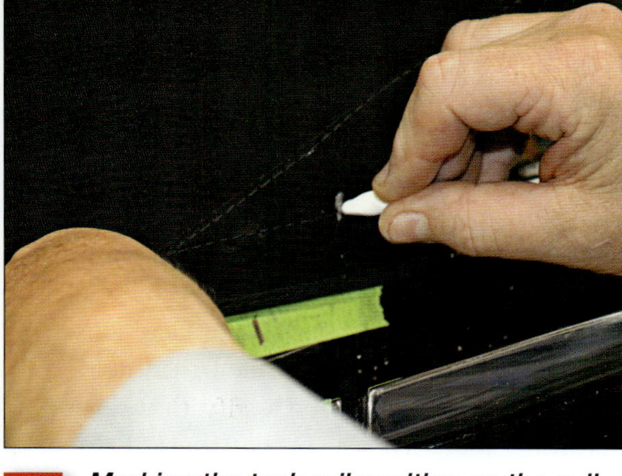

3 Marking the tack rail position on the sail panel material creates a reference point where the staples are going to be set. Determine the position by feeling for the edge of the tack rail and then marking it with a piece of chalk.

4 Once the sail panel has been positioned on the rear quarter of the top frame, use a temporary staple at the leading section of the rear deck tack rail to hold the sail panel in place. Use 5/16-inch staples to secure the sail panel.

5 While the rear quarter of the convertible top is temporarily tacked in place, the sail area of the convertible top can be positioned and secured to the rear deck tack rail. The sail panel is smoothed around the rear quarter pad, and it is attached to the tack rail with 5/16-inch staples.

6 Removing the excess slack in the top deck material requires the top material to be pulled taut and the edges aligned with the side rails of the frame. The fabric is then temporarily stapled to the leading edge of the header bow so that the stretch can be established.

Fitting the Top *Continued*

7 Use chalk to mark the edge of the header bow on the convertible top material. The line is used as a reference to help stretch and reposition the convertible top material. Without a visual reference, it is difficult to get an even stretch on the convertible top material.

8 After the top material has been stretched over the header bow, it is stapled in place across the leading edge of the header bow with small 3/32-inch staples. The staples will be covered and protected from the weather by the decorative stainless trim header molding.

Rear Bow Seam Staple

When the edge of the rear side flaps are aligned with the vertical side rails of the frame, the convertible top should be aligned so that the split in the rear bow seam will line up with the center of the rear bow. Hold the top material in place on the rear bow, and put a temporary 3/8-inch staple at the rear bow seam to keep the top from moving while the other side is stretched into position and temporarily tacked in place.

Deck Bow and Sail Panel Positioning

On the forward part of the sail panel, feel for the tack rail on the deck bow and use chalk to mark the leading edge. Now, use a 5/16-inch staple to temporarily hold the sail panel of the convertible top material in position onto the tack rail. Do the same for the other side.

Top Material Alignment

Now that the leading edge of the sail panel is in proper position, work the top material of the sail panel over the quarter pad until it lies smooth over the pad. The Velcro strip on the inside of the sail panel should line up with the Velcro strip on the outer edge of the rear curtain. Align the lower edge binding of the top with the lower edge binding on the rear curtain, and tack the sail panel to the lower tack rail with 5/16-inch staples. Do the same with the other side.

Stretching Out the Wrinkles

Move to the front of the top and pull the center of the top material over the header bow just enough to remove most of the wrinkles in the top deck. Temporarily tack the material to the front tack strip. Work the top material to the side, and when you have the front flap aligned with the edge of the side rail, temporarily tack the material to the front tack rail with a 1/4-inch staple to keep it in place. Align the other front corner of the top to match.

Header Bow Top Tension

Chalk a line across the top material all along the front edge of the header bow. Unlatch the convertible top from the windshield, lower the top frame enough to pull the top material about 1/8 inch past the edge of the header bow, and staple the top material just enough to keep it in place. Raise the top, latch it to the windshield, and check to see if the tension on the top looks correct. Make the adjustments necessary to remove any wrinkles in the top material. When everything looks correct, the top material can be stapled off to secure it in place.

Side Cables

Along the inside edge of the top is a cable sleeve that retains the elastic cord designed to help keep the convertible top material from buffeting. The elastic cord also prevents the top material from bunching up when the convertible top is lowered into the trunk of the car.

To install the side cords, lower the top halfway down to relieve the tension on the top material. Turn the edge of the top over to reveal the bow sleeve. Now, anchor the rear eye of the cord to the frame with the retaining screw.

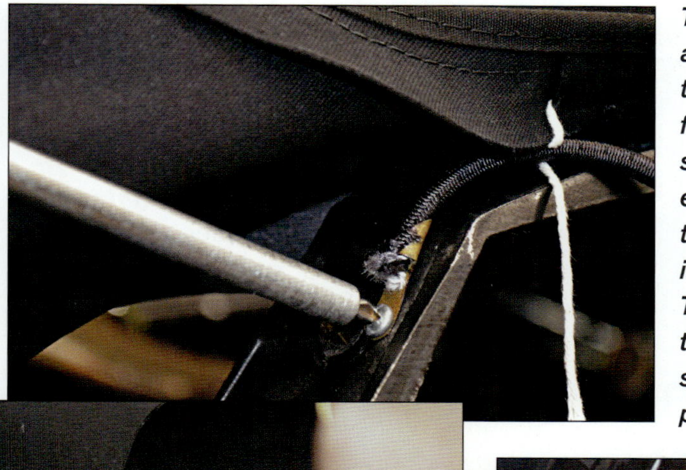

The rear side cord anchor is attached to the convertible top frame with a small screw before the other end is drawn through the side cable sleeve in the convertible top. The cord will be tied to the string in the cable sleeve before it is pulled through the top.

After the side cord has been pulled through the cable sleeve of the convertible top, the front anchor of the cord is secured to the side rail of the convertible top frame with a small machine screw. The elastic cord will help keep the top from buffeting and bunching up when lowered.

Insert the bow sleeve retainer into the bow sleeve of the convertible top. The bow sleeve is located on the inside of the top decking, and it helps keep the convertible top material from buffeting when the car is driven.

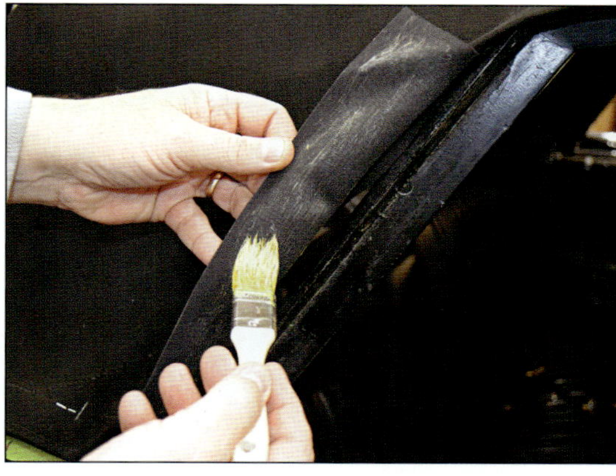

Applying glue to the rear vertical flap will help secure it to the convertible top side rail. The rear side flap keeps the top positioned correctly. The rear rubber weatherstrip molding will cover the side flap to aid in holding the flap in place.

Contact cement is being applied to the front side flap of the convertible top. This flap helps secure the convertible top material to the side rail of the top frame. The side flap also conceals the side cord anchor point hardware.

To get the side cord through the top cable sleeve, tie the string that the manufacturer put in the cable sleeve to the eye of the cord, and pull the other end of the string to draw the cord through the cable sleeve in the edge of the top until it emerges. Grab ahold of the cord to keep it from retracting back into the sleeve. Secure the end of the cord to the front of the side rail with a retainer screw. Straighten out the side material of the top, and proceed to the other side to repeat the cord installation.

Bow Sleeve Retainers

While the top frame is still half retracted, the bow sleeve retainers can be inserted into the bow sleeves. Center the retainer in the bow sleeve and then secure it to the cross bow with the small trim screws. Use a #2 Phillips screwdriver to tighten the screws snug to the cross bow.

Glue the Flaps

At this point, the top side flaps can now be affixed to the side rails. Raise the top and latch it to the windshield. Apply contact cement to the frame rail and the underside of the flap. When the contact cement is dry to the touch, press the flap onto the side rail. Make sure that the edge

of the top material is at the edge of the frame rail so that the binding on the top lies smooth and even along the side rail of the top frame.

Header Trim

To finish off the front of the new top, the stainless trim molding and rubber weather seal must be fitted across the header bow. The

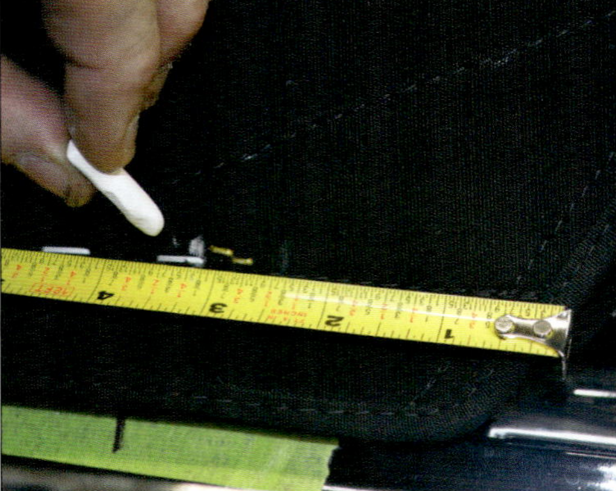

Fasteners and nuts are used to retain the weatherstrip to the side rail of the convertible top frame. A wrench is used to tighten the fastener of the weatherstrip seal to the side rail. The rubber weatherstripping helps keep out the wind and rain when the convertible top is in the up and latched position.

Along the bottom to the header bow is a rubber weather seal. The seal is held in place by a retaining strip and several machine screws. Once the weather seal is attached, it will also anchor the decorative stainless header trim in place.

convertible top needs to be unlatched and lowered enough to gain access to the front edge of the convertible top frame.

The stainless trim molding is fit over the leading edge of the top material and secured to the header bow from underneath with small machine screws. Before the trim can be secured, the rubber weather seal must be installed along the bottom of the header bow and over the stainless trim. Now, the machine screws can be inserted through the seal retainer and rubber seal. Evenly tighten the screws to hold the weather seal and trim in place.

Rubber Weatherstrip

While the top frame is still in the half-lowered position, the roof rail seals can be installed. Make sure that the special T-fasteners are inserted into the rubber seal and align the seal to the frame rail. Reinstall the nut fastener on the back side of the frame

rail. Do not overtighten the fasteners because that causes the rubber to distort. When the rubber seals are in place, the top frame can be lowered and then latched to the windshield.

Wire-On Welt

The last task that needs to be performed is the installation of the wire-on welt. This special trim is used to conceal the staples that hold the top material in place along the beltline and across the top of the rear bow.

Begin with the beltline wire-on. The wire-on runs from one side to the other along the rear deck bow. Each end of the wire-on finishes about 3 inches from the vertical rise in the sail panel. Locate the leading edge of the deck bow tack rail by feeling through the top material, and make a small chalk mark to indicate the end point of the tack rail. Repeat this procedure on the other side.

Place the wire-on welt onto the sail of the top about 3/16 inch inward from the chalk mark with the small bead on the bottom. Put a 3/8-inch staple in the end of the wire-on welt to secure it to the tack rail. Now, gently pull the wire-on welt along the lower deck rail to straighten the welt. Carefully staple the wire-on welt to

Take a measurement for a reference mark that will indicate a starting point for the attachment of the beltline wire-on welt. The setback usually begins at the forward end of the tack strip, which will allow the top material to move without damaging the top material when the top is folded.

the tack rail while keeping even spacing along the bottom edge of the convertible top.

Continue stretching the wire-on welt along the lower skirt of the rear curtain and onto the other sail panel. Cut the wire-on welt about 3/8 inch from the chalk mark and finish by stapling it. Use a plastic mallet to close the wire-on welt over the staples.

Locate the wire-on tips so that they do not extend past the chalk mark, and secure the tip to the rail

Make sure the stainless steel welt tip is in the correct place before it is fastened to conceal the cut end of the wire-on welt. This decorative element will complete the installation of the beltline wire-on.

Fasten a stainless steel welt tip on the end of the rear bow wire-on welt to cover the raw end and seal the welt from the elements. The tip extends only 3½ inches past the deck seam of the top, and it is fastened in place with a small finish screw.

with the tip screw. If the welt tip extends past the tack rail, it will create a hole in the top material, and it will also cause the tip to become loose, which will make a bigger hole in the top.

To finish off the top, the rear bow wire-on welt will need to be installed. This welt will cover the staples that hold the top material to the top of the rear bow. The end of the wire-on welt begins 3½ inches from the deck seam in the top. If it were any lower, the top would not fold correctly and the wire harness in the pad could be pierced.

Use 3/8-inch staples to attach the wire-on across the rear bow and flatten the wire-on to conceal the staples. Install the welt tips with a #1 Phillips screwdriver.

Clean Up

Remove the side drape and tacking guide tape from the car and clean away any fingerprints or smudges that you may have left behind. Vacuum the car, and remove any staples or debris that may have accumulated in it while you worked. It might also help to give the top a good steaming to help relax any box wrinkles and make the top look like it was just pressed.

With the new convertible top installed, it will need a quick steaming to help relax away any remaining box wrinkles in the material. Before the car goes out onto the street, it will also receive a coat of RaggTopp protectant to prevent UV rays from damaging the material.

THE SCISSOR TOP

By the early 1970s, the popularity of the convertible was waning due to the lack of creature comforts. Features such as air-conditioning and stereo sound systems were previously not offered in convertibles and were now desired by the consumer. Also, in an effort to appeal to the family, a larger car with a full-size rear seat was what Detroit thought would revive this slump in sales.

In 1971, General Motors released a whole new concept in the hideaway convertible top design. All five GM divisions offered the newly developed Hideaway Top in their full-size models. This style of folding top frame soon became better known as the scissor top because of the unique way it folds and stacks behind the rear seat of the car. Cadillac was the last of the American auto manufacturers to produce a convertible model car until the 1980s. The final Eldorado convertible was produced on April 21, 1976.

A reintroduction of the American convertible happened in 1982 with the Chrysler LeBaron. Next to offer a convertible top option was General Motors with the 1983 Buick Riviera, and soon after Ford with the Mustang convertible.

Replacing a Scissor Top

Putting on a new top and curtain in a full-size GM car is not an easy task. These frames operate much differently and require a much stronger skill set than any other convertible top. Correcting problems that have developed over the years can become expensive and frustrating.

I highly recommend that you contact Convertible Service and get a copy of the *GM Full Size Convertible Top Manual* before you begin. There are a lot of diagrams and procedural information in the manual that will guide you through the proper way to install your new top.

One of the first things that you will notice about the top frame is that there are no hydraulic cylinders used to move the top down and up. Another thing that jumps out at

This 1976 Cadillac Eldorado was one of the last American convertibles produced for the era. The unique way that the top folded was stylish and yielded more passenger space, but it proved to be very problematic and difficult to service.

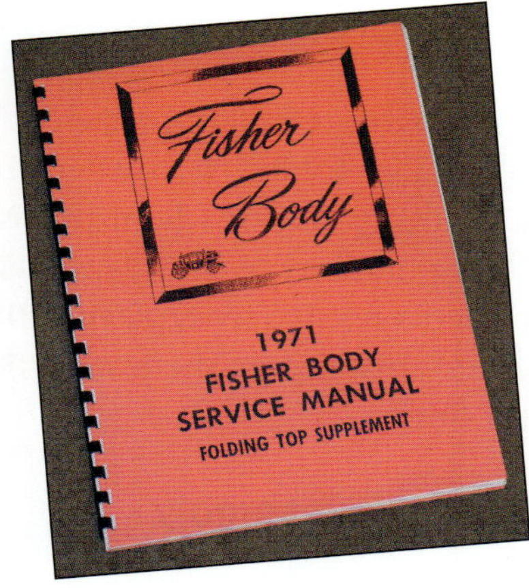

This excerpt from the GM service manual is a must-have item when working on the scissor top. Inside are many detailed drawings and step-by-step procedures that will help get your convertible back into proper working order.

you is that the top frame folds in upon itself as it folds away behind the rear seat of the car, almost like something from a *Transformers* movie.

Getting Started

Before unlatching the top from the windshield, check the trunk of the car and verify that there is nothing in the well area. Removing any and all objects from the rear of the car will prevent the rear glass from being broken when the top is lowered.

Drape the back of the car to protect the paint from damage before any work begins. Now, unlatch the

top and operate it through its complete cycle. Determine if there are any issues with the way it operates by lowering it and then raising it fully.

Begin by lowering the top into the well of the car. As the top folds, watch and listen to isolate any binding or grinding sounds that could indicate that there is a problem with the top frame. As the top frame begins to lower, the right side rail will fold inward followed by the left side rail. The rear window or curtain

Inside the trunk of the car we can see that there are spring-loaded retractors to aid in repositioning the rear glass window. The area under the well liner must be kept clear of all objects to prevent the glass from being crushed when the top is retracted.

This top actuator is one of two that work in unison to make the top go up and down. They have taken the place of the traditional hydraulic cylinders used on conventional convertible tops. Inside the device are gears driven by a square cable that is connected to an electric motor.

Taking the place of the hydro-electric pump on a traditional convertible is this small electric motor. The motor is activated by a small relay that tells the motor which direction to turn the square steel drive cables that connect to the top actuators.

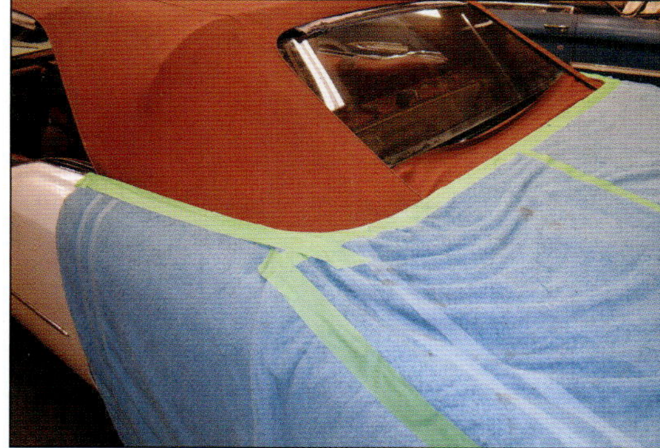

Before any work begins to replace the old convertible top, a protective padding is applied to the back of the car to shield the paint from any accidental damage that could happen while the new top is being installed.

will begin to retract into the well and make room for the top frame to nest or stack.

Raise the top and latch it to the windshield. Make notes on any problems that were encountered during the inspection of the convertible top. These issues must be corrected before the new top is installed.

One of the more obvious problems encountered during a test on a 1976 Cadillac Eldorado was a failure with the spring-loaded rear window retractor that resulted in a broken rear curtain. An unsuitable retainer pin clip was used to hold the retractor rod in place, and it broke, causing the spring-loaded retractor to jam and the glass to retract improperly. As the top frame folded, it crushed the glass. Nothing else was bent or broken, but it made a mess. The problem is simple to resolve by replacing the incorrect pins and washers with the correct ones.

Disassembly

To make access to the well area, remove the rear seat's bottom cushion by pushing in and lifting the cushion up and out of the car. A T50 Torx bit is used to remove the seat belt retractors that anchor the rear seat's backrest to the car before it can be removed and set aside. Now, use a panel clip lifting tool to remove the fasteners holding the boot retainer along the top of the well liner. Then, lift the retainer and well liner away from the backrest support.

Disassembling the Top

1 *A panel clip lifting tool is used to remove the small fasteners retaining the boot fastener along the top edge of the seat support. After the fasteners have been removed, the well area of the car can be easily accessed to reach other components.*

2 *Lower the convertible top into the well of the car to gain access of the rubber weath- erstrip. Use a screwdriver to remove the retainer screws from the outer corners of the rubber weatherstrip that are found on the underside of the header bow.*

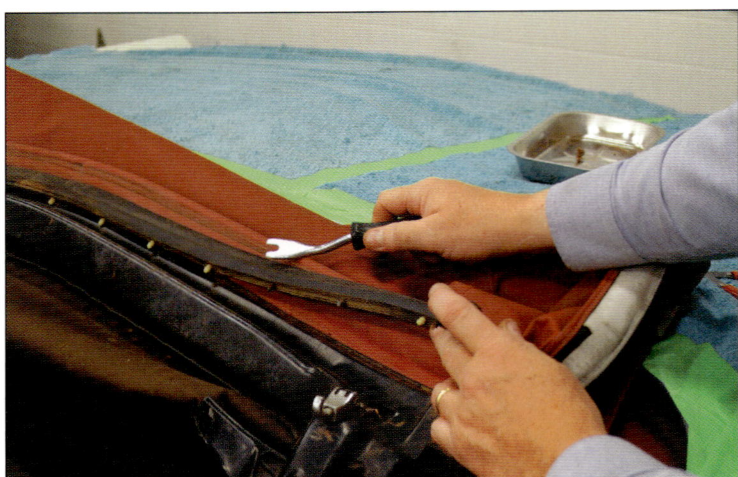

3 *While the convertible top is in the lowered position, a panel clip tool is used to access the small plastic T-fasteners holding the rubber weatherstrip onto the under- side of the header bow and lift them out of their retainer holes.*

Disassembling the Top *Continued*

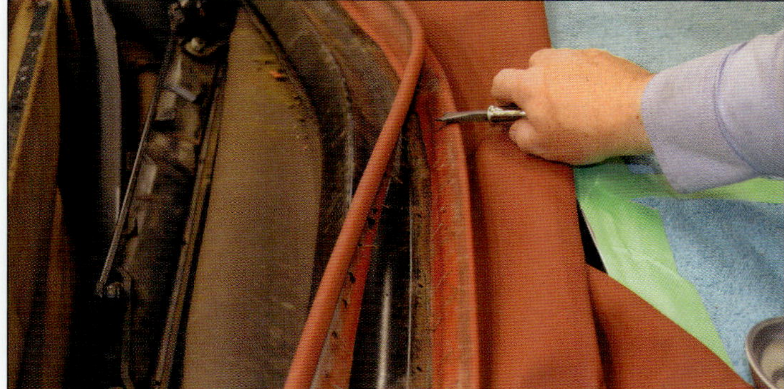

4 *Remove the front weather seal from the leading edge of the header bow with a staple puller. The weather seal has a 1/2-inch foam core, and it is the first line of defense to repel the wind and rain on a convertible top.*

5 *During the removal of the top material from the header bow, we soon realize that the tack strip material is damaged and no longer serviceable. Fortunately, the metal retaining tabs underneath are still in good condition and able to hold the new tack strip.*

6 *With the convertible top material pulled back from the header bow, the leading end of the side hold-down cable is visible. The cable end is released from the header bow by unfastening the trim screw that retains it in place on the bow.*

Lower the top into the well and remove the inner rubber weather seal from the underside of the header bow. The rubber weatherstrip is held on the head header bow with small retainer screws and little T-fasteners that are inserted into the rubber of the weatherstrip. Use a #2 Phillips screwdriver to remove the screws at the ends of the rubber weatherstrip. Use a panel-lifting tool or a small pair of pliers to lift the plastic T-fasteners holding the body of the weatherstrip from the header bow.

Stapled across the leading edge of the header bow is the front weather seal. Removal of the weather seal can be done with a staple puller. Once the weather seal has been removed, it can be discarded.

While the top is still retracted, remove the staples across the leading edge of top material to release the material from the header bow tack strip. The condition of the header bow tack strip is most likely marginal, so it will have to be replaced after the top frame has been stripped, adjusted, and cleaned.

Raise the top about a foot from the windshield and pull back the top material from the header bow to reveal the side hold-down cables. The cables are attached to the header bow with a trim screw. Remove the screw and lift the end of the cable free from the top frame. Halfway back there is another short secondary cable that is part of the main cable. This secondary cable controls the action of the first bow and keeps it stable as the top is lowered and raised. Remove the small screw that holds the secondary cable to the first bow.

Control Links

Connected to a small bracket on the lower corner of the rear window are spring-activated control links. This device helps retract the rear window deeper into the well of the car to prevent the glass from getting broken when the top is retracted. They need to be disconnected so that the rear curtain assembly can be removed from the car and replaced.

While the top is still about a foot off the windshield, move to the rear and disconnect the spring-loaded guide links from the rear curtain. At the lower corner of the window you will see a bracket on each side that has a small, metal rod pinned to the bracket. The control link is under tension from a heavy spring in the trunk, so be very careful when working with the control link.

Connected to the rear window is the control link. This vital component aids in the proper retraction operation of the rear window. A small pin clip retains a washer and the upper portion of the control link arm to the rear curtain bracket.

Removing only the required bolts from the rear curtain assembly can be somewhat challenging. Shine a flashlight to illuminate the main lower bolt on the frame assembly to isolate the correct fastener so that it can be removed easily.

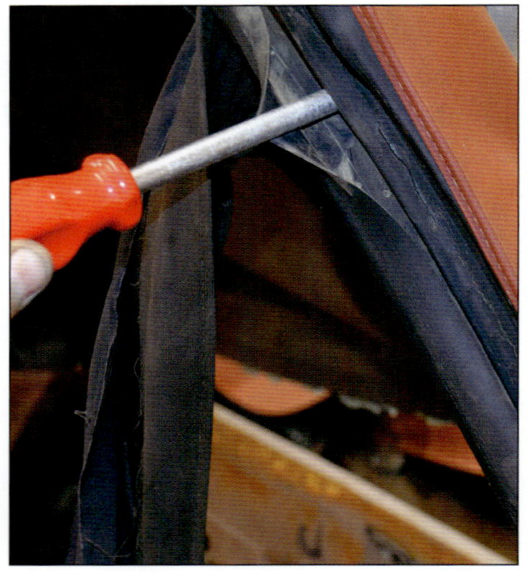

Use a Phillips screwdriver to remove the fasteners holding the side rail weather seals to the convertible top frame. Access to the lower screw sometimes requires the convertible top to be lowered about halfway down so that it can be reached.

control links have been disconnected from the rear curtain brackets, slide the control arms though the opening in the well liner and rest them on the floor of the well area.

Now, lower the top about halfway to gain better access to the rear rubber side rail weather seal fasteners. Use a #2 Phillips screwdriver to remove the three screws that hold the seal to the side rail. With the seals removed, you can now peel back the rear vertical side flaps that are glued to the side rail of the convertible top frame.

Rear Assembly Removal

Removing the rear curtain assembly from the car is not as difficult as it is cumbersome. Access to the mounting bolts is tight, and when they are removed, the entire rear frame section comes out of the well area as one unit.

Begin by lowering the top so that the header bow is a few inches off the windshield. Inside the rear quarter of the well are a lot of pivot points and many bolts that hold the convertible top frame to the car. Locate the lower main hinge bolt and use a 5/8-inch wrench to remove it. The retaining

Pull the pin that holds the control link to the bracket, and then remove the retainer washer. There is a small nylon bushing that a small rod goes through. Do not lose the nylon bushing when you remove the rod from the bracket. Hold the control link firmly and gently pull it from the bracket. Remember there is tension on the control link, so do not let it just snap out of control. After the

Important Tip

Be careful when removing or installing nuts and bolts so you do not drop the hardware into the forward wheel well. It is very difficult to retrieve anything that goes into no-man's-land. ◼

Remove the forward nut and bolt from the main hinge with two different wrenches. The locking nut requires a 9/16-inch wrench, and the pivot bolt uses a 5/8-inch wrench. It is a tight workspace, but it is easy to manage when the top is lowered about halfway.

nut for the bolt is permanently attached to the rear tack rail.

Lower the top about halfway to make access easier to the forward bolt and nut on the main hinge. Removal of the lock nut requires a 9/16-inch wrench. Loosen the nut and set it aside. The bolt can be loosened with a 5/8-inch wrench and unthreaded from the pivot point. The bolt passes through a bronze bushing. Do not lose the bushing because it must be in place when the unit is reassembled. Now that one side is unbolted, remove the same bolts from the other side.

Rain Gutter Clips

The scissor top has a soft cloth rain gutter that is made out of convertible top material. The rain gutter is attached with staples to the rear tack rail along one edge. It is attached on the other edge with a steel rod

From inside the trunk area, access the five retainer clips that hold the rain gutter to the beltline of the well opening. These clips can be opened to release the retaining rod inside the gutter so that the rear curtain unit can be removed from the car.

that runs through the length of the gutter, anchoring on each side of the top frame through a hole on the upper wheel well support.

To release the rain gutter from the car, crawl into the trunk to unclip the retaining rod from the beltline of the well opening. There are five metal clips that hold the gutter in place. There is a clip on each side of the trunk hinge and one in the center. Use a pry tool to bend the clip enough to release the gutter rod.

Move the front of the retaining rod forward to release it from the body of the car.

Lifting the Rear Assembly

To remove the rear tack rail and curtain assembly from the well of the car, use a pry bar. The pry bar helps you move the assembly far enough forward to come out of the well. Work one side forward and then the other until you can lift one rear corner of the assembly out. Then do the other. Rest the assembly on the protected deck of the car.

Removing the Rear Curtain and Accessories

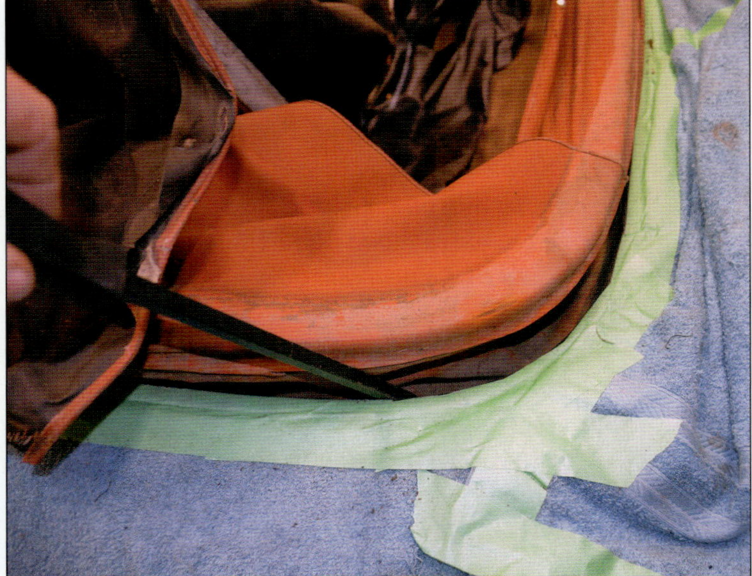

1 *Use a pry bar to assist in the removal of the rear curtain unit from the well area of the car. The unit is lifted from the well after moving it forward on both sides until there is enough room for the rear tack rail to clear the stainless outer molding.*

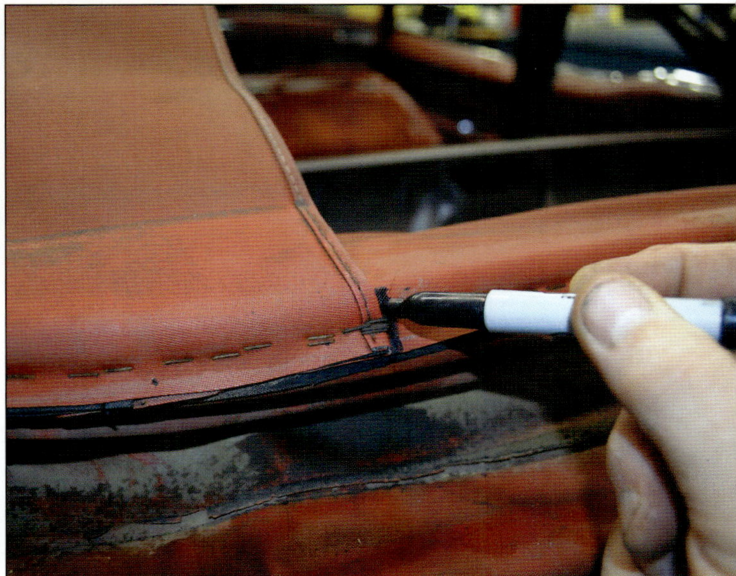

2 *To make installation of the new rear curtain quicker, make reference marks on the old top and curtain material to aid in the alignment of the new top components. A permanent marker is best suited for making the marks on the old material.*

Removing the Rear Curtain and Accessories *Continued*

4 *Before the old rear curtain material is removed from the rear tack rail, use a china marker to mark the leading edge of the rear curtain skirt onto the rear tack rail. This mark will help with the positioning and fitment of the new rear curtain when it is installed.*

3 *Along the edge of the rear tack rail are many staples that hold the old convertible top material, rear curtain, and other components in place. A staple puller makes quick work of lifting the staples to remove the old, worn-out material.*

5 *Side skirt material from the rear curtain extends around the rear tack rail to give support and help shape the sail area of the convertible top. Staples are removed from the lower edge of the rear curtain material with a staple puller.*

6 *An inspection shows that many cracks and small holes are compromising the integrity of the original rain gutter. Use a staple puller to remove the old rain gutter material from the rear tack rail so that a new rain gutter can be installed.*

Marking the Edge Positions

Before removing the old top materials, mark the end locations of the old top onto the curtain and rear tack rail. These marks can be used as a reference guide when you reassemble the top. Mark the end position of the old material with a permanent marker or china marker to indicate the edge position of the top panels.

For better transfer of the marker, it may be necessary to first wipe the dirt away from the surface of the top. Mark both the leading and trailing edges of the sail panel onto the rear tack rail and the rear curtain before removing any staples. The top material can now be removed from the rear tack rail with a staple puller.

Rail Staples

To remove the top material from the rear tack rail, use a staple puller to lift the staples along the edge of the rail. The staples and tool are sharp, so take care while working. You do not want to slip and gouge yourself or the car with the tool.

Curtain Markings

With the top material out of the way, you will be able to see the side skirts of the rear curtain. Mark the forward edge of the curtain with a china marker to indicate the end points of the curtain on the rear tack rail.

Lower Curtain Edge Staple Removal

Use the staple puller to lift the staples along the tack rail to free the lower edge of the curtain. Reposition the curtain material out of the way by moving it into the well area to allow better access to the remaining staples holding the well liner and rain gutter to the rear tack rail.

Well Liner and Rain Gutter

At this point you may need to replace the well liner and rain gutter. If the material is sun faded, torn, or damaged in any way, it would be a good choice to remove the old item and replace it with a new one.

Remove the well liner material from the rear tack rail by pulling the staples along the rear tack rail to release the old well liner material.

The final piece attached to the rear tack rail is the rain gutter. The scissor top has a soft floating rain gutter that contains a metal rod that is located inside the gutter sleeve. It acts as a shape retainer for the gutter and also gives the well clips something to hold on to. If the overall condition of the original rain gutter is poor, it should be replaced with a new one.

The raw edge of the rain gutter is attached to the rear tack rail with staples. Use a staple puller to remove the staples along the rear tack rail to release the rain gutter.

Removing the Old Top

Depending on the condition of the convertible top that you are working on, the cross bow listings may have already come loose from the inside top decking. The cross bow listings are the last remaining items that are holding the convertible top material to the frame.

To remove the old convertible top material, the rear section of the top is folded forward to expose the staples along the center bow of the frame. Remove these staples to release the listing. Do the same for the front bow. Fold the material back and remove the staples.

Before the convertible top material can be removed from the frame of the car, the side tension cable needs to be disconnected from the rear inner bow. The cable can be removed from the cable sleeve in the old top and reused if it is found to be in good condition.

Pad Removal

Because the old pads are torn and damaged, they are no longer serviceable and must be replaced with new, modern pads. Begin with peeling back the old pad material from the rear curtain assembly and removing the foam padding that is glued to the rear curtain stretcher. Remove the staples along the center bow that are holding the pad to the bow.

This convertible top was in very poor condition when it first arrived in my shop. It is not surprising that the underlying cross bow listings and support pads were in shreds. This top should have been replaced many years ago.

Anchored to the center bow of the top frame is the rear cross bow sleeve. It has detached from the convertible top decking and is now being removed. Inside of the bow sleeve is a foundational tack strip that helped keep the bow sleeve straight when it was stapled to the cross bow.

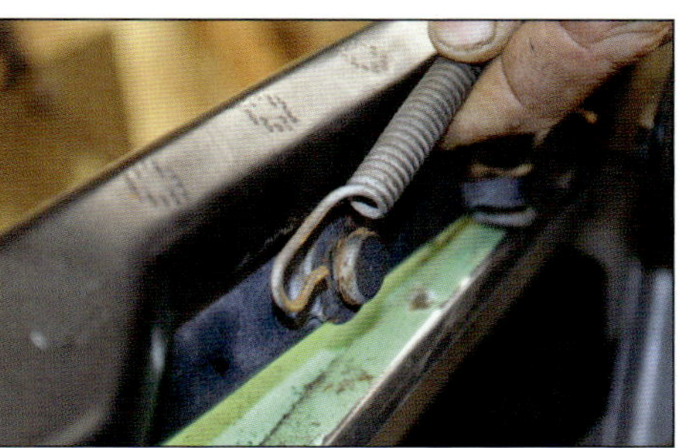

Unhook the side tension cable from the post at the inside of rear tack rail, and remove it from the cable sleeve that runs along the inside edge of the convertible top. The old convertible top material can now be set aside. You can use it as a reference guide when you are installing the new convertible top material.

The underlying foam of the convertible top pad has been damaged, and it will no longer be able to protect the convertible top from the frame. After the old pad cover material is removed, discard the foam filler along with the rest of the old pad materials.

The front of each pad is attached to the header bow with trim screws. The screws should be under a piece of protective body tape. Lift the tape to reveal the trim screws and remove them with a Phillips screwdriver. The old pad is no longer usable and it can be discarded.

Curtain Removal

A row of staples across the leading edge of the rear curtain extender are removed with a staple puller. Once the rear curtain is removed from the frame, the real work of adjusting, cleaning, and repairing the convertible top frame can begin.

Do not discard the rear curtain at this time. You will need to transfer the reference marks made earlier to the new top material. This will help with positioning during the reassembly of the convertible top.

Finally, remove the rear curtain from the top frame. The leading edge of the rear curtain extension is attached across the center bow with staples. Remove the staples with a staple puller, and lift the rear curtain from the top frame.

Servicing the Frame

With all the convertible top materials removed from the top frame, inspect it for damaged and worn parts.

The first thing I noticed was that the bolt for the front bow side pivot bracket was repaired, and the hold-down hardware did not fit properly. After disassembly, I noticed the stud that was welded had some bunged-up threads. When I chased the threads with a thread-cutting die, the stud came off due to the poor quality of the welding that was done. The stud should have never been welded in the first place, and now the side rail is in unusable condition.

First I thought this meant I would need to replace the side rail, and that can be a considerable expense. Instead, I machined a new hole in the bushing and tapped it with new threads to accept a new stud. A new bolt was threaded into the fitting and red Loctite was used to permanently retain the bolt. The head of the bolt was cut off, and the bolt was dressed down to match the height of the other bow stud, resulting in a perfect repair.

More typical problems include bent and worn components that result in the frame not preforming correctly. Procedures for checking for these issues are addressed in the white paper offered by Convertible Service. This guide, along with the Fisher Service Manual, will help resolve your ailing top frame issues.

The top frame should also be adjusted to accommodate the window operation and fit. This is done prior to fitting the new convertible top, and adjustments are made in the usual way. Replace any worn or damaged tack strips, and then clean and paint the frame to give it a fresh appearance.

When the old convertible top material and pads are removed from the frame, take a closer look at what needs to be repaired or replaced. Sometimes it shocks me to see what someone else has done to repair a top frame.

After all of the previous rework was removed, the side rail was machined, and a new stud was added to replace the broken unit. After the Loctite had set up, the head of the bolt was cut off, and the remaining stud was ready for finishing.

This is the completed repair of the side rail. The new stud was dressed down to the height of the original, and the hardware was added and secured just as it should be. This repair will outlast the new top and perform like it was never damaged.

Installing the New Top and Components

Now is a good time to check the movement of the top frame. You want to assemble the bare frame into the car and make sure that it performs properly before any new materials are added. If no other adjustments need to be made, the new top can be installed.

Rain Gutter

Prior to attaching the new rain gutter to the rear tack rail, the retaining wire will need to be inserted into the gutter sleeve. It is much easier to do this now compared to after the material is attached to the rear tack rail.

The new rain gutter is installed by stapling the raw edge of the material to the rear tack rail as it hangs downward across the rail. Beginning at the center point on the rear tack rail, the rain gutter is stapled in place by working from the center outward in both directions. Pull slightly on the gutter material to relieve any wrinkles as the fabric is stapled in place to the outer end of the tack rail.

Once the rear curtain assembly was removed from the car, we noticed that the condition of the original soft rain gutter was badly deteriorated and was no longer serviceable. A new rain gutter was made and stapled onto the rear tack rail.

Well Liner

The new well liner will drape over the top edge of the rear tack rail and hang down inside the well area of the car. Start stapling from the center point and move outward to the end of the tack rail in both directions. Keep the well liner material smooth and wrinkle free as you fasten it to the tack rail.

Rear Curtain Prep

Before the new rear curtain can be installed, some prep work is needed on the workbench to ready it for installation. The lower portion

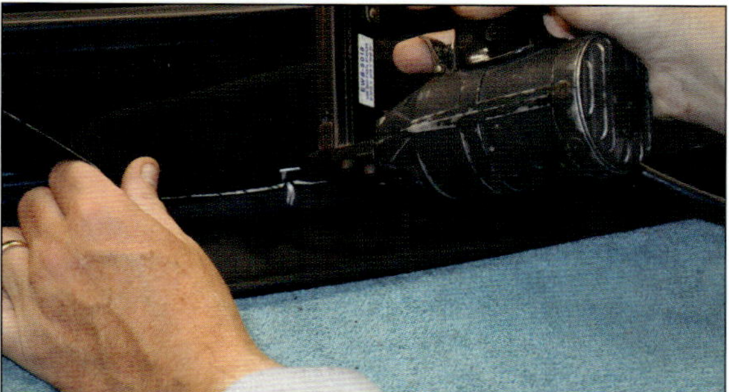

of the rear curtain is retracted into the well when the top is lowered by a pair of spring-loaded control links. The control links connect to the curtain by a small pin that passes through a metal bracket that is riveted in place along the lower corner of the glass window. The metal brackets can be reused or a new set can be acquired if the old set is damaged or deemed unusable.

Install the Link Brackets

First, remove the old control link brackets from the old curtain and transfer them to the new curtain.

Center the new well liner into position and staple it to the rear tack rail. Having a new well liner makes sense when the sun-faded and water-stained condition of the old well liner material left us no choice but to replace it along with the new top.

This is the new rear curtain unit that was just installed in the 1976 Cadillac. It took just a little more than two hours to prepare and refit the new curtain material to the convertible top frame. Great care was taken to make sure that the curtain will operate properly.

Installing the Link Brackets

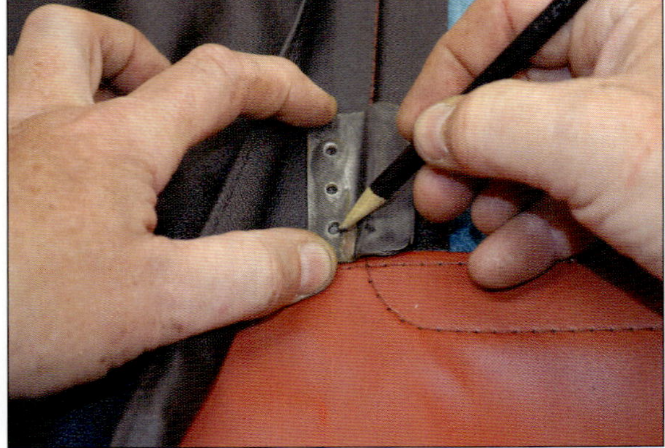

2 *When the correct placement of the control-link guide bracket has been established, use a pencil to mark the position for the through holes that will need to be made in the rear curtain material. The holes will allow the pop rivets to pass easily through the curtain material.*

1 *Remove the old retractor bracket from the old rear curtain. A 1/8-inch drill bit is used to drill through the old rivets that secure the bracket to the curtain material. After the bracket is removed, it will be attached to the new curtain.*

3 *Use a 1/8-inch punch to make a through hole in the lower portion of the rear curtain window material for a pop rivet. Use extra care when punching the through hole so that the glass window is not accidentally broken.*

4 *After the layout and positioning of the rear curtain window control link brackets have been determined, use three 1/8-inch aluminum pop rivets to secure each of the control link brackets to the lower portion of the rear curtain material.*

The brackets were held in place with 1/8-inch pop rivets, and they must be drilled out to release them from the old curtain material. Place a small scrap of plywood under the bracket as a backer when drilling through the old rivet. The bracket is made of two pieces of metal: a front and rear flange. Use a 1/8-inch drill bit to drill through the rivet without harming the bracket.

Now that the old brackets are free, lay the new curtain out over a protective cover on the workbench. Place the front piece in position on the new curtain and mark the location of the rivet holes on the curtain with a pencil. The correct position for the bracket is with the relief line of the bracket parallel to the glass and the bottom edge of the bracket just above the stitching on the skirt of the curtain. Do *not* try to mount the bracket on the glass because that will break the glass.

Pre-punch holes for the rivets in the curtain material with a 1/8-inch hole punch. Use a backer under the material when using the punch to get a good, clean hole. Be very careful that you do not hit the glass window because it will shatter.

Rivet the two bracket pieces together with three 1/8-inch aluminum pop rivets with a 1/4-inch grip range. Insert the rivet from the outside through the bracket and curtain material and into the inside bracket. Make sure that you have a good solid

Place the old curtain on top of the new curtain and transfer the alignment marks that were made before the old curtain was removed. Use chalk to mark the alignment positions onto the new material.

Only a few staples are used to temporarily hold the rear curtain extension in place to verify the correct positioning of the curtain material. After the lower portion of the curtain is secured, this top section can be adjusted to the correct tension.

Staple the rear curtain extension to the center bow of the convertible top frame. Notice that there are no staples in the pad flap of the extension material. This area will be filled with foam padding before it is finished.

connection. If the bracket is loose, it will eventually fail and tear out.

Once you are finished riveting the brackets onto the new curtain, line up the old curtain on top of the new curtain. Transfer the alignment marks made during the disassembly process to the new curtain. Use a piece of chalk or a grease pencil to mark the new position indicators on the new curtain material.

When the transfer of reference marks to the new curtain is finished, clean off any dirt smudges that may have been made by the old curtain, and move the new curtain to the car for installation.

Curtain Install

Begin by aligning the center mark of the rear curtain extension on the center bow. The edge of the material should be flush with the forward rib on the bow. Staple the material every 2 inches across the bow from the center point outward on both sides. Do not staple the top pad cover flap to the center bow at this time; it will be finished later.

Move to the lower skirt of the curtain, align the center point on

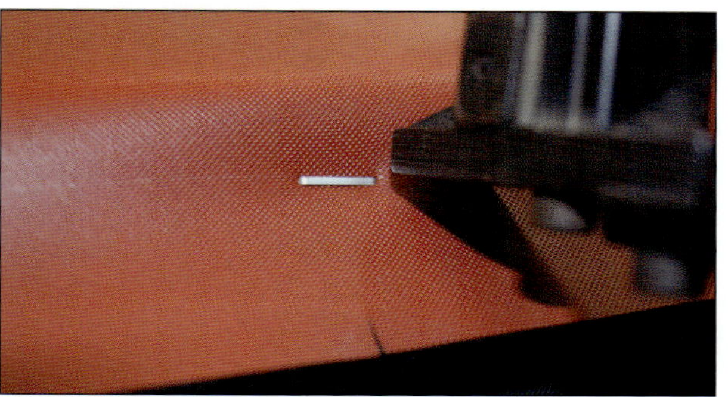

Place a staple at the center point of the rear curtain skirt after it is positioned in place along the rear tack rail of the top frame. The position of the skirt is checked for alignment and centering before additional staples are added.

the rear tack rail, and put a staple at the center point to hold it in position. Align and staple the skirt every 2 inches horizontally along the tack rail. Apply slight pressure on the skirt to give it a little stretch as you staple to help eliminate any wrinkles in the material. Do not over-stretch the material.

Staple the material up to the inside of the curtain flap, and then pull the material forward and over the staples to make the flap lie flat. Continue stapling every 2 inches until you reach the curtain end-point reference mark on the tack rail.

Protective Pad

After the curtain has been secured, the protective top pads can be installed. Normally, the protective top pads are installed first, but this is a scissor top, and nothing about this top is normal. The top pad is first secured along the center bow by opening the pad and stapling the deck material to the bow. Check the alignment of the pad by smoothing the pad forward toward the header bow, but do not attach it yet.

The pad is not secured to the first bow. This bow must be able to move without any additional restrictions. If the pad was attached to the bow, it would tear the pad and cause the top to bunch up, which would result in a broken rear window.

Insert the foam filler into the curtain extender pad flap all the way to the rear bow. Continue to fit it into the open pad up to the header

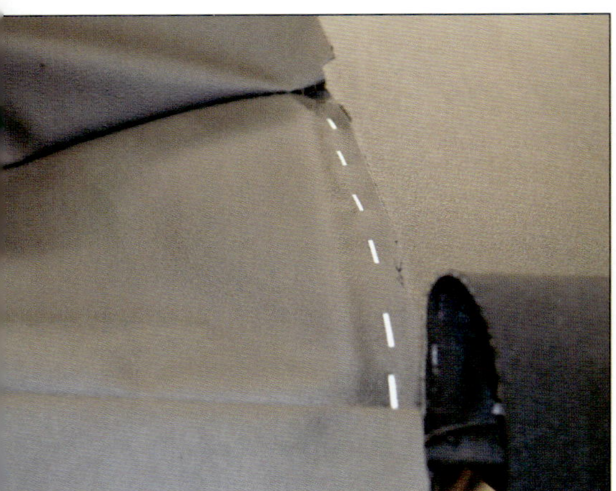

Use staples to anchor the base of the protective convertible top pad to the center bow of the top frame. The pad is applied on the inside of the rear curtain extension pad flap before it is filled with 1/4-inch foam padding.

Fit 1/4-inch foam padding into the open convertible top pad. The foam helps soften the frame against the convertible top material, preventing the top from chafing and abrasion while the top is run through the lowering and raising process.

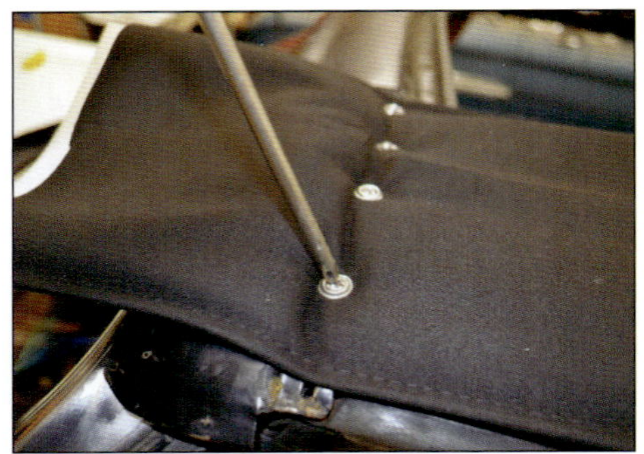

Washer-head trim screws are used to secure and seal the front of the convertible top pad to the header bow. Screws are used to fasten the pads in this application because they hold the material more securely and can take the stress of the folding top much better than the traditional tack strip and staples.

bow. The flaps of the pad can then be closed over the foam to hold it in place. Fold the inside flap first and then the outer to prevent any ballooning that may happen when the car is driven. Staple the end of the pad closed along the center bow to hold the foam in place. Carefully trim any excess pad material from the end of the center bow, taking care not to cut into the curtain extender.

There isn't a tack strip at the header bow that the pad would be stapled to. The front end of the pad on the scissor top is secured to the header bow by four 1/2-inch washer-head trim screws. You will notice that there are five trim screws holes and a small tab slot. The outer trim screw and tab slot will be used for the side tension cable.

Begin attaching the inside corner of the pad with a trim screw. Smooth the pad material forward to keep it wrinkle free and continue adding the trim screws.

Seal the edges of the pad flaps with contact cement. Brush glue onto both mating surfaces of the

Apply contact cement to the inside edge of the rear curtain extender flap by brush to seal in the 1/4-inch protective foam padding. Staple the leading edge of the flap closed to retain the foam padding in place.

After the rear curtain extender flap is filled with foam and glued closed along the outside edge, seal off the leading edge of the flap with a neat row of evenly spaced staples to keep the foam securely in place.

Apply a protective layer of Gorilla Tape over the tops of the center bow staples to prevent the top material from rubbing on the staples and causing abrasions during the folding process. The tape also smooths over the underlying surface to give the top a nice appearance.

pad and press them together to encapsulate the foam material. Also glue the rear curtain flap along the outer edge to seal in the foam pad.

The flap on the rear curtain extender is now secured to the center bow with a row of staples. The staples are then covered with Gorilla Tape to seal the staples from the weather and also protect the top material from rubbing on the staples.

Fitting the New Top

Before the new convertible top can be installed, there are a few items to address. The first is to locate the center point of the top so it can be properly positioned on the frame. Prep the new top by folding it in half, and use a china marker or pencil to mark the center point on the bow sleeves. This mark will be used to align the top to the frame.

After the bow sleeves are marked, a 1/2x36-inch piece of upholstery tack strip can be inserted into the bow sleeve. The tack strip material is a medium-weight tagboard that will

serve as a foundation for the bow sleeve to be fastened to the cross bow of the convertible top frame.

Rear Bow Sleeve

Lay the new top over the frame and fold the rear section of the top material forward to reveal the rear bow sleeve. With the sleeve material flat and smooth, align the center mark on the bow sleeve with the center point of the center bow of the convertible top frame. Attach the material to the center bow with one staple.

To keep the bow sleeve material straight along the edge of the cross bow and give something a little more substantial for the staples to hold on to, insert a piece of upholsterer's medium-weight tack strip material into the bow sleeve.

Place a single staple at the center point of the bow sleeve to hold the top material in position after it was aligned on the center cross bow of the top frame. The single staple will allow you to check the overall spacing and alignment of the top material.

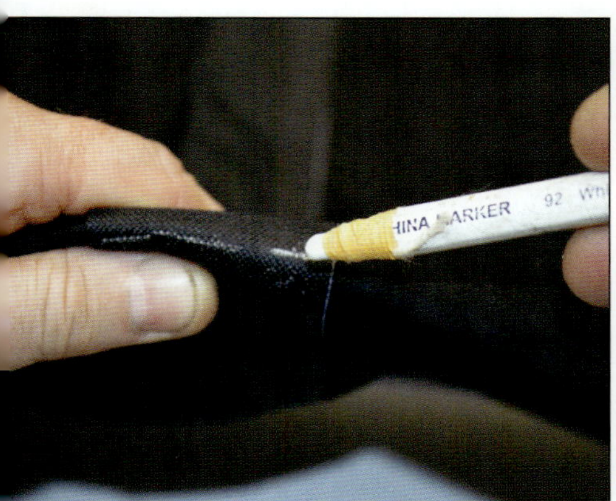

Before the new top can be applied to the frame, determine a center reference line by folding the top material in half to create the alignment point. Make a mark along the fold on the inside bow sleeves with a china marker.

The completed row of staples in the rear listing on the center bow of the top frame is shown. A slight adjustment was made to the center point of the listing to get an even margin of top material on both sides of the frame rail.

Check the fit and spacing at each frame rail to make sure that the top material is positioned equally on both sides. The top material must be in the correct position and fit squarely on the frame, otherwise the new top will not fit right. Make any adjustments necessary before proceeding.

Smooth the bow sleeve along the center bow. Give it a slight pull as you staple it in place from the center outward on both sides from the center point. Place the staples about 2 inches apart and keep them parallel to the center bow.

Side Cables

Before the top is attached to the rear tack rail, insert the side hold-down cable into the top cable sleeve. The cable sleeve runs along underside of the outside edge of the convertible top. The purpose of the hold-down cable is to help keep the convertible top material tight to the side rails of the frame, preventing the top material from buffeting as the car is driven down the road.

Tie the supplied string inside the cable sleeve to the front fastener of the cable, and pull the cable through the sleeve. If the manufacturer of the top did not insert a string, then use a stiff wire to hook the cable to pull it through the sleeve.

There is also a special shunt cable attached to each side cable that emerges about 18 inches back from the front of the top through an opening in the cable sleeve. This cable is about 2 inches long, and it attaches to the outside end of the first bow with a 1/2-inch long #8 pan-head sheet metal screw. The shunt cable helps keep the first bow in proper position as the top is lowered and raised.

Built into the convertible top is a cable sleeve that runs along the outside edge of the top. The side hold-down cable is drawn into the sleeve with a string left there for this purpose by the top manufacturer. When the string is tied to the cable end, it can be simply pulled through the cable sleeve.

Exiting the forward end of the cable sleeve is the front side tension cable anchor plate. A small trim screw will be used to attach this end of the side tension cable to the header bow of the convertible top frame, keeping it securely in place.

One very unique feature of the scissor top is the small shunt cable that branches off of the side tension cable. This short stubby cable emerges from the cable sleeve, and it will be connected to the outer end of the first bow to help control its movement.

Securing the Sail Panel

To secure the rear section of the convertible top to the rear tack rail, fold the top material back over the rear frame and align the inside edge of the window opening with the reference mark you transferred to the rear curtain. Center the material on the rear tack rail and place two staples in the material to hold it in position. Continue to move forward and fasten the sail panel material to the rear tack rail with staples about every 2 inches until the leading edge binding is 3/4 inch from the end of the tack rail. Place two staples at the end of the panel. Repeat this step for the other side of the top.

Install the rear curtain assembly into the well area of the car. Insert the ends of the rain gutter retainer wire into the retainer holes and lower the unit into the car.

For the rear curtain to perform as designed, the correct hardware must be properly installed to the rear curtain retainer bracket and lower control link–attaching stud. The hardware that was used on the top before we started working on it was not correct and had failed, leading to the glass window in our curtain to jam and break.

Reattach the rear window control links to the window brackets. Secure

A staple has been used to secure the new top material to the rear tacking rail after it has been properly aligned to the reference guide mark transferred from the original top. A minimal number of staples are used until the material fits perfectly.

A row of staples holds the front bow sleeve to the first bow. Inside the bow sleeve is a cardboard tack strip that acts as a foundation for the staples, allowing the bow sleeve to lie straight and smoothly across the surface of the first bow.

With the rear quarter sail panel of the convertible top aligned into position and properly adjusted to relieve any wrinkles in the material, the panel has been evenly stapled along the rear tack rail to hold the material securely in place.

Install a new hairpin clip on the upper control link stud to ensure that the control link will operate as it was designed to. Using makeshift hardware will result in an eventual failure of the control link, leading to a broken rear window.

the links to the window brackets with the correct hardware. The nylon bushing must be able to pivot in the bracket on the rear curtain, and the lower pin bushing must slide easily along the long slot in the control arm. Once the pin and bushings are inserted, use the retaining washer and locking pin to hold them in place. If you use the incorrect hardware, your rear glass curtain can malfunction and end up broken.

Secure the rear assembly to the car with the correct mounting bolts. Make sure that the pivot bushings are in place before installing the bolts. Raise the top and check the fit of the top material for wrinkles. You may need to remove the assembly to

make any necessary adjustments to the sail panels to remove any wrinkles that may still be in the panels.

Once you are satisfied with the look of the top material, the rain gutter can then be attached. From the inside of the trunk, reposition the rain gutter retainer rod back into the body, and secure the rod with the five retainer clips.

Front Bow Sleeve

Move to the front of the top and fold the material back to reveal the front bow sleeve. Adjust the tack strip so that it is centered inside the bow sleeve. Align the centerline of the bow sleeve with the center point of the bow, and place a staple through the bow sleeve and tack strip into the bow. Work your way from the center to the outer edges, stapling every 2 inches. The deck material of the top should be smooth and flat. Work out any wrinkles in the material before proceeding with the top installation.

Attaching the Cable

Lower the top about a quarter of the way down to give you enough slack to fasten the side cable to the header bow. Fit the tab of the side tension cable into the small slot in the header bow and secure the cable end with the correct trim screw. Cover the screw heads with Gorilla tape to protect the top from being damaged by the tops of the screws.

While the top is still retracted, attach the shunt cable to the front bow with a 1/2-inch #8 pan-head sheet metal screw. The screw goes into the end of the tack strip material

---

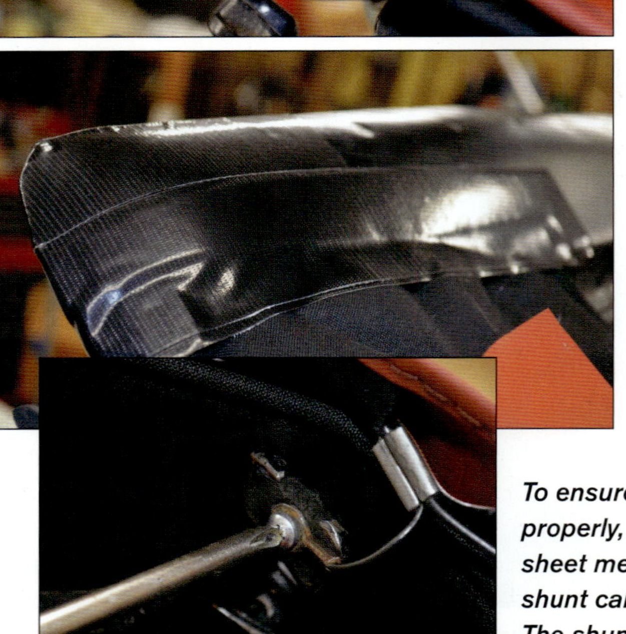

Side tension cables are used to help keep the convertible top material from buffeting when the car is moving at higher speeds. Fasten the cable end to the header bow with a trim screw to keep it from pulling loose when the top is latched.

A protective layer of Gorilla Tape is used to shield the inside of the top decking from the heads of the pad's fastener screws. Without the protective layer of tape, the top material can become damaged by rubbing on the screw heads.

To ensure that the first bow moves properly, use a small pan-head sheet metal screw to attach the shunt cable in the end of the bow. The shunt cable is part of the side tension cable that helps hold the top material tight to the frame.

Unlatch the top from the windshield and lower the top until it is almost vertical. Begin at a front corner and pull the top material over the edge of the header until the reference line is about 1/4 inch past the edge of the header bow. Align the bound outside edge of the top with the outer edge of the header and fold the front retainer flap inward. Tuck the flap under the top decking, and staple the top material to the tack strip that is on the underside of the header bow. Repeat this on the other corner of the top.

Work inward to the deck seam, keeping the same distance on the reference line, and add two more staples. Raise the top, latch it to the windshield, and then check to see how much more tension you may need to put on the top decking to relieve the slack in the top material.

Continue this process of adjusting the top decking until the top material is evenly tensioned on the top frame. Then, finish stapling across the header bow every 2 inches to secure the top decking to the header bow.

on the bow. The shunt cable is an important feature for the scissor top to function properly. If the cable is not attached to the bow, the bow will move incorrectly and damage the top and other parts of the top frame.

Bow Fix

If the shunt screw is too loose and does not tighten, it may be necessary to add a sliver of waterproof panel-board material into the hole to help give the screw some bite. In some cases, the tack strip material is severely damaged or missing altogether. If you encounter this condition, a small block of aluminum can be fashioned to fit into the end of the bow and staked into place. The shunt cable can then be attached by drilling a hole in the end of the aluminum block and tapping the block to accept a #8-32 machine screw.

Secure the Leading Edge

Raise the top and latch it to the windshield. Pull the top decking over the front of the header bow. With a pencil or chalk, mark the leading edge of the header bow onto the top material. This will give you a reference as to how much to pull the top when it is fastened to the header bow.

Make a chalk mark as a reference line across the leading edge of the top decking material to help with the tensioning of the top material. Without a visual guide, it would be very difficult to reposition the top material to eliminate unwanted wrinkles in the top decking.

The wrinkle that has formed in the top decking material at the center bow will need to be removed. Correcting this condition can be done by pulling the top material over the header bow and adding more tension to the top material.

Weather Seals

Size and fit the 1/2-inch rubber-core weather seal to the leading edge of the header bow. Lower the top until it is almost vertical, and attach the weather seal by blind stapling it to the tack strip on the underside of the header bow. Apply contact adhesive to the inside of the weather seal to protect and conceal the staples from the weather.

Install the rubber lower weather seal to the underside of the header bow. The rubber seal is held in place on the header bow with small plastic T-fasteners and trim screws. Snap the T-fasteners into the holes along the underside of the header bow, and use the correct mounting screws at the outer corners of the seal to anchor the seal in place.

While the top is still retracted, reinstall the rubber rear quarter roof rail weather seals. After the weather seals are secured to the top frame, the convertible top can be raised and locked to the windshield.

The Finished Top

At this point, inspect the top for any imperfections and clean away any smudges or fingerprints that may have been left behind while you were working on the top installation.

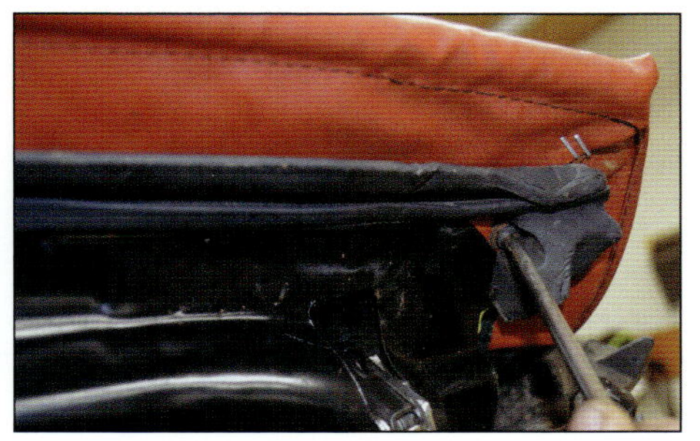

The main weather seal is blind stapled to the underside of the header bow to shield and protect the staples from rusting due to the elements. This larger rubber-core seal is the primary barrier to divert wind and rain from entering the car.

Give the top a good steam to help relax away any leftover box wrinkles. Carefully run the top through the down-and-up sequence, and make sure that the top folds correctly. Be

One of the very last things to do is refit the rear quarter rubber weather seal on the Eldorado. The top has been retracted to make the installation and access to the screws much easier. The weather seal also helped hold the rear side flap in position on the frame rail.

Small trim screws are installed at the ends of the inner rubber weather seal to keep it from shifting out of place. The main body of the weather seal is held in place by small plastic T-fasteners that push into small holes in the header bow.

absolutely sure that there is nothing in the trunk area that could possibly cause the rear curtain to jam, otherwise it will be crushed when the top is folded.

The new top installation has been completed and tested on the Cadillac Eldorado. After a final inspection and a little steam to remove some of the box wrinkles, this Detroit classic is ready for the open road and many more years of enjoyment.

TWO-PIECE TOPS

The most common top application found on an American-made convertible is the two-piece top. Logically, the name is derived from the two major components of the top: the main top decking and the rear curtain.

Installation of a convertible top is not as complicated as you may think, but it does take time and some skill to make the top fit and work correctly. Prior to any work being done, the convertible top mechanism and hydraulic systems should be checked for damage and repaired accordingly to ensure that the top will perform properly. After this inspection, parts for repair and the new top, curtain, and pads can be ordered. Work should not begin until all of the necessary components have arrived and are ready for installation.

Verify Correct Elements

Remove the new top from its packaging, and lay it over the old top. Verify that the item is the correct size, color, and fit for the make and model of the car that you are working on.

Before you begin taking the old top off, verify the current rear bow height by measuring from the center point on the rear beltline trim to the middle of the rear bow. Some people like to use a yardstick for this procedure, but I prefer using a retractable tape measure. Although a yardstick is rigid and easy to use, it also poses a

This 1967 Oldsmobile 442 came in after it was repainted, and it is now ready to have a new top installed. The rear portion of the top was removed from the body so that the body shop could get to the pinch-weld area for a better paint finish.

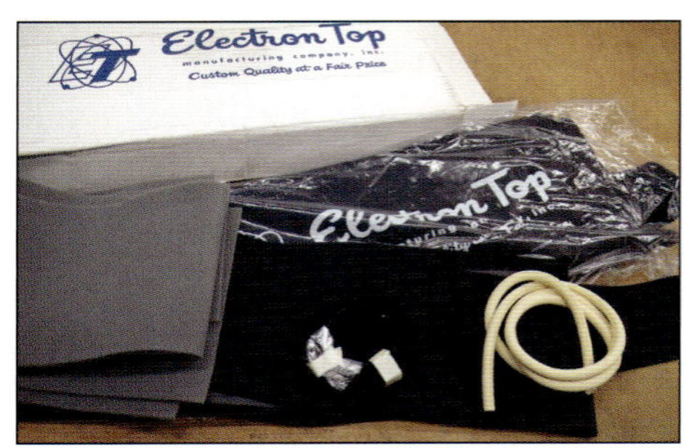

Inside the box of a premade convertible top, you would typically find all the new components needed to replace a top. The basic pieces that are needed include the main top, rear curtain, pads, front weather seal, and the wire-on welt with screws and tips.

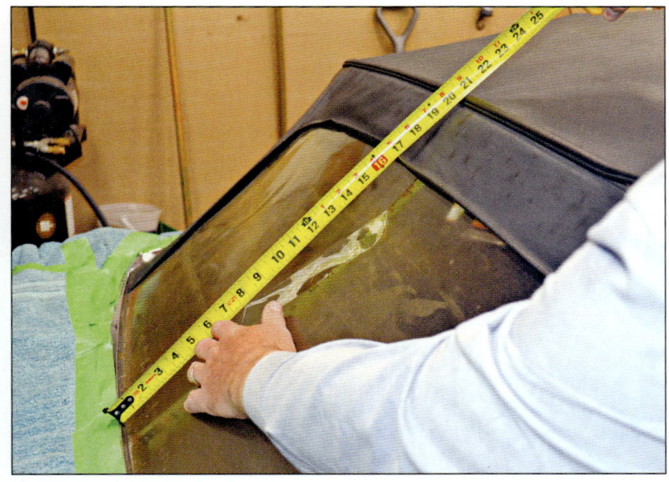

Before removing the old convertible top material, it is a good idea to check the rear bow height. This measurement can be compared to the manufacturer's recommended measurement to ensure that the new top material will fit the frame of the car properly.

possible chance that the car could be damaged if it comes in contact with the sheet metal.

Compare the existing measured bow height of the car to the measurement specified by the top manufacturer. They should be the same, but if there is a difference, call the top supplier to double-check the correct rear bow height. Now, roll the windows down on the car. This will make it easier to work on.

Protect the Car

To prevent any accidental scratches or damage to paint on the car, the work area should be draped with a soft but heavy padded material. Moving blankets make a perfect car drape. I use large bath towels that have been doubled up and sewn together to drape the car. The towels are soft and yet thick enough to protect the painted surface of the trunk and rear fenders of the car.

Attaching the drape to the car is done with quality painter's tape. The adhesive properties of painter's tape make it an ideal product to use for this application. While the adhesive on painter's tape is strong enough to hold the drape securely in place, the tape can be safely removed when the project has been completed. The adhesive on standard masking tape and duct tape are too aggressive and can damage the painted surface of the car, and they can also leave a sticky residue on the car.

The tape should be applied to the stainless beltline trim of the car if possible (any time you can tape to a solid surface is better than a painted surface) and to the edge of the drape.

The tape will also give you a place to make reference marks for the repositioning of the new top. After the draping has been applied and before the old top has been disturbed, make a reference mark onto the tape, indicating the location of the edge of the binding from the old top that will reference the curtain opening.

The adhesive properties of the painter's tape will allow for the safe removal of the tape when the project is completed. Other types of tape may harm painted surfaces.

Protecting the paint and finish is done with a soft, padded drape. The drape is secured to the stainless pinch-weld molding around the well area of the car with a quality painter's tape. Preventing damage to the car's painted finish is well worth the time and effort.

Remove Wire-On Tips

Running across the rear bow is the wire-on welt. Covering the raw ends of the wire-on are stainless steel welt tips. These pieces are held in place with 3/4-inch-long #6 oval-head trim screws. Remove the screws with a #1 Phillips screwdriver. A new top should have come with new tips and screws, so the old tips can be discarded. If the top did not include new tips, clean and reuse the old hardware.

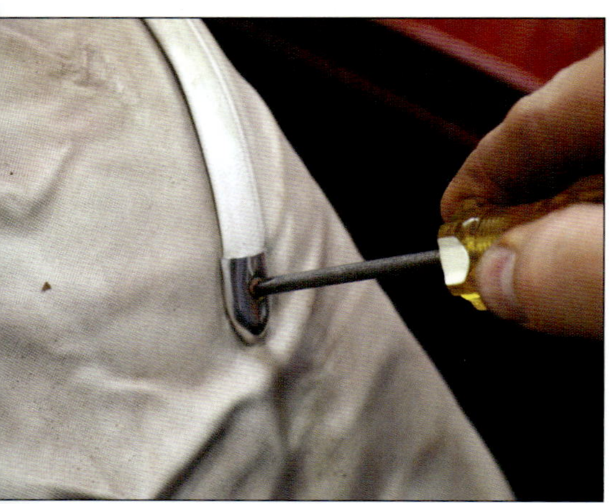

To reveal the end of the wire-on welt, the screw of the stainless steel tip is removed with a #1 Phillips screwdriver. Once the decorative tip is removed, it will reveal the raw end of the wire-on welt. New tips should be supplied with the new top, so the old one can be discarded.

Disassembly

There are several items to remove before you can move on.

Wire-On Welt

The wire-on welt is held in place by tacks or staples. The fasteners are concealed inside the wire-on, and they can be found by lifting the large part of the wire-on up to expose them. Remove the wire-on welt by pulling the staples that hold it to the

Folded inside of the wire-on welt are many staples or tacks that hold it in place along the rear bow of the top frame. A staple puller makes easy work of lifting the wire-on welt up for removal.

Magnetic trays are handy for collecting the staples, tacks, and trim hardware as it is removed from the convertible top. I prefer to keep the hardware that will be reused separated from the staples and parts that need to be discarded.

rear bow, and throw the old wire-on away.

With the wire-on off the car, more staples along the rear bow will be visible. Removal of these staples releases the top material from the rear bow.

As you work, the removed staples and hardware can end up everywhere. This is messy and can lead to other problems such as lost hardware and flat tires. The solution is to use a magnetic tray to collect the discarded items.

Rubber Weatherstrip

Now is a good time to roll all the windows down. It will be much easier to access the top frame with the glass out of the way.

Along the outer frame rails of the top are the rubber weather-

Removing the old, rubber roof rail weather seals is done by accessing and removing the screws and/or nuts that hold them in place along the perimeter frame of the top. This hardware should be retained for the reinstallation of the new rubber weather seals.

strip moldings. These moldings are attached with machine screws and sheet metal screws. Unlatch the top from the windshield and lower the top halfway to gain better access to the attaching hardware on the inside of the side rails.

Header Bow

Continue to lower the top frame all the way into the well of the car. This will clearly expose the many components that are attached to the underside of the header bow, allowing easy access for them to be removed.

A rubber weatherstrip seal is glued to the underside of the header bow. It will also most likely have a metal retainer strip holding it in place. Remove the screws and the metal retainer strip, and then scrape off the old rubber weatherstrip. Discard the rubber, but keep the retainer so that it can be reused.

Along the leading edge of the header bow is a thick weather seal. The weather seal is made of 1/2-inch rubber core covered in matching top material. This seal can also be removed and discarded.

Stapled to the header bow tack strip is the leading edge of the convertible top material. Pull the staples that are holding the material to release it from the header bow.

The leading edge of the convertible top is attached to the underside of the header bow. Removing the tacks and staples will free it from the header bow. The underlying tack strip material will need to be checked and replaced if it is in poor condition.

Side Flaps

Along the front and rear side quarters of the top are small flaps of topping material that have been glued to the side rails of the convertible top frame. These flaps need to be peeled off of the frame rails to reveal the side cables and the attachment hardware.

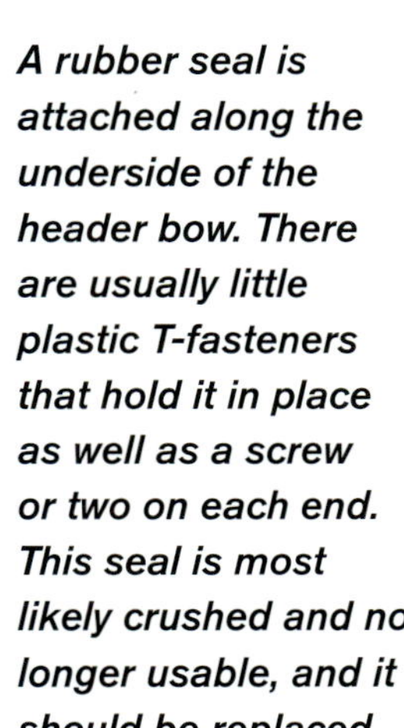

A rubber seal is attached along the underside of the header bow. There are usually little plastic T-fasteners that hold it in place as well as a screw or two on each end. This seal is most likely crushed and no longer usable, and it should be replaced with a new seal.

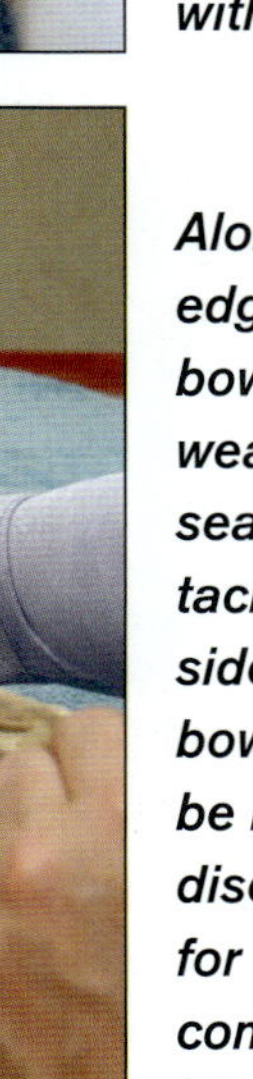

Along the leading edge of the header bow is the main weather seal. This seal is stapled or tacked to the underside of the header bow and needs to be removed and discarded. Materials for a new seal should come with a new top kit.

The front retaining flaps of the convertible top were glued in place. Before the top material can be removed, peel the flaps back from the frame. This will reveal the front side tension cable fastener.

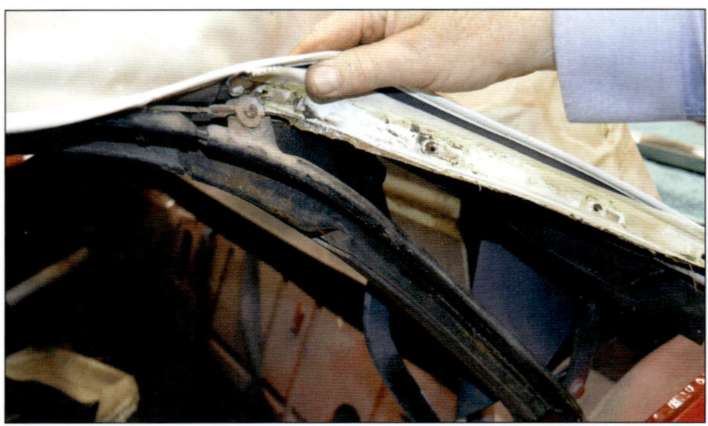

Glued along the vertical frame rail is the rear retaining flap. This flap is also peeled back from the frame to release the top material and expose the rear side tension cable fastener.

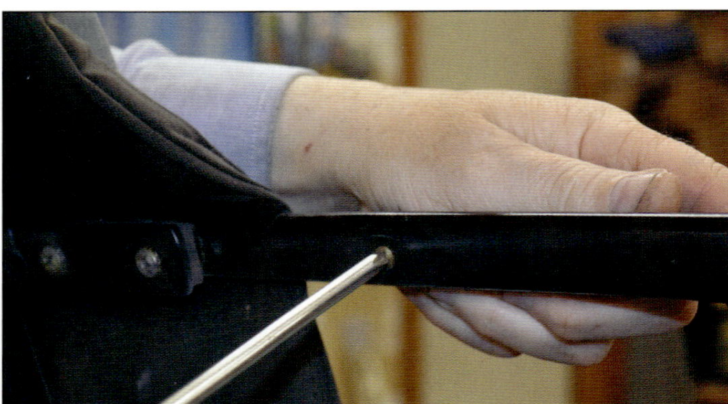

The second bow of this model of car has an inside bow sleeve with a retainer bow. Use a Phillips screwdriver to remove the four small screws that secure the retainer to the bow. Remove the inner bow retainer from the bow sleeve and set it aside.

Side Cables

A feature added to cars in 1963 was side rail cables. Earlier convertible tops did not have bow sleeves or side cables, and the convertible top would balloon up and slap against the frame, creating a buffeting effect when the car was in motion. To correct this annoying problem, cable sleeves were added to the outer edges of the convertible top and side cables were inserted to help hold the top material tight to the frame.

With the top frame halfway up, the convertible top material can be pulled out of the way to reveal the end of the side cable. The cable may be fastened with a screw or rivet, or it could have a ball end that slides into a retainer in the frame. Remove the cables from the top frame and pull them free from the bow sleeve in the top.

Bow Sleeve Retainer

Some cars have an extra blind bow sleeve built into the top. An inner bow retainer is inserted and screwed to the second and sometimes the third bows to help prevent the top from buffeting when the car is traveling at highway speed.

To remove the bow sleeve retainer, raise the convertible top halfway up, which takes the tension off the top material to gain access to the second and third bows. The bow retainer can now be removed by unscrewing the retainer screws from the cross bow.

Remove Rear Seat

Place a soft towel across the top of the windshield to protect the windshield molding from being

With the header bow unlatched from the windshield, the side tension cable screws can be removed. The tension cable can be removed from the cable sleeve in the top and inspected for possible reuse. If the cables show any sign of damage or wear, they should be replaced.

To gain better access to the rear well area and tack rail, remove the rear seat from the car. The rear panels may also be removed if you are going to service the hydraulic system with new cylinders and hoses.

scratched. Then, raise the top frame all the way up but do not latch the top.

Removal of the rear seat will give you better access to the rear tack rail. The bottom seat cushion is removed by pushing in and then pulling up along the lower edge of the seat. The backrest is anchored by metal tabs or sheet metal screws. Remove the fasteners at the bottom of the seat, and lift the backrest up and out of the car.

Well Liner

Separating the cab of the car from the trunk is a large piece of material called the well liner. This material conceals the rear tack rail and pump motor, giving the top a clean place to rest when it is in the lowered position.

Removal of the well liner begins by lifting the leading edge of the material that is attached along the top edge of the rear seat's backrest support. This material may be glued, screwed in, or have push-in fasteners holding it in place. Carefully remove

these fasteners. There may also be an additional piece of hardware that the boot may attach to. This hardware will need to be removed as well.

Some Ford models used special flathead screws to attach the well liner around the rear of the well opening. Remove these screws to release the well liner from the car.

Rear Tack Rail

Underneath the well liner is the rear tack rail. The tack rail is secured to the inner body of the car with 1/4-20 hex head machine bolts and/ or #14 hex head washer sheet metal screws that are usually 1½ to 2¼ inches long.

I found that it is best to use a 1/4-inch ratchet with a long extension to remove the bolts. With a 7/16 six-point socket, remove the hex bolts that are securing the tack rail to the car. Start removing the bolts from the center outward. Make note of the length and position of the bolts when you remove them. Some bolts may be longer, and if you put them back incorrectly, they will damage the paint and body of the car.

With all the tack rail bolts removed, push down and inward on the lower part of the curtain to help free it from the car. Lift the tack rail with the attached curtain and quarter sail panels of the top out of the well area and set it up on the padding covering the trunk of the car.

Now, it is clear to see the staples that hold the bottom of the rear curtain and quarter sail panel top material to the tack rail. Remove the staples from the quarter sail panels on both ends of the tack rail to free the top from the car.

Rear Pads

Under the quarter sail panel sections of the top, you may find a short set of pads that run from the tack rail to the rear bow of the top frame. Not all cars have these pads, but if your car does, remove them now from the rear bow and then the tack rail.

Rear Curtain

Still attached to the rear bow and tack rail is the rear curtain. Remove the remaining staples across the rear bow to release the curtain from the

The leading edge of the well liner is attached along the top edge of the seat back retainer with glue, screws, or spring-clip fasteners. Once the fasteners are removed, the well liner can be lifted for access to the rear tack rail bolts.

All along the rear tack rail are 7/16-inch hex-head sheet metal bolts. These fasteners hold the convertible top rear tack rail to the body of the car. The top material and rear curtain are fastened to the rear tack rail with staples or tacks.

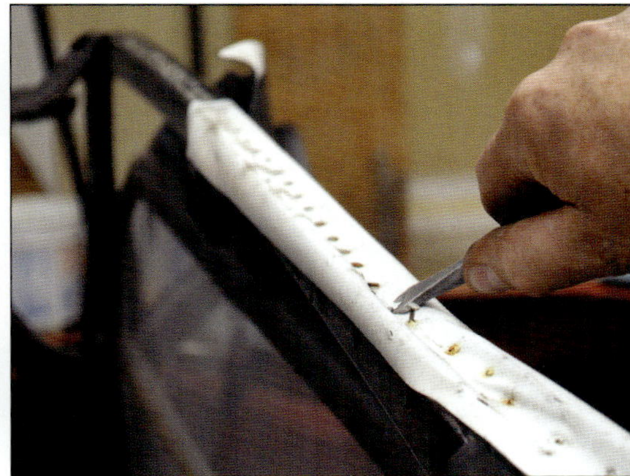

Before the rear curtain can be removed from the car, pull the staples running along the top of the rear bow. When the staples are removed, the old curtain can be removed from the car and then discarded.

top frame. Then, move the curtain and rear tack rail to a workbench where it can be further disassembled without risking damage to the car.

With the rear tack rail on the bench, the staples can be removed from the bottom of the curtain. The well liner staples can now be accessed and removed. Mark the rear tack rail *L* (left) or *R* (right) and with an *up* arrow in the center so that the bow can be returned to the car in the same position that it was removed.

Top Pads

The only components that should be remaining on the convertible top frame are the pads. Remove the staples along the rear of each pad, and then carefully lay the rear bow down into the well of the car.

At the front, the pad is attached to the header bow with staples or small machine screws. The fasteners are located under the protective tape that was applied to prevent them from harming or scratching the top material. Remove the tape by peeling it back to expose the fasteners. Remove all the tape that was applied to the bow and throw it away.

To access the staples holding the front edge of the pad, remove the protective tape. This tape was used to prevent the staples from rusting and help keep the staples from rubbing and creating holes in the top material.

Removing the Top Pad

1 *Staples are used to hold the front and rear ends of the pads in place. Removing the staples and opening up the pad will reveal a layer of padding material that cushioned the top from rubbing against the steel top frame.*

2 *With the top pad open and the cushioning material removed, remove the inner staples of the second bow. These staples held the pad in place and kept it from shifting when the top would be lowered.*

3 *Small screws and washers were used to hold the pad in place on the outer edge of the third bow. Remove these screws with a Phillips screwdriver; they can be reused when the new pads are fitted. Care must be used when removing these screws because they tend to break off due to age and corrosion.*

Remove all staples or screws that are holding the front end of the pad to the header bow. Open the pad and remove the padding material that is inside the folded fabric. Each pad is also attached to the second and third bows with staples or small screws with washers. Remove the fasteners to release the pad from the top frame.

If any of the small screws break or an incorrect fastener is found in the bow, make a proper repair before the new pad is installed.

Make Repairs

With the convertible top frame stripped down, make a complete inspection of the frame. Compile a list of all the issues that need to be addressed so proper repairs can be made. It is best to repair any damage to the frame while there is nothing in the way.

Look very close at the frame rails for cracks, bent bows, and rust. The header bow most likely shows signs of corrosion. This must be restored or replaced at this time. Refer to the section on restoration repairs for the proper procedures.

Clean the Frame

The frame is visible from inside the car, and it should look as nice as the rest of the car. Cleaning the frame of years of road dirt, grease, and wear is a good start.

Formula 409 sprayed on a clean rag will remove most of the grime from the frame. It may be necessary to use a stronger cleaner, but be careful; some solvents and cleaners can harm the finish on the car.

After cleaning the frame, wipe it down with a clean rag and water. This removes and neutralizes any cleaning-solvent residue that may

Now that the convertible top frame has been stripped of all material, it can be thoroughly cleaned. Years of built-up road dirt, oil, and grime can be wiped away with a cloth sprayed with Formula 409. After cleaning the heavy dirt, the frame can be wiped down with a damp rag and left to dry.

still remain on the convertible top frame.

Do not sandblast the frame. Sandblasting is too aggressive and will cause more problems than necessary.

Drape the Car

Protecting the finish on the car is vital. I use a 1 mil poly sheeting from bumper to bumper. The poly can be cut to allow for the frame mounts. Tape off everything that you do not want paint to get on.

Prep the metal as you would for any repaint by following the manufacturer's directions. Tack off the surface before you begin to spray to remove any dust that may still be on the surface.

Paint the Frame

I like to use satin black enamel on the convertible top frame. Satin is the best sheen for a top frame. It will allow the frame to blend with the lining of the new top and not stand out.

Before the convertible top frame can be painted, drape the car from bumper to bumper with 1 mil poly to protect the surface from overspray. A nice coat of satin black enamel will restore the frame back to its original luster.

Please do not powdercoat the top frame. The powdercoat finish is too thick and causes issues with the frame's ability to fold. Once the powdercoating gets into the bushings and joints, you will have even more trouble trying to get the top to fold.

Adjusting the Frame

Prior to fitting the new pads and top, the convertible top frame should be adjusted. The top frame should be checked for fit over the side glass, length from front to rear, and levelness from side to side. It is very difficult to make any of these adjustments once the top has been installed.

First, install the new rubber roof rail pieces to the header and side rails of the bare frame. Now, the top frame can be adjusted to fit the side glass.

By loosening the anchor bolts located at the base of the third rail section, the entire frame can be shifted. You can also loosen the two anchor bolts that hold the header bow in place to allow the frame to be adjusted forward or backward, giving a better fit to the rear quarter glass.

Move the frame so that the weather seals make contact with the side glass. When you are satisfied with how the convertible top frame is adjusted to fit the glass, tighten all the bolts to lock the frame in place.

Operate the top frame all the way down and all the way up and make any necessary adjustments so the frame operates smoothly. The rubber weather seals can now be removed from the frame.

Lubricate the Frame

Now is the time to lubricate the joints of the frame before installing the new convertible top. Because of its viscosity and applicator bottle, I like to use three-in-one oil. Care must be taken when applying the lubricant to the frame joints. Too much oil will become a dripping mess, and you do not want oil all over your new top or passengers.

New rubber weather seals are installed along the frame rails, and the windows are raised so that the newly restored convertible top frame can be properly adjusted. This is the time to get the frame right before installing the new pads and top.

Adjusting the height and tension of the frame is done from the rear anchor points of the frame. By loosening the three anchor bolts, the frame can now be easily moved to fit the glass. After the adjustments have been made, properly tighten all bolts to prevent unwanted shifting.

Lubricating the convertible top frame is vital to it performing without future problems. A quality three-in-one oil is all that is necessary to ensure good performance.

Each joint on the convertible top frame should be oiled before installing the new pads and convertible top. It only takes a drop or two of oil to get the job done. Wipe away excess oil with a clean rag.

Just a drop or two is all that is required on the bronze bushings. The nature of the bushing is to absorb the oil, keeping the joint lubricated for a long period of time. Take the time to oil every moving joint on the frame and use a rag to catch any excess oil that may run off.

Installation

After the convertible top frame has been stripped, reconditioned, prepped, and painted, begin the installation of the new convertible top. A new foundation of convertible top pads must be installed on the frame, and that will be done next.

Install the Pads

With the header bow latched to the windshield, position the pad on the frame and center it from front to rear. Place a temporary tack or staple in the front corners only. Pull gently on the rear end of the pad and line up the inside edge of the pad with the depression in the rear bow.

Pad Installation

1 *Setting the new pads on the frame begins with temporarily tacking the corners of the leading end of the pad to the frame. Once the length and position are established, an additional staple will be added on the inside to keep it in place.*

2 *Use staples to secure the pad to the second bow of the convertible top frame. These staples are the only fasteners that keep the pad in place when the top is lowered into the well of the car. Without fastening the pad to the bow, it will shift and damage the top material.*

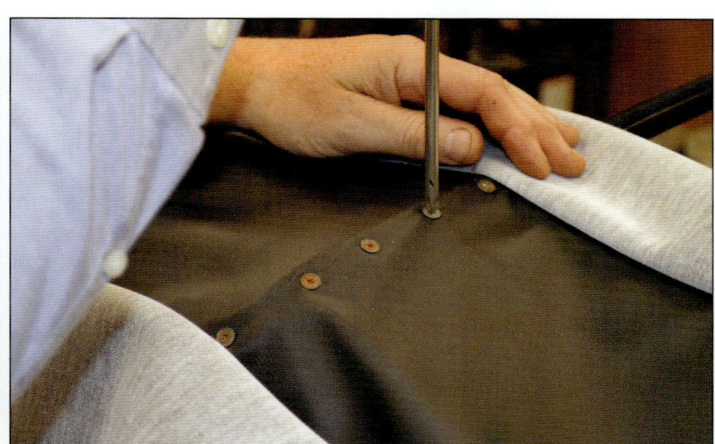

3 *The third bow on most GM cars is constructed from round hollow tubing. Attaching the pads to this bow requires five small machine screws and washers to keep the pad in place. The screws are essential to keeping the pad in position on the frame.*

4 *With the pad properly in place, it is opened up and a thin layer of padding is added inside the pad. Originally, the pad material was a cotton coach wadding, but foam is used today. The foam gives just enough protection without adding bulk to the contour of the top.*

Temporarily tack or staple the rear corners of the pad to the rear bow.

Open the pad and staple the lower panel to the cross bow tack strip. Keep the pad stretched taut to prevent wrinkles while stapling.

Attach the pad to the third bow with #6-32 machine screws and tiny washers. To find the holes in the bow, feel for the dimple in the bow under the material, and use the tip of your screwdriver to make a hole in the pad material. Insert the screw and washer and snug the screw down. Be careful not to overtighten the screws; they are prone to breaking off or stripping out.

After the pad is secured in place, the foam filler can be inserted into the open pad casing. Without the filler, the pad would not be as effective protecting the top from rubbing on the frame, and this could lead to a premature failure of the top.

Rear Bow Height

Now, the rear end of the pad can be fully secured to the rear bow. This step requires the bow height to be set to the specified measurement. Some people use a block of wood cut to length to set the rear bow height. I prefer to measure, temporarily tack the pad in place, and make adjustments until the desired bow height is achieved.

Once the rear bow height is set and the pads have been stapled off on both ends, the pad can be glued shut. Logic says that the outside flap should lie on top of the inner flap. This layering works best because if wind gets under the top material, it will flow over the pad and not cause it to balloon.

Contact cement is applied to both mating surfaces of the pad flaps. When the glue is tacky, press the flaps together to seal in the inner padding.

Check the rear bow height before the trailing end of the pad is secured. This is the most critical part of the whole project. If the bow height is off, the top will not fit the frame correctly. Make adjustments until the bow height is perfect.

To keep the padding from falling out, glue the flaps on top of the pad down. To prevent ballooning of the pad, secure the outer flap over the inner flap. Brush contact cement along the edges of the flaps and then press them together.

Excess pad material can now be trimmed to the edge of the rear bow with a sharp utility knife. The front edge of the pad is also trimmed to fit the contour of the header bow. Once the pads are trimmed, they provide protection to the top material from the frame without any unsightly bulges.

The staples along the leading edge of the pad are covered with two layers of Gorilla Tape. The tape is an added measure of protection to prevent the pad staples from rubbing the fabric side of the convertible top.

The excess length of the pad can now be trimmed with a utility knife. A fresh blade can cleanly cut through all the layers of the pad material. Try to trim the pad evenly and very close to the leading edge of the tacking strip on the header bow and along the back edge of the rear bow.

Cover the exposed staples on the leading end of the pad with heavy tape to protect the staples from moisture and to prevent the staples from rubbing against the inside decking of the convertible top.

The cloth body tape originally used by the factory has become cost prohibitive, and I have switched over to Gorilla Tape to cover the staples. The Gorilla Tape is weatherproof and will not dry out or fail like other tapes. Two layers of the tape will cover the staples and give a smooth appearance to the top.

Well Liner

The new well liner will be stapled to the rear tack rail, and it drapes over the front to conceal the body bolts when it is installed in the car. With the rear tack rail on the workbench, begin stapling the well liner to the rear tack rail from the center point and work your way outward.

Keep even tension on the well liner material as it is pulled sideways and then stapled.

After the material is attached, carefully cut material to reveal the through hole in the tack rail. It is better to make a rounded cut in the material, as the material tends to tear at the corners of a straight or sharp cornered notch.

Attach the Rear Curtain

Along the lower edge of the new curtain are reference marks made by the top manufacturer. These marks are there to aid in the positioning of the curtain. The marks are very accurate and should be observed. Start attaching the curtain to the tack rail from the center outward.

Pay attention to the installation marks as you go, and use as few staples as possible to hold the curtain in place. More staples can be added later, but if an adjustment is needed, fewer staples to remove is better.

Cut out the curtain material to reveal the through holes in the tack rail. Be sure to make an arched top to help prevent the material from tearing. Unlatch the header bow from the windshield, and use a spacer to

Center the new well liner along the rear tack rail and staple it in place. The well liner will cascade over the top of the tack rail and this will conceal the tack rail once it is installed into the well of the car.

lift the frame. This takes the tension off the frame and allows the rear curtain to be tensioned properly.

Fit the rear tack rail with the attached curtain/well liner assembly into the well of the car, and install every other tack rail bolt. Line up the center of the upper curtain with the center point of the rear bow, and begin to attach the top of the curtain to the rear bow. Again, use just enough staples to hold the curtain in place.

Remove the spacer block and latch the top frame to the windshield. Check the fit of the rear curtain. There will most likely be some wrinkles to deal with, and the rear bow height may also need to be corrected.

Apply a strip of masking tape along the lower section of the curtain, and make reference marks to indicate where the adjustments need to be made. Unlatch the top and insert the spacer before removing the tack rail. Remove the rear tack rail, make the necessary adjustments, and then reinstall the tack rail.

Now, remove any staples across the rear bow, and make the upper adjustments by pulling and repositioning the upper curtain material. Latch the top to verify that the curtain is wrinkle free. When you are happy with the fit, additional staples can then be added to secure the curtain in place.

Staple placement is very important along the rear bow. Many components are attached to the rear bow, and you can actually run out of staple space if you are not careful. Refer to the staple guide image on page 162.

Rear Pads

If your car has rear pads, they can be installed after the rear curtain

Fitting the Curtain

1 *Secure the bottom edge of the rear curtain to the rear tack rail. Align the reference marks that the manufacturer made so that the curtain will fit the car correctly. Place staples sparingly so that future adjustments can be made.*

2 *With the header bow unlatched from the windshield, place a spacer block between the header bow and the top of the windshield. This spacer takes the tension off the frame to allow the proper amount of stretch to the curtain.*

3 *Attach the top edge of the rear curtain to the rear bow. Staples are used sparingly to hold the curtain in place so the fit can be adjusted before the curtain is permanently secured in place.*

4 *After a few adjustments, the top has been latched to the windshield, and the rear curtain is now wrinkle free. Apply additional staples to secure the curtain to the top frame, holding it permanently in place.*

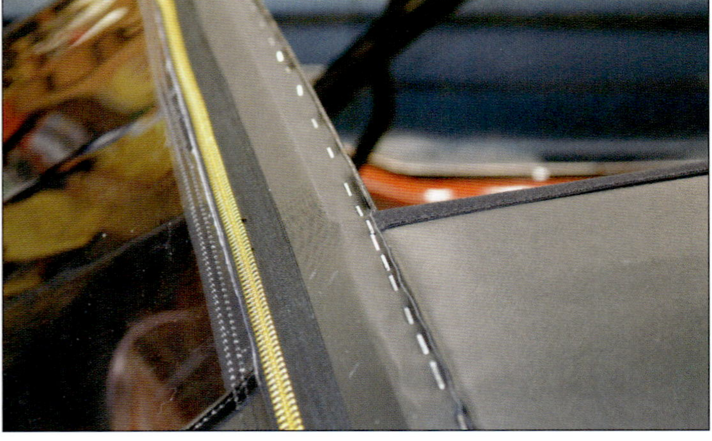

5 *Notice the finished row of staples along the top edge of the rear curtain. By pre-planning the placement of the staples, unwanted misses or bent-over staples will be prevented when further layers of top material are applied. Neatness ensures a better-looking finished top.*

has been secured in place. Attach the lower edge of the pad to the rear tack rail, and then fit the upper portion to the rear bow.

Fitting the Top

With the top frame latched to the windshield, dry fit the new top over the frame and verify that there are no more adjustments that need to be made. Check that the inside bow sleeve lines up with the second bow and that the top fits side to side. Also, set the rear bow corners of the top and see if the top of the curtain is covered by the top. Correct any issues that you are not happy with before you proceed.

Unlatch the top and use the spacer block. Remove the rear tack rail bolts and lift the assembly from the well. Start at the front edge of the rear tack rail and begin to attach the lower edge of the sail to the tack rail. Work your way to the rear of the sail panel material by aligning the reference mark to the tack rail while keeping tension on the material. Use as few staples as possible when fitting the top to the rear tack rail because adjustments will be necessary to remove wrinkles.

With the top material in place, make more arched cuts to reveal the through holes in the tack rail. Do not make the cut any larger than necessary; if the top material needs to be adjusted, the void can become too

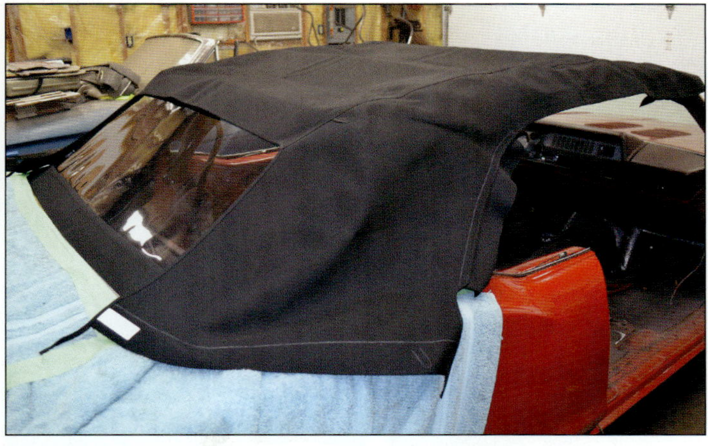

Dry fit the top to the frame to ensure that the rear bow height and curtain are set correctly. Now is the time to look for any other adjustments that may need to be made to the underlying materials to ensure a smooth and tailored look.

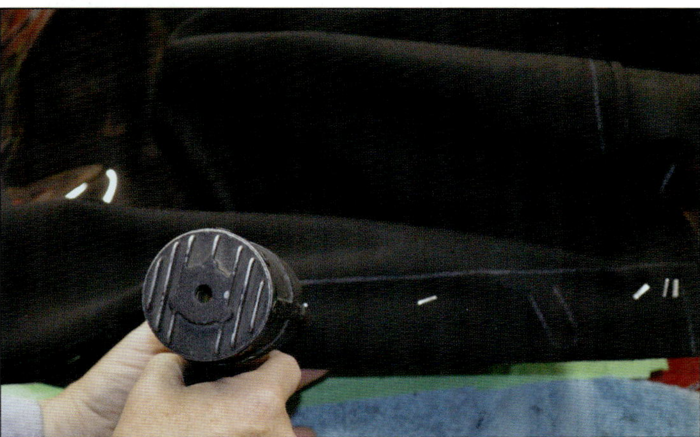

The rear tack rail has been removed from the body, allowing for the alignment of the sail panel placement marks and preliminary tacking of the sail area of the convertible top onto the rear tack rail. Only a few staples are used at this time.

Reveal through-bolt holes in the track rail by cutting a rounded access point in the top material. The sharp edges of a square-cut hole can cause the top material to accidentally tear out during the installation and adjustment of the new top.

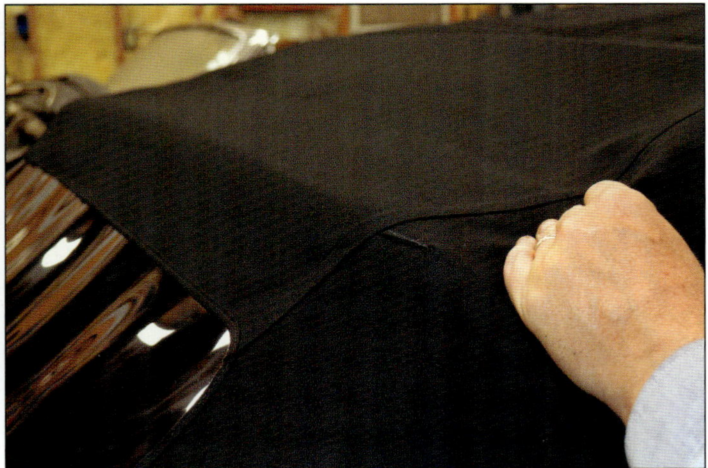

Adjusting the top material into position over the rear bow takes stress off the top material before the frame gets latched to the windshield.

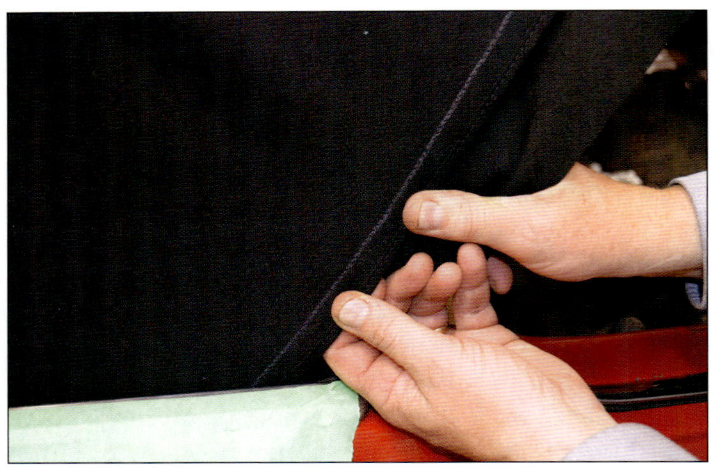

Check for proper sail area tension by pulling on the vertical edge of the top. When the tension is correct, the sewn seam should run along the vertical frame rail, and all the wrinkles will disappear from the sail material.

large, and you will not have enough material to staple onto the tack rail.

Fit the rear tack rail assembly into the well and secure it to the body with every other tack rail bolt.

Grab the top material and adjust the rear corners of the top to fit the contour of the rear bow. Some tops are split, and the division should line up with the center of the rear bow tack strip. Other tops may have a dart or seam in the corner. Align the seam with the center of the rear bow, and place a staple there to hold the top material in place. Repeat this for the other side.

On tops that are split across the rear bow, carefully staple the upper rear window section of the top to the rear bow first. Make sure to keep the top material smooth and even with a consistent measurement over the top of the rear curtain. Next, staple the top decking to the rear bow by overlapping the material onto the rear bow, covering the staples that you just put in. Refer to the stapling diagram on page 162 in the repair section on how to maximize the rear bow tack strip.

Pull the leading vertical edge of the top forward and down to align the flap seam with the leading edge of the third side rail. This will help the top material take the correct shape and position for a proper fit.

First Stretch

With the top frame unlatched, pull the top material to the front corner of the header bow. Square up the edge

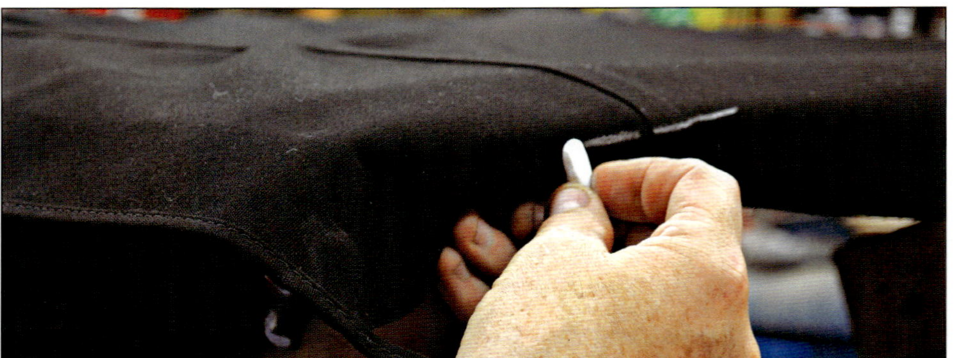

Use chalk to make a reference mark along the leading edge of the top material. This mark will help guide the tensioning of the top material over the header bow when it is temporarily tacked in place.

binding and front side flap so that the seam fits nicely along the outside edge of the header bow. Now wrap the top decking material over the leading edge of the header bow and fold it over the tucked under side flap on the underside of the header bow.

Use a piece of chalk or a pencil and make a reference mark along the leading edge of the header bow. Do the same on the other side of the top.

Lower the top to access the underside of the header bow and reposition the top like it was, but pull the top material about 1/4 inch past the leading edge of the header bow. Staple the material to the header bow tack strip to keep it in place. Repeat this with the other front corner of the top.

With the front corners of the convertible top secured in place,

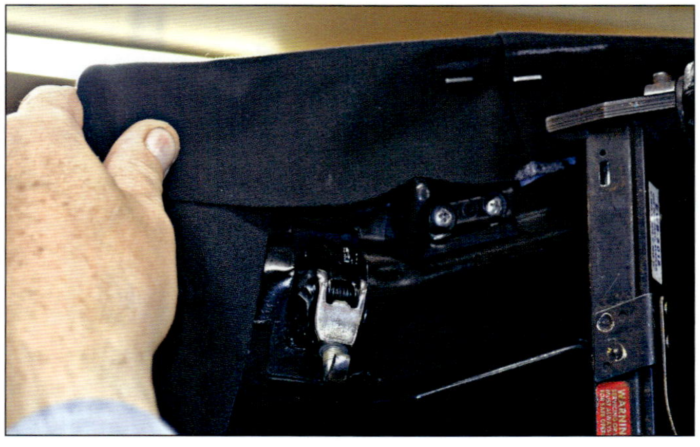

Tensioning begins by pulling the top material a 1/4 inch past the leading edge of the header bow and stapling the material to the underside of the header bow. The top frame can now be latched and the top can be checked for fit.

the top frame can now be latched to the windshield. This first stretch will be the hardest to latch, and you may want someone to help work the inside latches while you pull on the top. Do not pull on the header bow because this can cause damage to the top frame. For better forward leverage, grab the frame at the third side rail and pull forward to assist with the first stretch.

After you have the top latched, check its fit. You may need to pull and tug at the material to get it to settle into place. This is normal for the new top material to not want to lay down nicely. The top material was made flat and it wants to be flat. You are now training it to curve and contour and act like a convertible top. Let the top sit in the latched position for about an hour. This will give the topping material some time to learn its new shape.

Removing Wrinkles

Wrinkles in the sail area of a convertible top are not good for a number of reasons. First, wrinkles look bad and are a sign of someone who did not take the time to do a good job installing the top on the car. Second, wrinkles can lead to creases, and creases collect dirt. Dirt will act like a saw and cut into the protective outer layer of the top material, and this will eventually turn into a hole. Removing the wrinkles in the sail is not difficult. When you increase your effort by investing the time and have a little know-how, the wrinkles will disappear.

When the top is latched, run a piece of painter's tape across the sail area close to the pinch well molding. Use a pencil to make reference points on the tape where you need to make an adjustment. It may only take a 1/16 inch or maybe 1/4 inch of stretch to make the wrinkle go away. Always start with less, and do not overtighten the material. The material may also need to be pulled forward or toward the rear. It takes a lot of practice to know how to pull the material to get it to lie smooth.

Begin by unlatching the top and putting in the spacer to relieve tension on the top. Remove the tack rail bolts and remove the rear rail assembly. Beginning with one side, carefully remove a few staples at a time. Reposition the top material on the rear tack rail by following your reference marks on the tape, and then staple the material in its new position. When you have made the corrections to both sides, reinstall the tack rail and latch the top.

Keep checking your progress and repeating the procedure until your top is wrinkle free. It may take one adjustment or five. Do whatever it takes to make the top wrinkle free.

Side Cables

The problem of driving down the road and having the convertible top material beating against the top frame has long been an annoyance to the driver. Inner bow sleeves were used to help secure the top material to the inner cross bows, but the problem and noise of the top buffeting needed a better solution.

To help keep the top material from buffeting, the convertible top

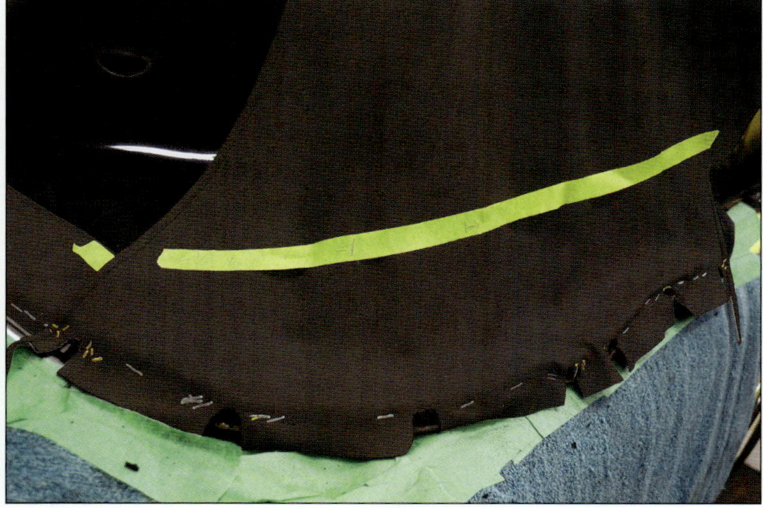

Correcting wrinkles in the sail area of the convertible top is done by repositioning the material on the rear tack rail. Make reference marks on a piece of masking tape to indicate where and how much adjustment is needed to make the wrinkle go away.

Side tension cables are used to help keep the outer edges of the convertible top tight to the frame. Without the side cables, the convertible top will catch too much air and buffet when the car is driven.

A cable sleeve runs along the underside of the outer edge on the convertible top. With the convertible top frame lowered in the half-down position, use a stiff wire to pull the side tension cable through the cable sleeve.

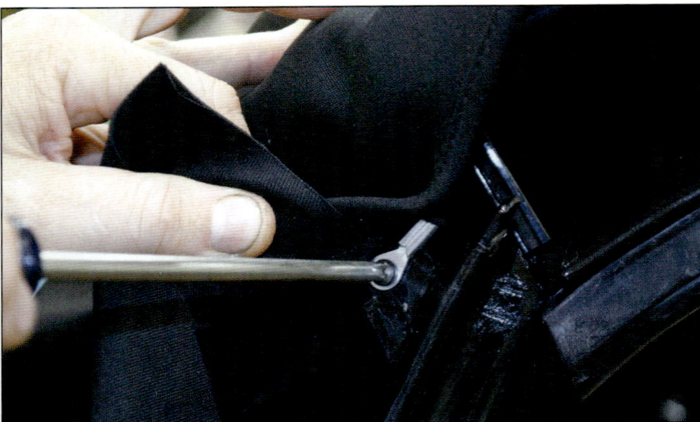

Use small screws on both ends of the side tension cable and secure it to the convertible top frame. The top material will have some ability to move as the top is raised or lowered, but it will be held snugly in place when the convertible top is latched.

material needs to be held tightly to the frame. Because the top frame folded, the topping material could not be attached along the perimeter of the frame, otherwise it would tear. The challenge was to still have the top frame articulate and have the convertible top material unattached along the sides of the frame. This was accomplished by adding cables into the outer edges of the convertible top material. The cable would be inside a sleeve along the edge of the top, and the ends of the cable were secured to the frame.

When the top was in the raised position, the cables would be taut, holding the top securely in place and keeping it from buffeting. Once the top frame was unlatched from the windshield and lowered, the cables would allow the top to move, allowing the top frame to fold properly without tearing the top material. In 1963, almost all manufacturers of convertibles began using this method of keeping the top material tight to the top frame.

To install the side cables into the top, insert a stiff wire through the cable sleeve. Another option is to tie the string that is in the cable sleeve to the cable and pull the cable through the sleeve, leaving the cable exposed on both ends.

The side tension cables are either secured to the side rail of the frame with a small sheet metal screw or a pop rivet. To fasten the cable, lower the top about halfway down to relieve the tension on the top material and give enough slack in the cable so it can be anchored to the side rail. Use the appropriate fastener to attach each cable end to the side rail.

Weather Seal

Across the leading edge of the header bow is a thick bead of mate-

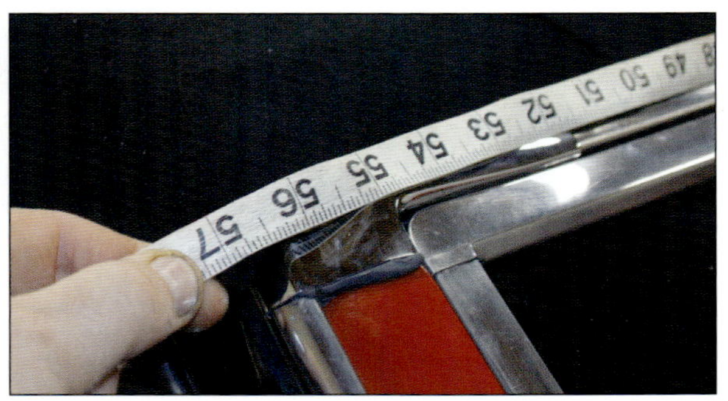

rial. This is the weather seal. Its primary purpose is to block wind and water from entering the car at the connection between the top and windshield. The weather seal is constructed from 1/2-inch rubber foam core and wrapped in matching convertible top material.

Making the Weather Seal

A tape measure is used to establish the distance across the leading edge of the header bow from the bound edge of the top to the other side. Make an accurate measurement so that the seal will fit exactly and not hang over or be short on the ends.

Your top kit should have included a 4-inch-wide strip of matching convertible top material. This material

Take an accurate measurement across the front of the header bow for the front weather seal. This measurement will tell us how long to make the weather seal. The sewn ends of the seal must line up with the outer edges of the top material.

With the weather seal material turned inside out, sew each end of the material closed with a back-bevel tapering to the back edge. This will allow the finished weather seal end to fit under the header bow without showing when it is stapled into place.

will become the new weather seal. Some top kits come with a premade seal, and sometimes the ends are sewn closed, but most are not. The ends should be sewn closed to give the top a professional appearance.

Begin by folding the top material in half with the inside fabric facing the outside and the outside weatherproof surface on the inside. Starting on the folded edge, sew a line 5/8 inch straight across, and then turn the material to about a 35-degree angle and sew inward to the outside edge. Trim the excess material to 1/8 inch. Measure from the seam, and mark the other end of the seal with the measurement taken from the header bow. Sew this end closed and trim it just like before.

Turn the seal material inside out again. All the seam allowances should be on the inside of the seal, and the weatherproof surface of the material is on the outside. Insert the 1/2-inch foam core material tightly into the end of the weather seal.

The weather seal can now be sewn closed with a right-facing zipper foot. Begin sewing on one end, and sew the foam core snugly into the seal as if it were a large welt cord.

Use a piece of 1/2-inch rubber foam core to fill the header weather seal casing. The foam core is fit tightly to the inside end of the weather seal before it can be sewn into the casing.

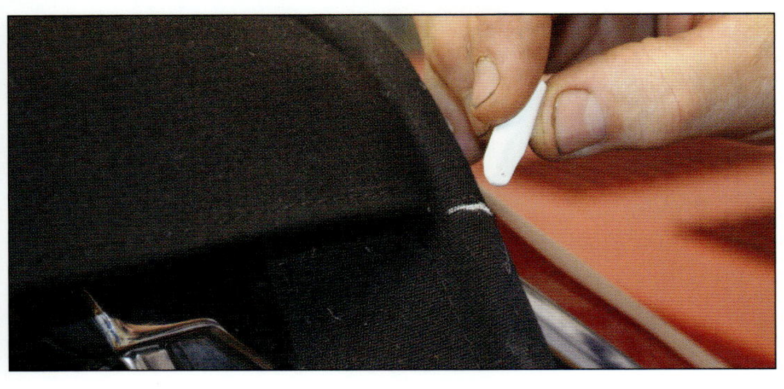

The rubber weather seal is sewn into the header seal casing with a right-facing zipper foot. The sewing will need to pause about 6 inches from the end so that the foam core can be trimmed to fit the casing end before the stitching can be completed.

An alternate method to get a weather seal measurement is to latch one finished end of a partially sewn weather seal in place under the header bow. Mark the unfinished-end seam position with chalk, and once it is sewn, we will have an exact fit.

Another method of getting an exact fit for the weather seal is to sew one end closed and then sew the 1/2-inch foam core into the weather seal. Fit the weather seal to the header, and chalk a reference mark on the seal to indicate where to sew the end closed.

Weather Seal Installation

Your convertible top frame should be in the half-lowered position to install the weather seal. Fit the weather seal to the header bow by making sure that the sewn seam is positioned tight against the leading edge of the header bow. Open up the seal and begin stapling inside of the seal. (It also looks a lot better not having a row of staples showing).

Apply contact adhesive to both surfaces on the inside of the weather seal, and after the glue has tacked, press the edges together. This will conceal the staples from the weather and prevent them from rusting.

Side Flaps

To secure the quarter flaps to the side rails of the frame, apply contact

Apply contact cement to the frame rail and onto the top sealing flaps. When the glue flashes, press the flaps into place. Trim the excess material of the flap to give the top a neat, finished appearance.

cement to the side rail and to the backside of the flap material. When the glue flashes, press the flap into the glue and smooth out any wrinkles that may have formed. Trim the inside edge of the flap even with the recess on the frame side rail.

Rubber Weatherstrip

It is easier to position and fasten the side rail rubber seals onto the side rails after the holes have been located and cleared. This can be done by feeling for the opening through the flap and then using a small awl or upholsterer's regulator to create the through hole in the material.

Fit the rubber weatherstrip section in place, and replace the screws and fasteners to keep it in place along the side rail. It may make this task easier if you lower the top halfway to access the lower screw holes.

With the top lowered into the well of the car, the rubber header weather seal can be attached. Depending on the car you are working on, the rubber seal can be held in by a metal retainer and screws or small plastic T-fasteners and screws on the ends.

With the header weather seal in place, open the weather seal, and place staples on the inside of the weather seal to hold it in place. The purpose of blind stapling is to protect the staples from the weather, and the finished seal looks better without fasteners showing.

By applying contact cement to the inside of the weather seal, a weather-tight seal is made, protecting the staples from getting wet and possibly rusting. The glue also makes the seal stronger and it will lay flatter under the header bow.

Fit the new rubber weatherstripping to the roof rail and hold it in place with screws. The rubber not only seals out the weather, it also helps lock the sealing flaps in place.

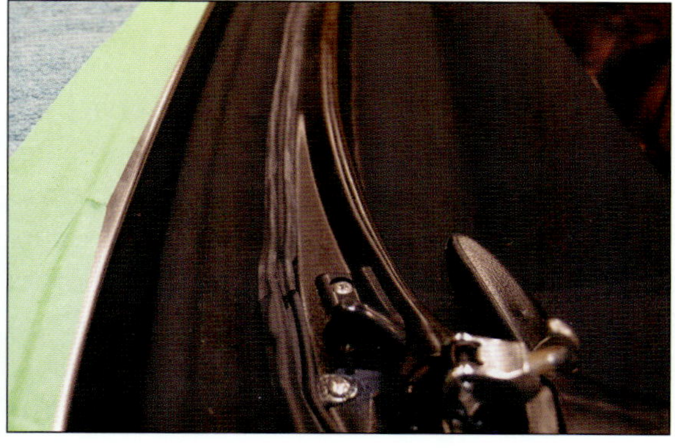

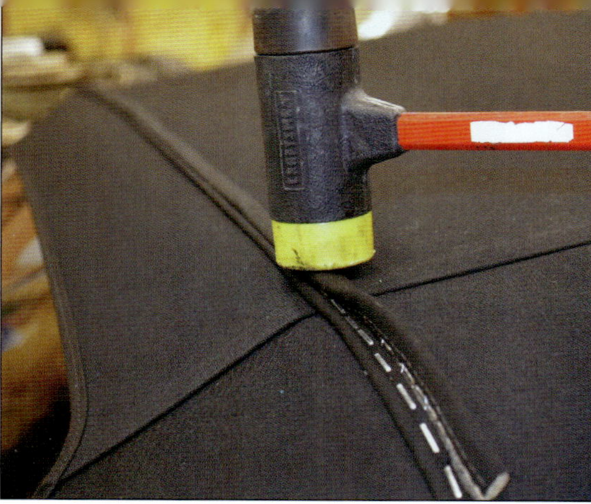

Fully retract the top to make the installation of the rubber header seal easier. Small plastic fasteners hold the seal in place along the underside of the header bow along with small sheet metal screws on each end.

Installing the Top

Raise the convertible top and latch it to the windshield. The top material should now be wrinkle free, and the rear curtain should be smooth. Check the position of the rear bow seam to see that it is dead center across the top of the rear bow.

Before the wire-on welt can be installed, a measurement is made from the deck seam. Use chalk to make reference marks on the top material to indicate the ending position of the wire-on welt.

Installing Welt-On

Use a tape measure to make a reference mark about 5½ inches from the deck seam. Repeat this measurement on the other side of the convertible top. These reference points will be the beginning and ending points for the wire-on welt. You may also know that on some models the top manufacturer will specify a distance from the deck seam. Do what the top maker suggests to avoid problems with the top.

Some tops may have a split in them and are stapled across the rear bow; the wire-on welt is used to hide and protect those staples. Start on one side of the convertible top beginning at the reference point with the smaller bead of the welt facing to the rear. Center the wire-on welt on the rear bow so that it will cover the staples and begin to staple the wire-on welt up to the deck seam.

Move to the other side and stretch the wire-on welt tight enough

Use staples along the inside of the wire-on welt to keep it in place along the top of the rear bow. The staples are evenly spaced, and any bent staples are removed to prevent a wavy appearance when the welt is finished off.

The purpose of the wire-on welt is to conceal the staples that are on in the inside. This is accomplished by folding the wire-on over and tapping it closed with a small plastic hammer. The internal zigzag wire keeps the wire-on closed and seals out the weather.

to remove any wrinkles, and place one or two staples in the wire-on at the deck seam to hold it in place. Stretch the wire-on down to the reference point, and cut it off with a scissor. Secure the wire-on by stapling from the deck seam down to the end of the welt. Add a few more staples in the middle to stabilize the wire-on, and then fill in across the length until the wire-on on is fully attached to the rear bow of the car.

Seal the wire-on closed by folding the top half over to meet the lower half, and gently tap the wire-on closed with a small plastic hammer. Do not mash the welt, just gently tap it closed.

Wire-On Welt Tips

Finish the raw ends of the wire-on with the chrome tips supplied with the new top. Place the welt tip over the end of the wire-on with the screw hole of the tip just over the wire-on. Use a small awl or regulator to make a pilot hole in the rear bow tack strip through the hole in the welt tip.

Insert the 3/4-inch-long #4 oval-head screw into the hole, and tighten the screw with a #1 Phillips screwdriver until it firmly holds the

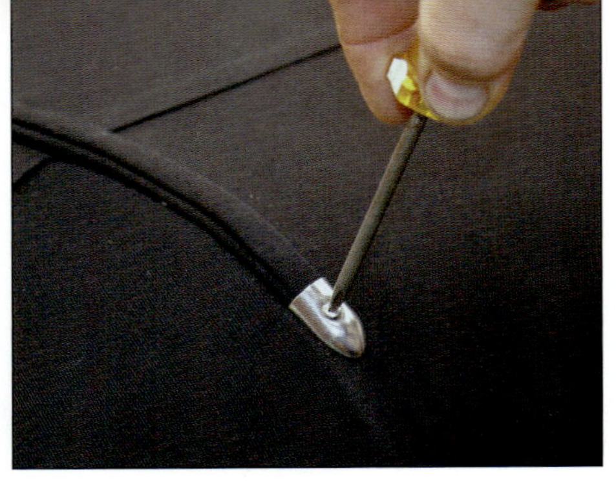

This decorative device not only looks nice, it neatly finishes off and conceals the raw cut end of the wire-on welt. The welt tip is held in place by securing it with a #1 Phillips screwdriver and a 3/4-inch #4 screw that is supplied with your new top kit.

welt tip in place. Do not overtighten the screw.

Bow Sleeve Retainer

The bow sleeve retainer can be easily inserted into the bow sleeve by unlatching the top and lowering it about halfway down. This will give you plenty of room to insert and align the retainer into the second bow.

Make sure that the bow retainer sits at the bottom of the bow sleeve with an equal amount of fabric on both sides. The ends of the retainer should sit on top of the convertible top pad when it is aligned correctly.

Secure the bow sleeve retainer with the correct hardware. The screws need to be fastened snugly without overtightening.

The top can now be raised and latched to the windshield. Check the top for anything that does not look right and make corrections as necessary.

Well Liner

On the inside of the car, the forward edge of the well liner can be attached to the rear seat's back support. Apply contact cement to the metal support and on the underside of the well liner material. Align the well liner material with the seat support, and press the material into the glue.

If the car was equipped with a boot channel retainer, refasten it to the rear seat's support using the correct screws.

Rear Seat

Reinstall any of the rear panels that may have been removed to service the windows or hydraulic system. Now, the rear seat can be fitted back into the car. Hang the backrest and secure it in place with the correct anchoring fasteners. It is important that the seat back is not going to loosen because it can possibly be thrown from the car while driving with the top in the down position. Set the lower cushion into position, and then make sure that it snaps securely in place with a firm push.

Remove the drape from the car by carefully lifting the tape that holds it in place. Spot clean any fingerprints from the top, trim molding, and paint before you take the car out for others to admire. It is also advised that you do not lower the top for at least two weeks after the new top has been installed. This will give enough time for the top material to stretch and retain its new shape. It will also help the top to latch with less strain.

Fasten the bow sleeve retainer to the second bow with four #8 1/2-inch trim screws with a #6 oval head. Snug the retainer screws with a #2 Phillips screwdriver.

With the top frame unlatched and lowered halfway, lift the top material enough to easily slide the retainer into the bow sleeve. Once inserted, the bow retainer can be centered into the bow channel and secured with the proper screws.

The newly installed top looks great! It will need to be left in the latched position for the next two weeks until the material will settle in and retain its shape. A light steaming will help relax the new top material and make this top look even better.

SCRATCH-BUILT CONVERTIBLE TOP

It is a great convenience to order a convertible top for your car from a reputable manufacturer, but sometimes the top you need may not be available for your particular car. There are many early cars that a premade top is not available for, or your top frame may have an irregularity, and a standard top just will not fit. So, what do you do?

Well, back in the early days, you would take the buggy to the local blacksmith shop, and he would fashion a new canvas top to fit your top frame. Today, a modern car requires a lot more finesse and skill to fashion a tailor-made top.

If you can take accurate measurements and operate a sewing machine, you can create your own custom convertible top in a color and design that will fit the car.

Prep the Frame

Before you can start the process of fashioning a new top, the top frame of the convertible must be put in order. Just like any other project, the convertible top frame must be adjusted to fit the side glass, the hydraulics inspected for wear, and the tacking strips checked for viability.

Begin by inspecting the hydraulic lines for leaks and cracks. Check the cylinder rods for any pitting or rust. Also look at the rod seals for excessive buildup of hydraulic oil and accumulated dirt, which is a sign of a failed seal. Run the pump motor, and listen for any unusually high-pitched or grumbling sounds that may indicate a low-fluid condition. With an older car that most likely has had several top replacements over the years, the tack strip material should probably be replaced at this time. Correct any issues that you find to ensure worry-free operation of the top mechanism.

This 1949 Chevy is the perfect candidate for a custom-tailored top. The top frame is wracked and the frame binds as it is raised. The car is riddled with many non-standard issues and problems that would not allow a premade top to fit or operate properly.

Too many times, this is what I see and have to work with. The rear beltline tack strip was not installed prior to the new paint on the car. The challenge here is to make and install the tack strip without causing any damage to the paint.

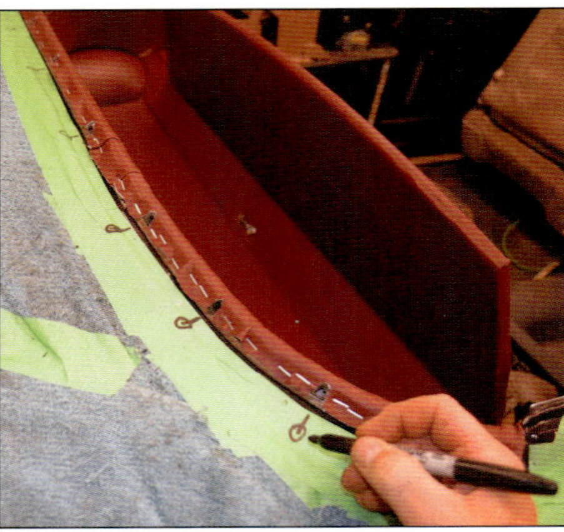

Protecting the paint on the car from accidental damage is a priority. The masking tape used to hold the draping in place also serves as a notepad. Fastener positions and alignment marks can be made on the tape to help with the top installation.

Before a new top can be installed, remove the header bow from the car to avoid accidental damage to the car as it is being worked on. A new tack strip is an essential foundational element to the longevity of a convertible top installation.

Make adjustments to the convertible top frame prior to fitting a new top. Here, the top frame has been adjusted, and the door glass correctly fits the new roof rail weatherstrip. With a fresh coat of paint and a few drops of oil, this frame is ready for a new top.

Adjust the Top Frame

As with all convertible top replacements, the frame must be in proper alignment before the new top is put on. Install the new side rail rubber on the top frame, and then adjust the side glass and top frame as well as possible before cleaning and painting the convertible top frame. After the prep work has been completed, the process of making a new top can commence.

Measure for Materials

You will need to take some measurements of the top frame so that the correct amount of materials can be ordered for the new convertible top. Because the cost of the top material is significant, do not make mistakes or waste material and order too little or too much.

The top is made in sections, and each section is laid out on the unrolled material and then cut. After

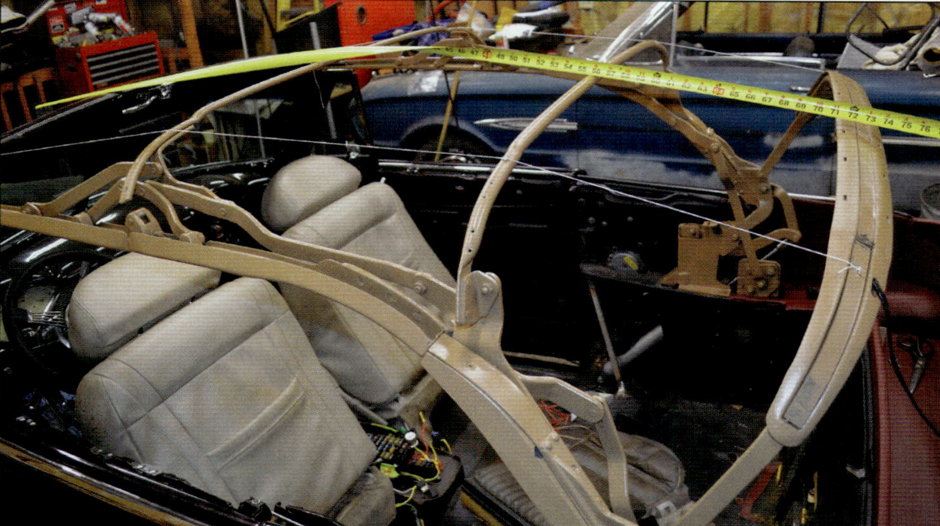

Because the cost of the convertible top material is high, it is important to get accurate measurements before ordering materials. Use a tape measure to get the decking measurements that run from the header bow to the rear bow.

Run a string from the header bow to the rear bow to temporarily set the rear bow height for the new convertible top. The correct bow height will help while measuring the top frame to determine how much convertible top material should be ordered.

The top side panels need to be adjusted to fit the contour of the convertible top frame. For this reason, the starting point of the tape measure is extended 2 inches past the leading edge of the header bow.

Having an accurate measurement is great for the fit of the top panel but not when measuring for a material order. Adding a few extra inches to the length of the panel will prevent the possibility of not having enough material to make the panel.

Although the convertible top pads are not really seen, they are visible from the inside of the car, and the base material should match the top material. Allow additional material for the length of the pads by measuring from the header bow to the rear bow.

Visualizing the layout of the rear curtain will help provide an idea on how to measure and assemble the individual components that make up the curtain. Always remember to add extra material for seam allowances and the attachment of the curtain to the car.

This is a perfect example of what happens to a zipper after it has been abused and neglected by the owner. Someone had replaced the original zipper and now this one has a missing tooth and appears to be jammed up, preventing it from being fully closed.

cutting the individual pieces, they will be sewn together to make the convertible top.

The center section of the convertible top is called the decking. This section is measured from the leading edge of the header bow to about 5 inches past the rear edge of the rear bow. Add an additional 6 inches to the length of the decking for attachment and sewing. The width of the decking is determined by measuring across the slight depressions on the header bow and adding an additional inch for a seam allowance and then between the pad depressions of the rear bow.

The side panels are measured from the header bow to the rear deck beltline; add another 8 inches for attachment. The widths of the side panels are measured from the seam line down along the rear bow to the beltline; add another 5 inches for attachment and sewing.

Take measurements for the base material to make the top pads. The length of the pad runs from the inner header bow tack strip to the rear bow plus 4 inches. The width of the pad runs from the depression in the rear bow to the outer end of the tack strip with an additional 1½ inches per pad for sewing.

A rear curtain for the top needs to be made. The size of the window is defined by the rear bow height and the placement of the rear quarter pads. Measure the distance between the depressions on the rear bow, and then subtract 1 inch from each end to get the width of the window. When factoring the height of the rear window, the curtain area is divided into five equal sections. The upper fifth connecting to the rear bow is the top valance, and the bottom fifth will be the lower valance. The remaining three-fifths in the center of the curtain becomes the clear-vinyl window.

A zipper in the rear curtain is an option. Some convertible models use a heavy-duty brass zipper to allow the rear window to be dropped into the well. There are pros and cons for the zipper, and I personally do not like them. Too many times, the zipper will fail and create more problems for the car owner. Unzipping the curtain can lead to many difficulties in reconnecting the ends. Misalignment of the zipper halves can cause the teeth to jam and fall out. Too many times, I have seen the pull talon come off from tugging to get the zipper closed. For these reasons, I urge my customers to omit the zipper whenever possible.

Materials Needed

Now that you have an idea of how much convertible top material is needed, figure out all of the other supplies necessary to complete the project. Finishing materials are also needed to complete the construction of a convertible top.

Use bias binding to finish the outer edges of the top and around the rear curtain opening. To cover the staples along the rear bow and across

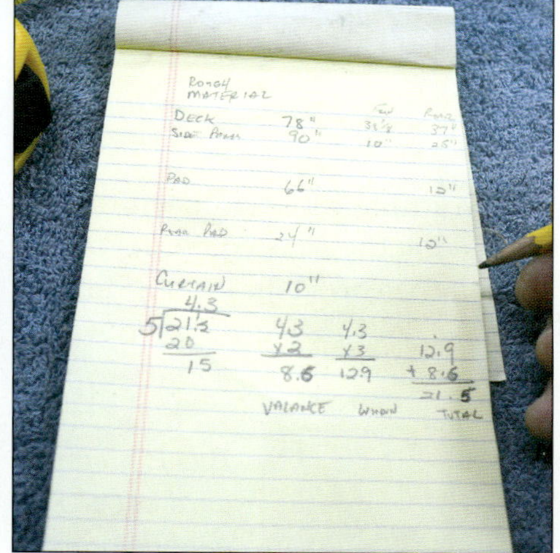

Keeping track of the panel dimensions on a note pad will help you place an accurate order for the materials needed to make a new convertible top. It can become costly to order more top material than necessary, and it can delay a project if not enough is ordered.

The raw edges of the convertible top must be finished to give the top a sharp and clean appearance. A tape measure run along the side frame rail and rear window opening provides an idea of how much bias binding is needed for the order.

The top material is fastened to the very front of the header bow on this car with staples. To cover them, a length of wire-on welt is needed. To get an idea of how much to order, double the measurement from the center of the header bow outward.

As with most convertible tops, the rear bow needs a piece of wire-on welt to cover and protect the row of deck staples securing the top. Double the measurement taken from the center point on the rear bow down to the end of the tack strip.

the header bow, wire-on welt will be needed along with two sets of wire-on tips and screws. The convertible top protective pads require 1/4-inch foam and bowdrill fabric or automotive-seat vinyl for the cover flaps.

A 40-gauge, double-polished, clear vinyl window; 6 feet of 1/2-inch foam core for the front weather seal; and a set of universal side tension cables will round out the required materials. Because the top is exposed to sunlight and UV rays, use a quality polyester marine-grade thread.

Placing an Order

There are many places to get convertible top material and supplies. First, check with your local upholstery supplier and pick up what you need. You can also go online and order supplies from any of the preferred convertible top vendors listed. Call ahead and ask them questions before you place an order to make sure you are getting exactly what you are expecting. After you have all the supplies for the project on hand, the work of making the new convertible top can begin.

Pads

As long as you are making the top, also consider making custom pads. Yes, you can order pads from a convertible top manufacturer, but by making the pads yourself, you can get a better fit. Pads are not difficult to make, and they are a good way to get started.

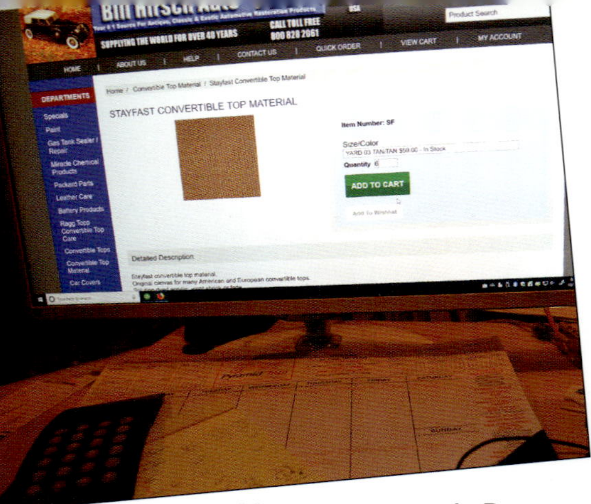

My go-to source is Pyramid Trim Products in St. Paul, Minnesota; they carry a lot of what I need, but the internet is also a great source for just about everything. With just a few mouse clicks, convertible top supplies are sometimes easier to get from an online supplier.

This is a standard set of generic premade convertible top pads that you may order from any convertible top manufacturer. Sometimes they just do not fit the top frame the way a custom set will. It is always worth the effort to make your own pads.

This is what a custom convertible top looks like before it is assembled and installed on the car. All the raw materials needed to make a convertible top are checked and verified before they are cut, sewn, and shaped into a tailored masterpiece.

Measuring for Pads

1 *The length of the convertible top pads starts with a measurement taken from the header bow to the rear bow. An additional 2 inches are allowed on each end of the pad so that the pad can be adjusted to fit the frame.*

2 *On each end of the header bow, there is most likely a depression that acts as a relief for the convertible top deck seam. Take a measurement from this line to the outer frame rail to establish the width at the front of the pad.*

3 *From the header bow to the rear bow, the width of the pad gradually gets bigger. To achieve maximum coverage, a measurement for the width of the top pad is taken at the rear bow from the ridge outward to the end of the tack strip material.*

First, determine the correct rear bow height. Then, measure from the inner top header bow tack strip to the rear bow and add 4 inches to allow for adjustments. The width of the front of the pad is measured across the outer end of the header bow from the ridge line to just above the side rail of the frame. The width of the pad at the rear is measured from the dip in the rear bow down to the end of the tack strip.

Unroll the top material faceup onto the workbench, chalk out the dimensions of the pad, and add 3/4 inch to each edge for sewing. Cut the base of the pads from the top material, and then fit the pad base to the top frame.

To get the pad fitted, temporarily staple the pad base to the header bow and then the rear bow. The pad must lie smoothly over the cross bows of the top frame. Align the chalked edge line of the pad to the recess in the second and third bows, and add a staple or screw to hold the pad in position. Pull on the pad material until it is wrinkle free across the bows. Pull the pad to the rear bow, adjust the material to lie smoothly, and retack the material to the rear bow while maintaining the correct bow height.

Reposition the front of the pad material across the header bow tack

Transfer measurements to the convertible top material for the base of the top pads. Use chalk to mark the surface of the top fabric to indicate the cut and folding lines of the pad base. After the marking is complete, the pad base is cut from the roll of material.

Place a temporary staple on the lower corner of the top pad to anchor the material to the top frame. The pad material will be stretched over the cross bows and tacked to the rear bow. After the wrinkles have been worked out of the pad base, it can be sized to the frame.

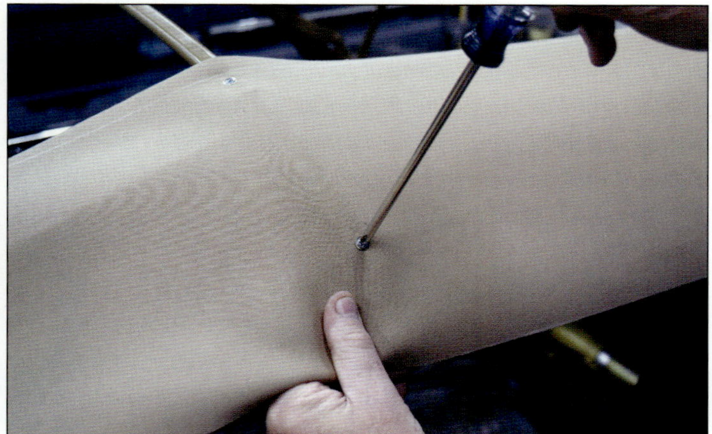

Small screws and washers are used to anchor the pad base to the second and third cross bows of the convertible top frame. The screws will keep the material in position as it is pulled and marked for a custom fit.

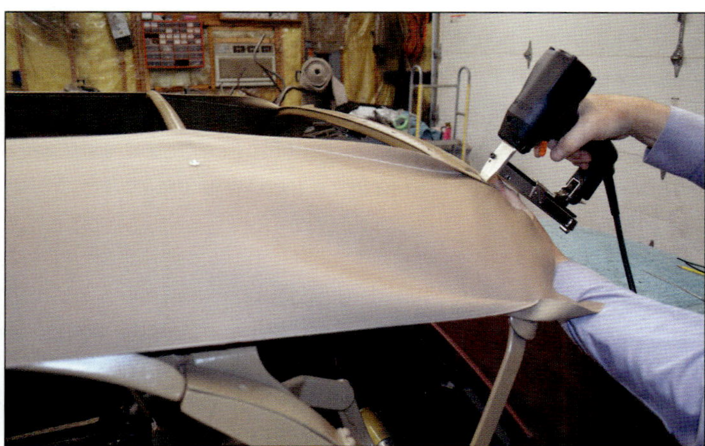

Reposition the top edge of the pad base to fit the contour of the rear bow, and use a staple to hold the material in position as the front of the pad is adjusted for fit. Use chalk to mark the new edges of the pad material.

After the base material of the pad has been custom fit to the top frame, remove the material and place it on the workbench so that new cut lines can be added to the material. The pencil lines will indicate where the pad should be trimmed.

Measure and cut strips of upholstery vinyl to create the top flaps for the new pads. Make each flap wide enough for them to have a 2.5-inch overlap. The extra material provides a place for contact cement to be applied, sealing the pad.

Each half of the pad flap has been fit to the fold line of the pad base with the proper overlap. The fold line is transferred to the flap material, and the extra material is then trimmed away. After the pad is sewn together, the pad will be able to lie smooth and wrinkle free over the convertible top frame.

Each edge of the top pad will have the base material folded over the top of the flap material and sewn with a simple stitch to keep the flap material locked in place. The finished pads can then be fitted to the top frame, filled with foam padding, and then sealed.

strip until it is snug and smooth. Fold up the lower edge of the pad material to reveal 1/2 inch above the side rail so that it runs parallel with the side rail. Mark the fold with chalk at each cross bow position. After you have the pad sized and wrinkle free, it can be removed and placed on the workbench.

Use a straightedge ruler to connect the newly chalked width marks. Now, measure 3/4 inch from the outside of the width line and make a new cut-mark line. Trim the excess material from the pad base.

To make the top flaps for the pads, cut the top flap material from auto-seat vinyl. Make the pad flaps equal to the length of the pad base material with a width that will allow a 2½ inch overlap when they are fit inside the pad base. The outer edge of the flap must be trimmed to fit flush with the fold line on the inside of the pad base.

Before sewing the pad, align the flap section along the inside of the fold line of the base material, and fold the 3/4 inch of base material over the top of the flap. Sew along the edge of the pad to lock the flap in place. Repeat this for the other side section and the other pad.

Take the new pads to the car, and install them onto the freshly reconditioned frame along with the 1/4-inch foam filler. After the pads are installed, take measurements and start patterning the rear curtain.

Rear Curtain

The option is available to make a full-view curtain or a double-blind curtain for this 1949 Chevy. Either curtain would be correct, but the customer requested a full-size vinyl window, so that is what we will make. It may be easier to order a premade curtain, but it is not difficult to cut and sew a custom-made curtain. With the top pads already installed, we already have the rear bow height set, and the measuring can begin.

This owner wanted a more personalized look and opted to have a mail-slot window installed in a double-blank curtain for his 1949 Chevy. The car had several body modifications and the standard full-view rear window was not going to work with the overall customization of the car.

Vinyl Window

The rear window is 40-gauge clear double-polished vinyl. The vinyl is available on long rolls and can be purchased as cut yardage. Rear windows can also be ordered in precut sizes to meet your needs. The precut windows are also embossed with a Kal-Glas Department of Transportation (DOT)-approved logo.

The precut blank needs to be squared up and cut to a usable size for your particular project. I have found that the logo looks best when it is framed with a 1-inch margin in the finished top. To achieve this margin, trim the raw blank 1½ inches from the bottom of the logo and 2 inches from the left of the logo. The distance is greater on the left because

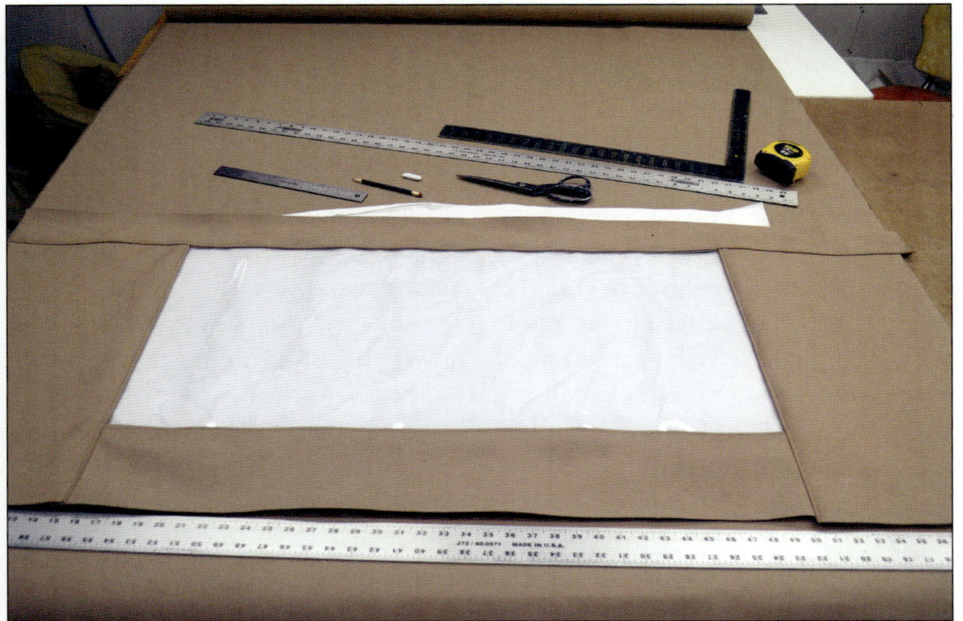

Here is the finished rear curtain that will be installed on our top project. The large, clear vinyl window and simple design will give the 1949 Chevy a timeless and classic appearance, which is the look the owner requested.

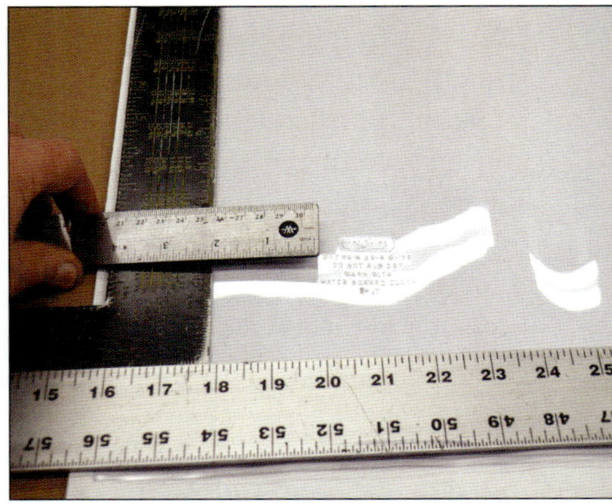

Take careful measurements before trimming the window blank to size. Be sure that the embossed Department of Transportation (DOT) logo ends up in the correct position on the finished curtain. Take extra care to prevent accidental scratches from happening to the clear, soft, vinyl window.

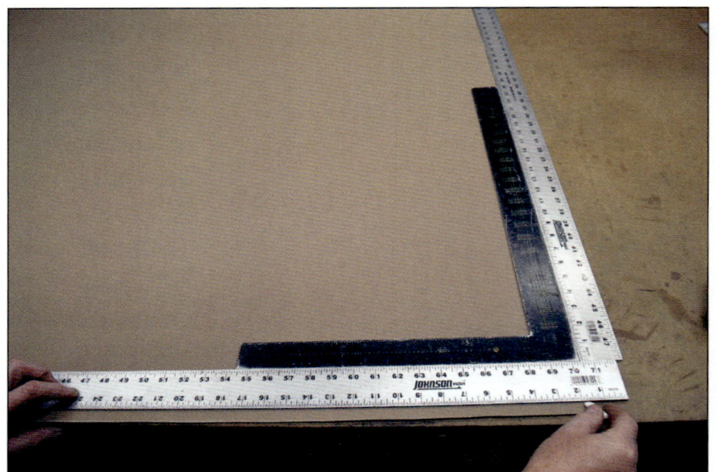

An essential part of making a convertible top is to properly align the panels. Before the convertible top material is cut, square up the fabric to give an absolute true edge to work from. If the material is skewed, the top will not look right.

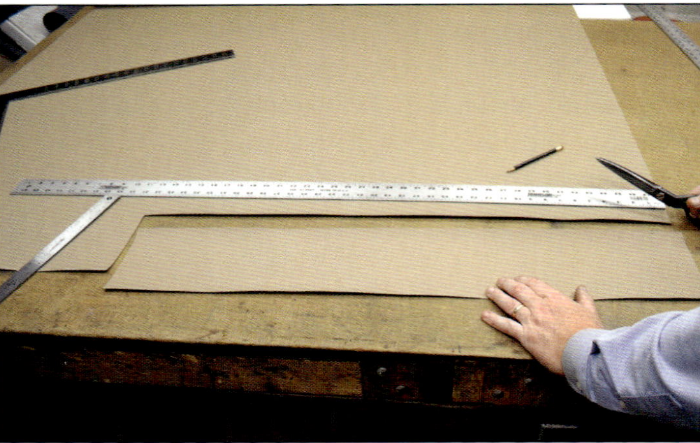

Precisely measure and carefully cut each panel needed for the top from the roll of top material to get the maximum yield from the fabric. Errors made from incorrect measurements and sloppy cutting can be very wasteful and end up being quite costly.

the top will overlap the edge of the window and reveal a nicely finished window.

Square Up the Top Material

Unroll the top material on the workbench and place a straightedge ruler along the selvedge edge of the roll to verify that the material is straight and true. Place the longer edge of a framing square against the straightedge, and then lay a 6-foot straightedge ruler across the material and flush with the short edge of the square. Reposition the 6-foot ruler up or down the roll until it reveals less than a 1/4 inch of top material, and then mark the fabric with a pencil. Now, the material can be trimmed to make it square.

The first thing to cut from the roll is a 4½-inch wide strip of top material for the front weather seal. If this is not done now, the piece may not be wide enough at the end of the project. This piece will be the last thing sewn up and installed; so, after it is cut, label it and then set it aside.

Two layers of top material are needed to encase the clear vinyl win-dow. Mark the lower valance pieces of the curtain and then cut them out. Do the same with the side panels and upper valance. When all the pieces are cut, the assembly of the rear curtain can begin.

Cut and Sew

The clear vinyl window is prone to scratches and must be protected while it is being sewn. Use the paper inner liner that the window was rolled up with as a backing guard.

Begin by aligning the top edges of the lower valance pieces with the lower edge of the vinyl window. Place the outer panel facedown on the face of the window and the inner valance panel, facedown under the clear vinyl. Sew the three pieces together with a 1/2-inch seam allowance. Turn down the panels, and run a cap stitch across the top of the lower valance.

Now, fit the side panels to the end of the vinyl window just as you did for the lower valance, and sew the panels together with a 1/2-inch seam allowance. Again, turn the panels down, and then add a cap stitch

Carefully check orientation of the lower valance panels prior to sewing them in place along the bottom edge of the clear window. Assembly of the individual components can be a little confusing because of the inner and outer panels.

down the edge of the fabric panel. Repeat the process to the other side.

Attach the upper valance panels just as the others and finish with a cap stitch. Temporarily tack the rear curtain in place, and mark the outer edges of the side panels to the end of the rear bow tack strip and beltline tack strip for trimming. Remove the curtain and use a straightedge to connect the trim marks. Sew the outer

Add a wide-width cap stitch along the upper edge of the valance panel. This cap stitch is not only decorative, it also serves as a reinforcement to strengthen the attachment of the valance panels to the vinyl curtain material.

After applying some heat to the clear window, all the wrinkles have been worked out of the rear curtain, and it is ready for the rear quarter pads to be installed. The rear dome light wire will be encased inside of the rear quarter pad.

Installation of the rear quarter pads has been completed. Inside of the left pad is the dome light wire along with the foam cushioning pad. Marking the location of the dome light wire onto the tape at the beltline reminds us to avoid stapling the wire.

edge of the panel together just inside the trim line, and then cut away the excess material on the outside of the sew line.

Install the curtain by first centering the upper valance to the rear bow, and work outward to the inside edge of the pad. Unlatch the top frame from the windshield and add a spacer under the header bow to take the tension off the rear bow. Attach the lower valance to the beltline tack strip, and then latch the top to the windshield. Make any adjustments necessary to remove the wrinkles from the rear curtain. Apply a little heat to help relax the heavy vinyl window as you make the adjustments in the curtain. Trim the upper and lower valance panels flush with the edges of the tack strips.

After the rear curtain is adjusted and you are happy with the fit, the rear quarter pads can be installed. The rear pads aid in the support and shape of the rear sail area of the convertible top.

Top Lay Out

Having the foundation components of the convertible top installed, commence construction of the new top. Start by taking a set of accurate measurements for the decking and side panels. This is an important step to get right, otherwise it can become costly to replace improperly cut topping material.

Begin measuring at the header bow by finding the center point. Measure across the header bow and determine the deck width. As a general guide, the depressions in the header bow allow a relief for the deck panel seam in the top. The distance of the seams should be an equal distance from the center line and also lay inward of the edge of the protective pad to hide the deck

Measuring for the Decking

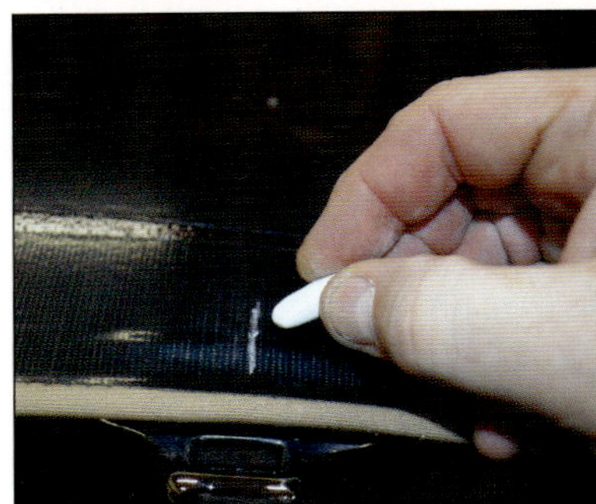

1 *Use chalk to make a reference mark at the center point of the header bow for the layout of the top decking. This central point allows for the accurate positioning and measurements needed to create and install the convertible top.*

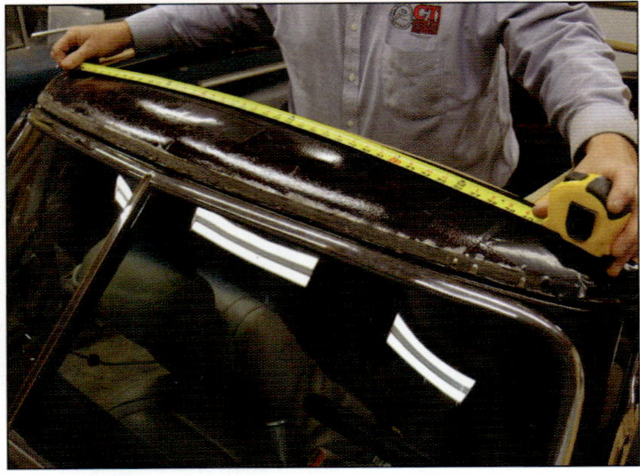

2 *While standing inside the car, use a tape measure across the header bow to determine the width to make the convertible top decking. This position allows for a great view of how the pieces of the top material will lay after they have been sewn together.*

3 *Make reference marks for the decking seam an equal distance from the center point of the header bow. Each deck seam should be concealed from view by the pad and is let in about 1 inch and marked onto the header bow.*

4 *To keep the width of the decking consistent, use a tape measure to locate the seam line on the rear bow of the convertible top frame. Make a chalk mark on top of the top pad to reference the location of the seam.*

5 *By running a tape measure or string from the center point of the header bow to the center point of the rear bow, all the cross bows can be accurately marked at their respective center points. This will help when measuring for the width of the decking.*

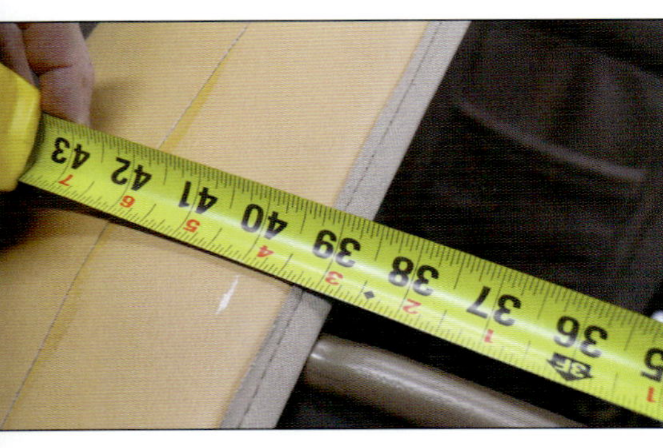

6 *To get the proper decking width, measure each cross bow from the center point outward and mark it on the top of the protective pad. The measurement must be the same from the front of the top all the way to rear to keep the deck seam straight.*

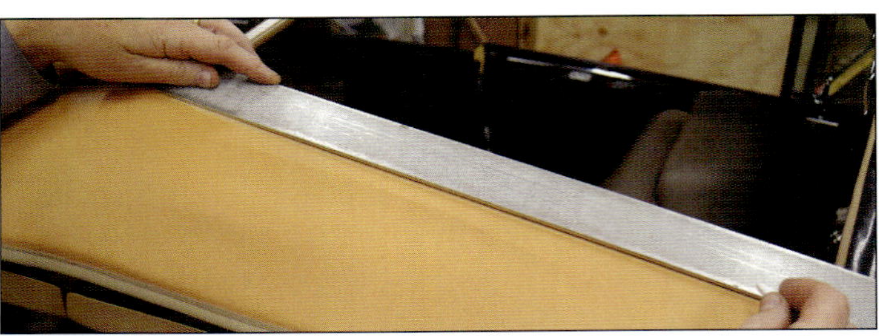

7 *Chalk a reference line from front to rear along the top of the protective pad connecting the decking width marks. This line will be used to mark the actual sewn deck seam in the top material. Keeping the line straight will result in the top having a professional appearance.*

seam from view when inside of the car.

The width of the decking at the rear bow should be the same as the header bow or at least within 1 inch of the measurement at the front of the top. After the decking width has been established, mark the centerline of the convertible top frame onto the cross bows by running a straightedge or tape measure from the header bow to the rear bow, and then mark the center point onto each cross bow. The decking width can now be marked on the top of the pads from the center point outward. Use a straightedge and chalk to connect the marks from the header bow to the rear bow along the tops of the pads.

Top Decking

Before the top material can be cut, it is necessary to know exactly how much material is needed for the individual panels. To get the correct measurements for the decking panel, measure from the front center edge of the header bow to the center line of the rear bow and then add 4 inches. This will be the length of the center decking panel.

To get the width of the decking, take the measurement across the rear bow and add 4 inches. The additional material will allow for the seam allowance and adjustment to the panel to accommodate the curvature in the top frame.

The upper panel over the rear curtain can also be cut the same width as the center decking. The length of the panel from the center of the rear bow down is generally one-fifth of the rear bow height, plus 2 additional inches. This piece can either be added as part of the decking panel or as a separate component. In our case, it will be a separate component.

Take a measurement from the leading edge of the header bow to the center point of the rear with a tape measure to determine the over length of the decking panel. Add 4 inches to the measurement to allow for attaching the panel to the top frame.

A smaller panel is measured for the upper rear valance that covers over the top of the rear curtain. This panel is about one-fifth of the overall height of the rear bow height and is as wide as the main decking for the convertible top.

Side Panel

We also need to get the side panel dimensions. These measurements should be larger than the actual size of the panel so that a cloth pattern can be made. The cloth will then be fit to the top frame, cut to the exact size of the side panel, and used as the cutting pattern for the actual side panel. Begin by measuring the length 3 inches past the end of the header bow, and continue all the way over the top frame to the rear beltline tack rail. Make adjustments to the length of the pattern material for the rear tack rail attachment.

The width of the panel tapers from the front to the rear. Take a measurement from the front of the side panel across the header bow from the seam line outward, and then 2 inches are added on both sides. At the rear quarter, take a measurement from the rear bow deck seam down the outside of the top. Allow enough material for the top to be attached to the appropriate inside or outside attachment points. The combination of these measurements will give you a rough idea of how much pattern material is needed to make the side panel.

Side Panel Measurements

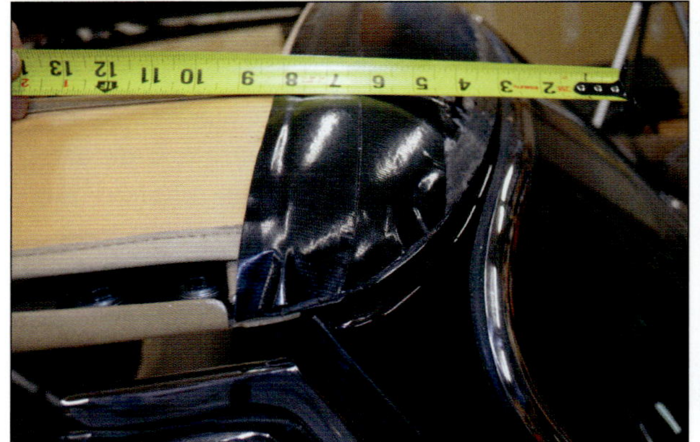

2 Allot an additional amount of material to the rear measurement for adjustments and attachment of the pattern to the rear tack rail. The pattern will cost only pennies and save on the amount of the expensive convertible top material that will be used.

1 Take measurements for the side panel pattern from the header bow on back to the rear tack rail of the car. Extra material is allowed in the pattern making to compensate for curvature of the convertible top frame and attachment points.

3 Take more measurements at the header bow to establish the width of the leading portion of the side panel. The dimensions of the raw-cut pattern material must be larger than the actual size of the finished panel to ensure a proper fit.

4 Naturally, the rear section of the side panel is wider than the front because the material must cover the entire sail panel area of the top. Rough dimensions are taken at the decking seam line at the rear bow, down past the beltline attachment point.

Sizing the Deck

Unroll the top material faceup on the workbench, and square up the material before chalking out the new deck and upper valance panels. Measure out the panels onto the top material and mark the cut lines with chalk. Connect the marks with the aid of long straightedge rulers. Double-check that the panels are the correct size before you carefully cut the panels from the roll.

Remove the cut panels from the workbench, take them to the car, and place the deck panel over the top frame. Align the deck material evenly over the top frame, and temporarily staple or tack the material to the center point of the header bow and likewise at the rear bow. This keeps the decking panel in position as it is marked for size.

Turn up the outer edge of the deck material to reveal the chalk line on the pad. Fold back the material to make a slight crease in the material at the chalk line, and transfer the seam line to the outer surface of the topping material with chalk. Do this along both outer edges of the deck panel from front to rear.

Fold the upper valance panel in half and notch the center point of the panel. Center the rear upper

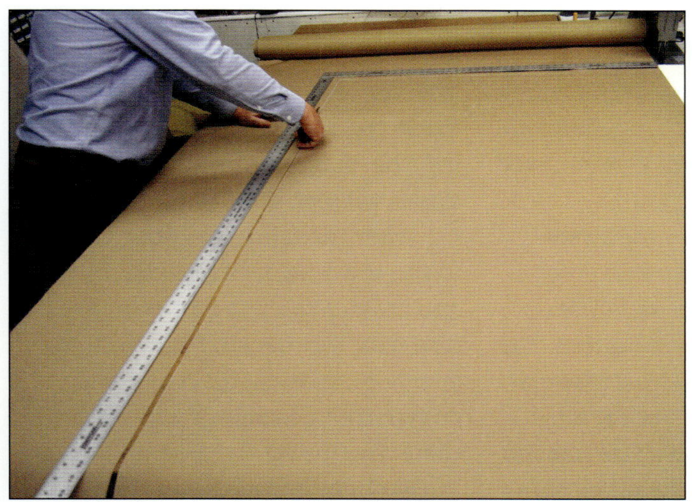

The deck panel is the first piece to be cut from the roll of convertible top material. The dimensions were carefully transferred to the top side of the material and then cut lines were made using chalk and a straightedge on the surface of the material.

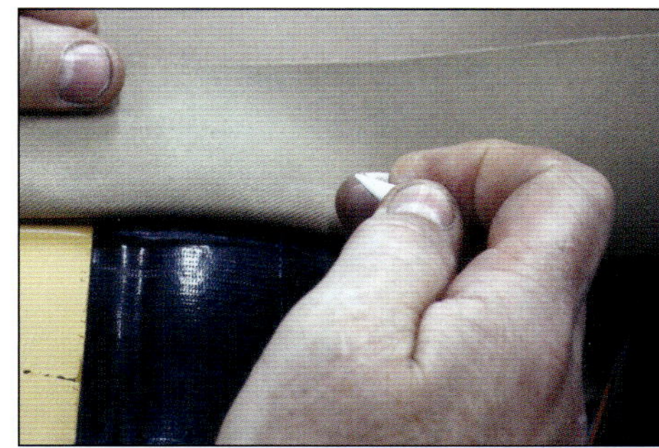

Put a crease into the edge of the top material at the seam line before it is marked with chalk. This method gives an accurate position of the line underneath the decking so that the surface of the material can be marked.

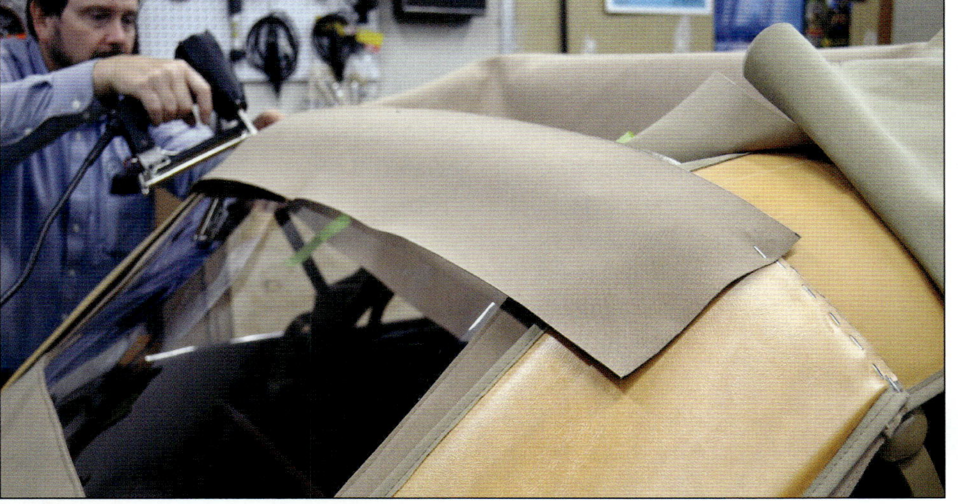

Use temporary staples to hold the upper rear valance panel in place so that it stays in position as it gets marked for sewing. When done correctly, the finished panel will line up exactly in this same position after all the top panels are sewn together.

Chalk a diagonal line on the upper valance panel to connect the window opening and deck seam points. The center of the rear bow tack strip will become the intersect point between the valance panel and top decking panel.

valance on the rear bow, and attach it by temporarily tacking it to the bow with staples. Locate the center line of the rear tack strip and chalk a reference point on the panel. This will later be lined up with the turning point of the side panel.

To create the rear window opening in the convertible top, measure across the top of the clear window of the rear curtain and subtract 2 inches from that dimension. Divide this number in half and make a reference mark from the center point outward

on the lower edge of the valance panel. This will be the opening size for the rear window.

Chalk another line on the upper valance panel from the seam mark on the pad to the center line of the rear bow tack strip. Notice that the upper and lower reference marks on the valance panel are offset. Connect the two points with a straightedge and create a seam line with chalk.

Realign the decking panel over the rear valance panel and check that all the reference marks intersect

correctly at the center point of the rear bow. Temporarily staple the deck material in place on the rear bow.

Side Panel Pattern

To get an accurate measurement for the side panel of the top, we will need to make a pattern. I like to use heavy-weight upholstery denim for this. The cost is minimal, and it works just fine for this purpose. Simply cut the denim to the length you previously measured, and then lay the fabric on the top frame.

You may wish to temporarily tack the material to the header bow and the rear bow to keep it in position while you are working. The material should lie smoothly over the top frame and pad without stretching it. Begin by trimming the upper edge of the material even with the chalked seam line on the pad and decking material. This will become the sew line for the side panel. When you reach the rear bow, continue following the diagonal sew line down the upper valance panel.

After the fabric has been trimmed to the sew line, fold back the cut edge and make reference marks on the pattern and top decking material about every 5 inches. These marks will ensure that the panels will be aligned correctly during the assembly stage.

To help refine the pattern, chalk out the lower sail area and rear tack rail attachment. Only trim the denim to within 1½ inches of the chalk mark. Do the same with the side glass area, and leave about 3 inches of extra material below the lower edge of the convertible top frame side rail. Do not trim the lower section too close at this time, otherwise the panel may not fit. On the other hand, if the pattern is made too big, you will waste expensive top material.

Remove the panel pattern and fit it to the other side of the car. The side panels should be symmetrical, but they are not always. If the pattern fits, transfer the witness marks to the top decking. Sometimes there is an irregularity in the pattern and it does not fit, and you may need to create a second patterned piece that will.

Cut and Assemble

Take the denim pattern to the workbench and lay it on top of the rolled-out top material. The pattern must lay out flat and smooth on the table to get an accurate transfer. Trace the lower perimeter of the pattern onto the top material.

Add a seam allowance to the seam line. To do this, measure 1/2 inch from the edge of the pattern and mark the top material. Use a straight-

Trim the upholstery denim for use as a side panel pattern. The low-cost material will be cut the exact size needed to make the side panels for the top. This will help prevent the possibility of a costly mistake with the top material.

Our pattern has been trimmed to the seam line on the deck and valance panels. Because this line is visible after the top panels have been sewn together, it is important to make the deck seam as straight as possible.

Make witness marks along the edges of the top decking and side panel pattern to ensure the proper alignment of the panels when they are sewn together. Without the witness marks, the panels will not come together correctly due to the curvature of the top frame.

Measuring and Marking

1 Lay the pattern out on top of the convertible top material and position it to get the best yield out of the material. After this panel has been transferred, flip it over and make an opposite panel for the other side of the convertible top.

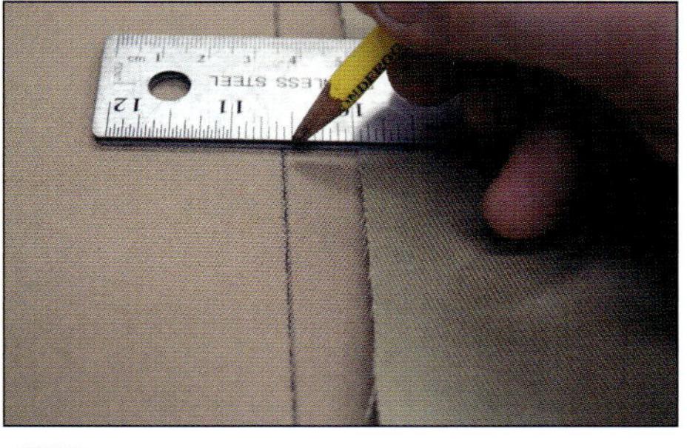

2 Add extra material to the seam line as a sewing allowance. This extra 1/2 inch of material helps prevent the thread from tear out and causing the seam to fail. The seam allowance also helps with smoothing the shape of the deck seam.

3 Witness marks are essential to the reassembly of the individual top panels. Without matching up the small marks, the panels can become skewed and cause the top to be sewn unevenly. This will create unsightly wrinkles because the top material will not lie correctly over the top frame.

4 After one side panel has been cut, it can be used as the pattern for the opposite side panel. Time can be saved since all the seams have already been lengthened and smoothed. Place the panel facedown and trace it along with the witness marks.

5 Apply seam tape to the face of the deck panel to help keep the pieces properly aligned during the sewing process. This special double-sided tape not only helps hold the fabric together, it helps make the seam waterproof as well.

6 After the adhesive of the seam seal tape has been exposed, align the witness marks of the side panel with the marks on the decking, and then press them together. The perfectly matched seam can now be sewn without any slipping or distortion.

edge to connect your marks. Notice that the sew line is not straight and that it has a slight curve to it. This is caused by the curvature in the cross bows of the top frame, which is normal. If you notice that the sew line is wavy, you must straighten it out, otherwise the seam will not lie straight.

Transfer the witness marks that you made from the underside of the denim to the top material. Do not cut notches for the witness marks, but rather make small marks along the edge of the material. The marks should not show after the panel is sewn.

Cut the panel out and then flip it over facedown on the top material. Use this panel as the template to trace the other side panel. Remember to add the witness marks to the newly traced panel. Cut the panel out of the top material and then set them aside to prepare the decking for sewing.

Lay the decking panel facedown on the workbench. Make a sewing guide on the back side of the deck panel. Measure and mark a 1/2-inch seam line along the outer edges of the

Seam Tape Tech Tip

Do not substitute and use general-purpose double-sided tape to align the panels. The base material and adhesive of the general-purpose tape is not compatible with the top material, and it will give you unsatisfactory results. ■

Use an even stitch to sew the deck and side panels together. Following close to the seam line as the panels are sewn will ensure that you will end up with a straight seam that will look nice when the top is installed over the top frame.

A decorative cap stitch is added to the deck seam to give the panel seam strength and keep it from tearing apart while the new top is in service. Take extra care to make the stitches as uniform as possible because this cap stitch will be seen after the top is installed.

panel on the back side of the material. Transfer the witness marks from the front to the seam allowance.

Seam Tape

Turn the deck panel over and apply a strip of 1/2-inch-wide seam tape to the face of the material along the outer edge of the deck panel. The seam tape is a double-sided transfer tape that helps keep the top panels perfectly aligned while they are being sewn. The tape also helps seal the seam and prevent leakage. You can get seam tape from your local upholstery supplier.

Make sure that you press the tape firmly onto the top material and then remove the backing paper to reveal the adhesive. Align the witness marks of the side panel over the deck panel while keeping the edges even. Press the two panels together and you are now ready to sew.

If you have a top like the one we are making, it has an upper valance panel that is separate from the decking and runs across the rear bow. This panel needs to be added when you get to the intersect point of the rear bow.

Sewing

With the deck panel on top, begin sewing the panels together with a UV-rated, marine-grade or polyester thread and a medium-length stitch.

Sew along the inside of the seam line to avoid the seam tape being exposed. Keep the material flat as it is fed into the sewing machine, and do not stretch the material, otherwise it will pucker. When you reach the intersect point where the top lies across the rear bow, align the upper valance panel and continue sewing until you get to the end of the side panel. Repeat this step for the other seam.

The deck seams need to be reinforced to prevent them from pulling apart. To do this, turn the top faceup, and pull the deck panel over the top of the seam allowance. Now, sew a cap stitch along the inside of the panel seam on top of the deck panel. This will lock the seam allowance under the deck and allow the side panel to lie smoothly over the top frame.

Use a guide foot to keep the stitch parallel with the edge of the seam. The cap stitch will be visible, so take your time and make the seam as straight as possible. Be sure to check your bobbin before you start to sew the cap stitch to ensure that you can make the stitch in one pass. Now that the

core of the top is sewn together, proceed with the rear window opening.

Window Opening

Lay the top facedown on the workbench, and mark off 1/2 inch from along the top and sides of the window opening. Radius the upper inside corners of the window opening to allow the binding to flow without causing any sharp bends or creases. When you are satisfied with the shape of the radius, trim the edge of the rear window opening to the new opening line.

Before the window edge can be bound, it must be reinforced with an additional layer of top material to give it strength and some bulk for the binding to wrap around. To make the reinforcement strips, place a piece of top material facedown under the top and trace the outer edge of the top onto the material below. Remove the top material and add 2 inches parallel to the line to create a reinforcement strip. Now, cut the strip from the material.

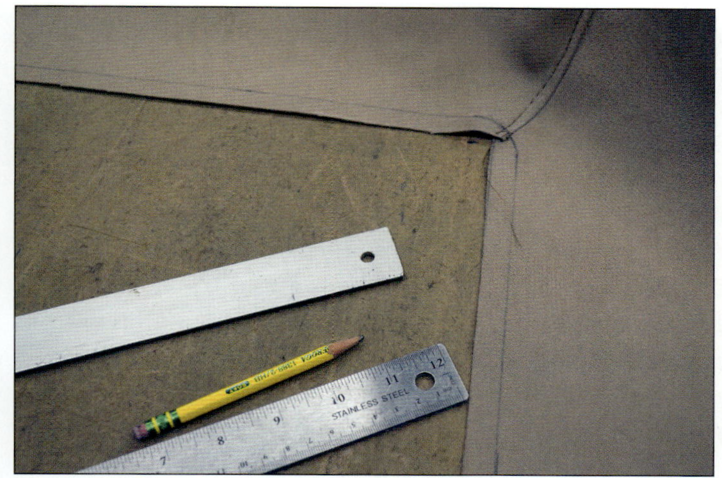

Add a rounded corner to the inside of the window opening to help the edge binding lie smoothly around the opening of the rear window. Without the radius in the corner, the edge binding will kink and spoil the look of the rear curtain.

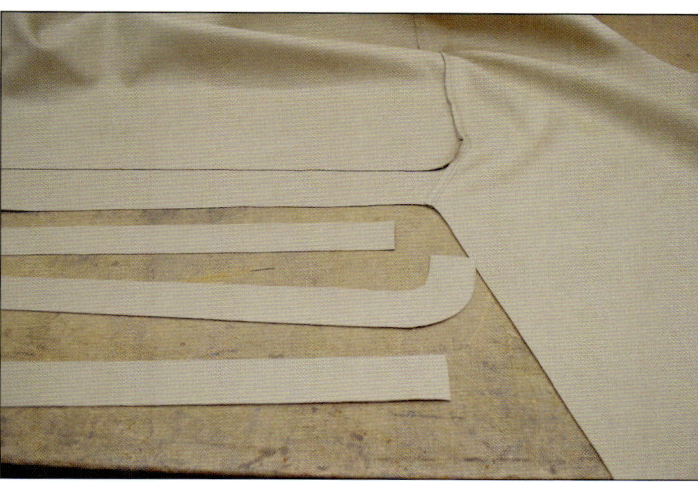

Pattern and cut reinforcement strips to give strength to the edge of the rear curtain opening. The additional layer of top material helps the opening retain its shape and it will also provide a base for the edge binding to be sewn to.

Brush contact cement onto the back side of the top material and reinforcement strip and allow it to tack before the pieces are pressed together. The glue keeps the material from shifting position while it is being sewn together.

Sew a stitch parallel to the rear window opening of the top to secure the edge of the reinforcement strip material in place. This stitch is decorative and it helps strengthen the outer edge of the top material.

Lay the reinforcement strip on the back side of the window opening and lightly mark the outer edge of the strip to the top material. This will show where to apply the glue to the top material. Remove the strip after tracing, and brush contact cement onto the mating surfaces of the top and the reinforcement strip. After the glue flashes, align the reinforcement strip to the top and press the pieces together.

Now turn the top over and chalk a line 1½ inches from the raw edge of the opening all the way around the window opening. This will become the sew line to secure reinforcement strip to the top. Place the top under the sewing machine and carefully sew on the chalk line. Again, check your bobbin before starting to sew, and make the stitch as straight as possible because it will be visible.

Binding

To finish the raw edge of the top, apply a bias binding by folding it in half over the edge of the opening and sewing it onto the top. This can be done by hand, or a binding appliance can be used if one is set up for your sewing machine. The trick here is to keep the bias binding centered and maintain an even stitch throughout the run of the

A decorative matching bias binding is folded around and sewn in place to cover the raw edge of the convertible top material. The binding not only protects the top material from fraying but also gives the top that professionally finished appearance.

binding. Work a little at a time and it will turn out fine. If you rush the binding process, you can end up with a wavy mess that will look terrible.

Pre-Fit

Now that the binding around the window opening is complete, the basic shape of the top is ready for the detail shaping and trimming. We will pre-fit the top over the frame and check for any alterations that may need to be made. Anchor the key points of the top along the rear bow and pull the lower edges snug to define the rear window. Add a few more staples along the beltline tack rail to keep the top material from shifting. Pull the leading end of the top forward, align the deck seams with the chalk marks you made on the header bow, and temporarily tack the top material to the header bow.

Chalk

After the top material has been set in position, use chalk to mark the lower edge of the sail area on the

Chalking, Cutting, and Reference Marking

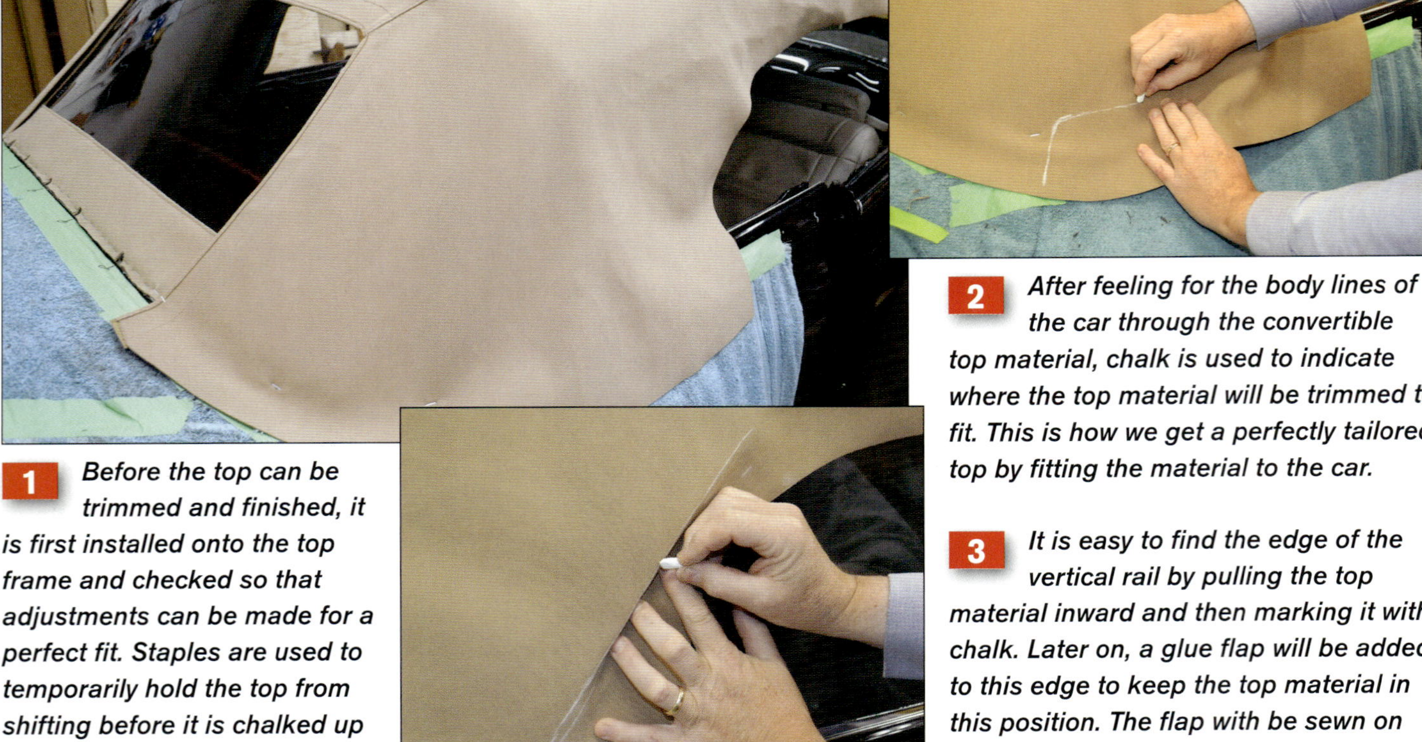

1 Before the top can be trimmed and finished, it is first installed onto the top frame and checked so that adjustments can be made for a perfect fit. Staples are used to temporarily hold the top from shifting before it is chalked up for completion.

2 After feeling for the body lines of the car through the convertible top material, chalk is used to indicate where the top material will be trimmed to fit. This is how we get a perfectly tailored top by fitting the material to the car.

3 It is easy to find the edge of the vertical rail by pulling the top material inward and then marking it with chalk. Later on, a glue flap will be added to this edge to keep the top material in this position. The flap with be sewn on the underside of the top material.

Chalking, Cutting, and Reference Marking *Continued*

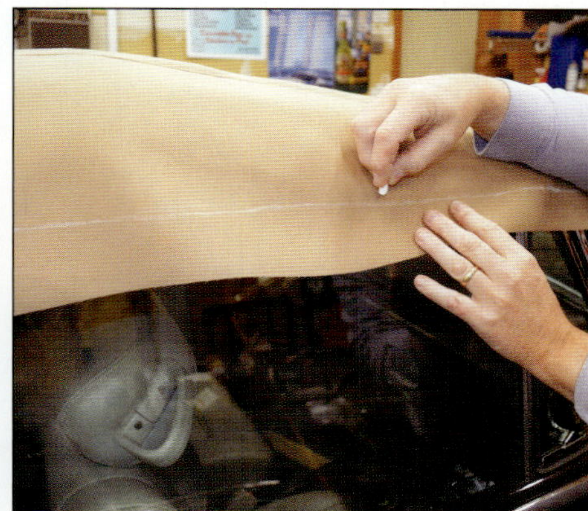

4 *With the side windows in the up position, mark the top material to cover the rubber weatherstrip while it just clears the top of the glass. This is what gives the top the tailored appearance that cannot be achieved with a premade top.*

5 *This is the pre-finished result after the top material has been carefully trimmed to fit the contour of the car. Take the same steps to make the other side of the top match the profile of the car. After the top is trimmed to size, it will be removed and finished.*

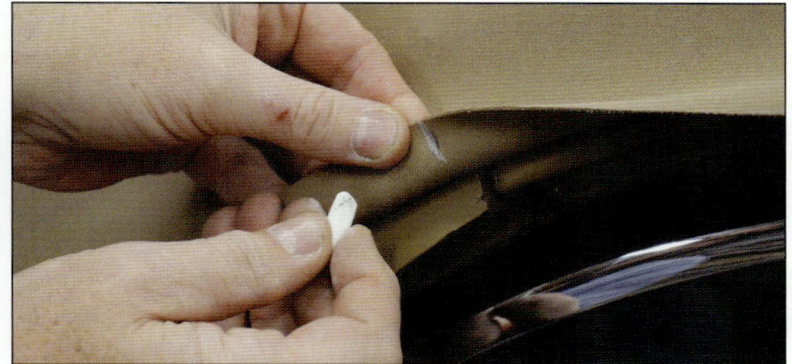

6 *Add a reference mark to the underside edge of the top material for the top of the vertical glue flap. These marks will guide us to correctly position the additional attachment features needed to fasten the convertible top to the frame.*

7 *Make alignment marks along the lower horizontal edge of the top material to define the length of the stainless steel retainer. This area will be the location for the banana peel fastener that tucks into the retainer, holding the sail panel in place.*

top. Feel for the body line and run the chalk on the ridge of the body to define the shape needed to make the top look right. Work the material over the edge of the vertical rail and mark the material for the placement of the rear glue flap that will secure the top to the frame.

Roll the side windows up and mark the position of the top edge of the door frame or glass onto the top material. The top material should cover the side rail of the frame and come within 1/4 inch of the top of the side glass. It is ideal for the top material to be as close to the top of the door glass without being touched by the glass when the door is opened. A straightedge can also be used to help straighten out the line.

Cut

Once the edge of the top has been defined, carefully cut the mate-rial along the chalk line. It is better to have the material too long and end up retrimming the edges to make it fit better than cutting too much and having an undesirable gap along the edge of the top.

Reference Marking

When you are satisfied with the way the top material lies along the frame rail, turn the edge up and mark the underside of the top material

Chalk reference points onto the inside of the top material for the side tension cables that will help hold the top tight to the frame. A cable sleeve is also needed to house the cable as it runs through the lower part of the side panel along the frame rail.

for key attachment points. The top of the third section of the top frame will need a reference mark to indicate the stopping point for the rear vertical flap. The lower end of the rear flap is marked at the body line. Another mark is placed along the lower horizontal edge of the sail area to show the beginning and end points of the sail panel retainer. There is a blind fastener that will be attached between these two points.

Cable Sleeve

Moving forward on the side rail,

just as the frame straightens out, is the mounting point for the side tension cable. The cables are an added feature to help keep the top from buffeting as it is driven. Mark the top material for the end position of the end of the cable and then about 2 inches forward for the end of the cable sleeve. The other end of the cable sleeve is marked about 2 inches from the front of the side rail.

After the reference points have been made, the top can be removed and laid out on the workbench to have the edges reinforced. Apply the 2-inch strips of top material to the edges of the top just as it was done for the rear window area. When you get to the cable sleeve area, make this variation. The front and rear sections of the edge reinforcement material should extend about 1 inch under the cable sleeve area. The cable sleeve material should be cut to fit between the two marks you made on the top.

When you are ready to attach the cable sleeve to the top material, only apply glue to the top 1/4 inch of the cable sleeve material and top before setting the material in place. The rest of the sleeve must be able to have the tension cable run through it. Also consider adding a length of string inside of the cable sleeve at this time

The forward end point for the cable sleeve is marked in chalk on the underside of the top material. The side tension cable will exit the sleeve and be anchored to the side frame rail 1 inch in front of the cable sleeve.

Only the top edge of the side rail reinforcement strip is glued and sewn to create the side tension cable sleeve. The bottom of the sleeve is sewn closed when the bias binding is applied, and this allows the cable to slide freely inside the sleeve.

to facilitate the insertion of the tension cable later on.

Hidden Fasteners

To allow the top to fold without the top material tearing, a section of the sail panel material is released to give the top more flexibility. Some models use snap fasteners along this section of the top, and others have a blind fastener called a banana peel. The banana peel is a thick section of material that tucks under the sail panel retainer. This gave the top a cleaner outward appearance, but the fastener was not always that secure, and it was eventually changed in later models.

Making the banana peel is simple. The core material of the banana peel is made from a piece of the 40-gauge, clear vinyl window material wrapped in matching convertible top material. Take a scrap of the window vinyl a little longer than the panel retainer and square an edge. Slide the vinyl

Making the Banana Peel

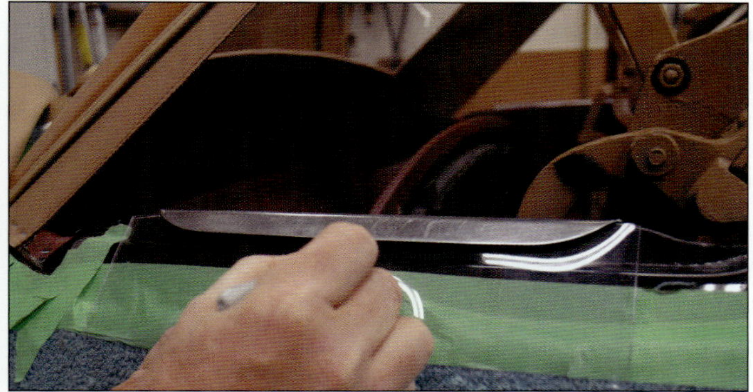

1 *A scrap piece of 40-gauge vinyl window material is used to create the blind banana peel fastener for the top. When the vinyl is inserted into the retainer, a marker is used to trace the exact shape and size needed for the new fastener.*

2 *Brush contact cement on the vinyl base material before it is wrapped in matching convertible top material. The wrapped piece of vinyl will then be trimmed from the material and brought to the sewing machine to be reinforced.*

3 *A simple stitch is made across and back on the retainer strip to fortify the fastener. The stitching not only keeps the top material in place but the stitches also give the fastener more strength by stiffening the entire length of the fastener.*

4 *After the banana peel fastener has been sewn, trim the top material closely to the vinyl core along the outer and lower edges of the fastener. A pair of these fasteners will need to be made with one attached to each side of the convertible top.*

5 *This small fastener is attached to the lower edge of the convertible top sail area with bias binding. When the fastener is slid under the retainer, it will hold the top material in place without the top lifting. The fastener can be easily removed from the retainer when the top is folded.*

up into the retainer and use a marker to trace along the lower edge of the retainer flap.

Cut the vinyl along the drawn line, and apply contact cement to the vinyl and on the back side of a piece of convertible top material. Set the vinyl on the glued material and apply more contact adhesive to the vinyl and fabric. Fold the material over the vinyl and press it together. To make the piece stronger and stiffer, sew through the piece from end to end and then turn the fastener and return the stitch. Trim the fabric close along the ends and the bottom, but do not trim the folded edge of the material.

Additional material is added to the underside of the top to be used as a glue flap. The flaps are attached at the front of the top and along the vertical rise in the rear quarter section. These flaps are what will be used to secure the top to the side rail of the frame.

Align the banana peel fastener with the bottom edge of the sail panel between the reference marks made earlier, and sew it to the top material very close to the bottom edge so that the binding will cover the stitches. This will keep it in position and make the binding process easier.

Cut pieces of top material 3 inches wide to be used for the glue flaps. The front flap begins 1/2 inch in front of the end of the cable sleeve and runs to the end of the top on both sides. The rear vertical flap is applied between the marks made previously.

The edges of the top can be bound with the bias binding just as the rear window area. Take the time to make the binding look tight and keep an even stitch along the edge. When the binding is finished, the top is complete and ready to be installed on the car.

Wire-On

This should be the final time you need to install the top. You have patterned, fit, and finished a tailored top. Installation is the same as it was

Apply the wire-on welt to conceal the staples and seam at the rear bow. These small tips are the finishing touch used to complete the task. Apply the chrome tip over the raw end of the wire-on welt and fasten it in place with a small trim screw.

before with the exception of the staples not being temporary. Attach all the key points and work the wrinkles out as you go. Finish off the rear edge of the decking with wire-on welt and chrome tips. Do not glue the side flaps at this time. There are a

few more items that we need to take care of.

Tension Cable

Modern convertible tops all came with side tension cables. They are going to be added to this top to help with the known buffeting issue. Universal top tension cables are available from almost all retailers of convertible tops. Installation is not hard, and once they are installed, the car will be more enjoyable to drive.

If the frame has never been fitted for cables, drill some holes in the side rails of the top frame. Begin with the rear mounting point. Unlatch the top frame from the windshield to relieve the tension on the frame and top material to make it easier to access the frame rail. Lift up the outer edge of the top material to expose the rear section of the second or center side rail. The tension cable

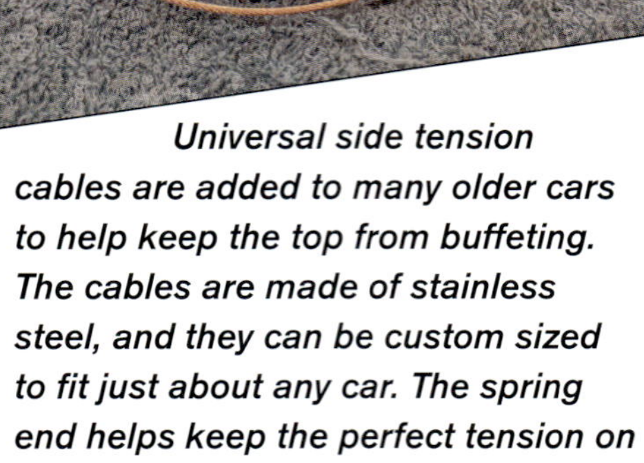

Universal side tension cables are added to many older cars to help keep the top from buffeting. The cables are made of stainless steel, and they can be custom sized to fit just about any car. The spring end helps keep the perfect tension on the installed cable.

Installing the Tension Cable

1 Sizing the tension cable to the car requires a small hole to be drilled into the side rail to accommodate a rivet or screw to anchor the cable to the side rail. Now, stretch the cable forward to the front mounting point and check for length.

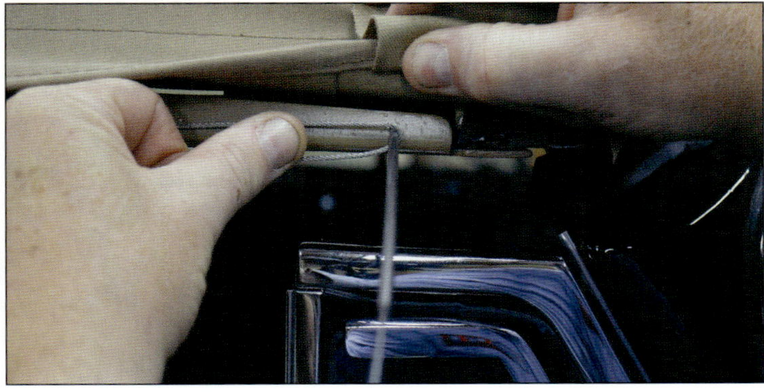

2 An upholsterer's regulator has been placed into the front mounting hole so that the side tension cable can be properly sized to fit the car. After the cable has been wrapped around the regulator, form a loop to terminate the cable.

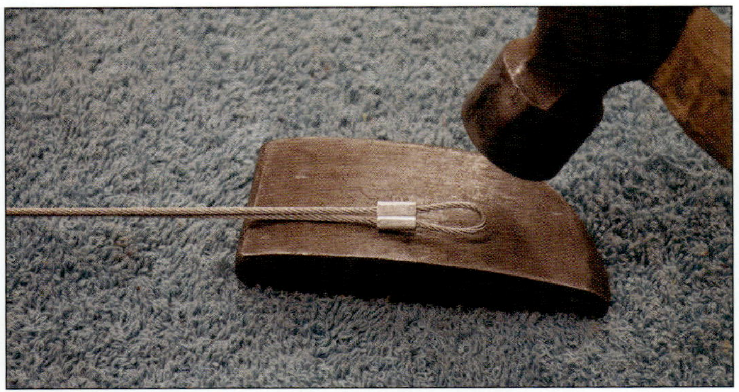

3 Make a loop in the end of the side tension cable by threading the cable through the thimble fastener and then crimp it to retain the loop. Variations in length require each side cable to be custom made to fit the car.

4 Apply heat-shrink tubing to the trimmed end of the cable to help prevent the cable from fraying and possibly damaging the convertible top material. The smooth vinyl covering also gives the cable a professional and finished appearance.

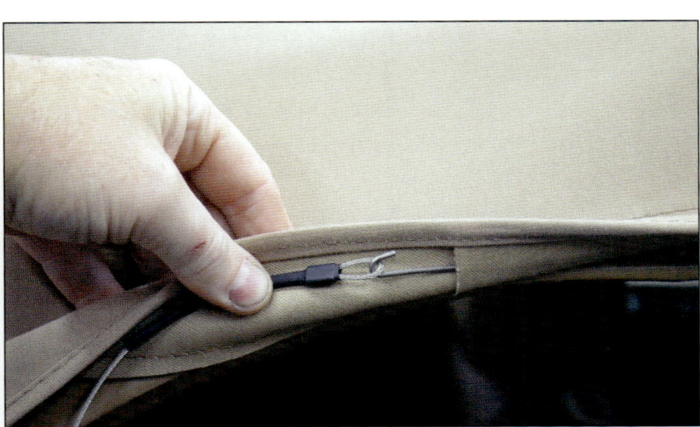

5 Threading the side tension cable through the cable sleeve is easy when you use a stiff wire that has been inserted from the opening in the front of the top. Hook the tension cable, and then pull it carefully through the cable sleeve until it emerges from the opening.

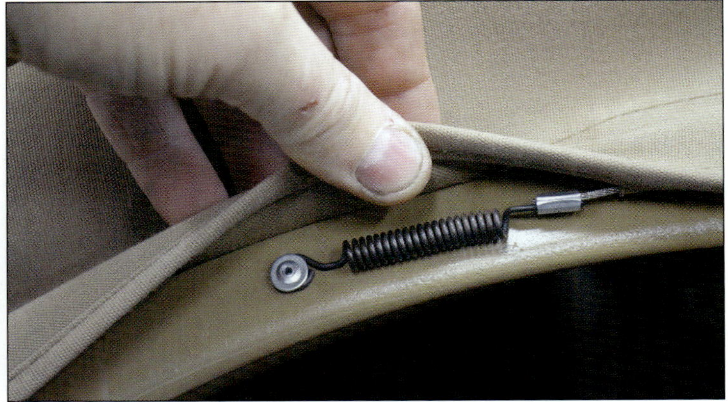

6 Use a 1/8-inch rivet along with a small retainer washer to hold the spring end of the side-tension cable to the rear section of the side rail. The low profile of the spring makes it undetectable under the edge of the convertible top.

will be attached to the side rail with a pop rivet. Make a 1/8-inch hole in the side rail to accommodate the rivet. Drill the hole on the center of the side rail at the predetermined point. Now, lift the top material at the front rail close to the header bow, and drill a hole in the side rail about 1 inch in front of the end of the cable sleeve.

To size the cable for the proper fit, insert a rivet with a washer through the spring end of the cable into the side rail, but do not fasten the rivet. Put some tension on the cable to hold it in place as you stretch the cable forward to the front mounting point. Insert an upholsterer's regulator into the rivet hole, and wrap the cable around the regulator to produce a small kink in the cable. This will be the new end of the cable.

Remove the cable from the car and feed the end of the cable through one side of the retainer thimble that came with the cable set. Loop the cable back through the other side of the thimble until you have a small loop about 1/2 inch in size. Place the thimble on an anvil or hard surface, and crush the thimble with a hammer to lock the loop in place. Trim the excess wire about 3/4 inch from the thimble.

To keep the cable smooth and prevent it from scratching the top material, I like to cover the thimble and cable end with heat-shrink tubing. Tape might work, but the heat shrink stays in place and is much nicer to work with. The heat shrink can be purchased at any hardware store. A 1/4 inch is the correct size, and it will fit over the thimble and seal everything when it is heated with a heat gun.

To get the cable through the cable sleeve, you could sew a string into the sleeve during the fabrication process and tie the string to the cable to pull it through. Otherwise, use a stiff wire and insert it into the front of the cable sleeve until it emerges at the rear of the sleeve; hook the cable end and pull it through the sleeve.

Attach the spring end of the cable to the frame rail with a 1/8-inch pop rivet and a 1/4-inch grip range. Use a retaining washer with the rivet to keep the end of the spring from coming off the rivet. Use the same setup for the front of the cable and rivet the cable in place. When the top is latched to the windshield, the cable will tighten enough to help keep the top from buffeting.

Front Weather Seal

A 1/2-inch round rubber-core weather seal needs to be added across the front to the header bow. Use the strip of material that was first cut from the roll of top material to cover the rubber foam core.

To get the correct length of the seal, measure across the front leading edge of the header bow. If you have help holding a measuring tape, this

1 *Before the front weather seal can be sewn, take an accurate measurement along the front edge of the header bow with a tailor's tape. This weather seal will help to deflect wind and rainwater from entering the interior of the car.*

2 *Mark a sewing guide on the inside of the weather seal strip. The measurements taken from the header bow show where the seams for the ends of the seal need to be sewn. After the ends are sewn, the material will be prepared for the rubber core filler.*

Creating the Front Weather Seal *Continued*

3 Make relief cuts to the seam allowance to eliminate some of the bulk that will be inside of the seal once the material is turned and filled. There must be enough room inside the seal for the 1/2-inch rubber-core material to lie without being crushed.

5 Place the tapered end of the rubber core inside of the seal as the seal is sewn along the edge of the rubber core like a large piece of welt cord. The zipper foot allows for sewing very close to the rubber core without distorting the shape of the rubber.

7 Apply a length of wire-on welt across the front of the header bow to conceal staples and the raw edge of the weather seal. Add chrome tips to finish off the ends of the wire-on welt, completing the installation on the header bow.

4 Cut a taper on the end of the rubber-core material to allow the weather seal to fit closer to the header bow. This is a custom-fit seal, and the end should be as close to the header bow as possible to avoid a square-ended seal.

6 With a little contact cement applied to the front glue flap and bottom of the side rail, secure the flap to the top frame. After trimming, the front weather seal can be applied along with the inner weather seal and retainer.

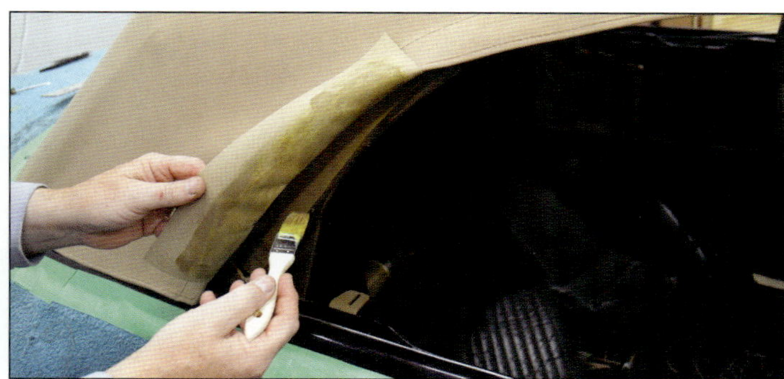

8 At last, the rear glue flaps are cemented in place on the vertical rails of the convertible top frame. This final step in the installation of the convertible top removes the small remaining wrinkles in the rear sail area of the top.

step is much easier. I usually tape one end in position, and then pull the tape across the header bow to get the measurement. If the seal is too long, the door will hit it; if it is too short, it won't seal properly.

After the dimension is taken, transfer the dimension to the strip of material first cut from the roll of topping material. Sew the ends of the weather seals closed instead of just folding them over; I think they look better. To do this, add a 1/2-inch seam allowance to the material. Normally, the seal has a squared-off end, but on this project the seal will taper in and curve into the header bow.

After the material has been marked and trimmed to size, sew the ends closed. First, fold the material in half with the weatherproof side inside. Sew the end at an angle to help keep the material from bulking up on the end of the header bow. Then, trim the seam allowance closer to the stitching to relieve bulk, and then turn out the material to keep the seam inside the seal.

Use 1/2-inch foam core to fill the weather seal. Because we are tapering this seal, the rubber core is also trimmed at an angle to allow a better fit of the final seal. Only trim one end at this time. The other will be trimmed closer to the end of the sewing process. This is because if the core was cut to size before it was sewn, it may end up longer or shorter due to stretching. It happens because the core is soft rubber.

Use a right zipper foot to sew the weather seal. The foot allows a tight fit against the rubber without crushing it. A 5/8-inch welt foot would give us the same result if it were a straight piece, but I like to use the zipper foot when I have to taper the ends. The rubber core is inserted into

the folded weather seal material and sewn to hold the core securely in place. When the sewing approaches 5 or 6 inches from the end, the foam core can then be trimmed to fit the end of the weather seal.

Take the weather seal back to the car and lower the top enough to reveal the underside of the header bow. Apply glue to the front flap and frame rail to secure the top to the frame. Before the weather seal can be attached on this car, the ends have to be split to allow the flaps on the seal to go over the front edge of the header bow and along the bottom side under the header bow. Apply glue to the lower flap and the bottom edge of the header bow. After the contact adhesive flashes, put the weather seal in position, and secure it to the header bow tack strip with staples.

The front edge of this top is finished off with the wire-on welt to cover the staples along the front header bow tack strip. The wire-on welt is then finished off with chrome tips to conceal the raw ends of the wire-on welt. An inner rubber weather seal and retainer are then applied to the underside of the header bow with small flathead screws to help seal out wind and rain.

Now, the top can be raised and latched to the windshield. Glue the rear vertical flaps into place. The rear flaps help hold the top material in position, and the forward tension on the seam allows the wrinkles in the sail panel to disappear.

The last details to address are the installation of the side rail weatherstrip retainers and rubber seals. After a good steam, the custom-tailored top will be ready for the road.

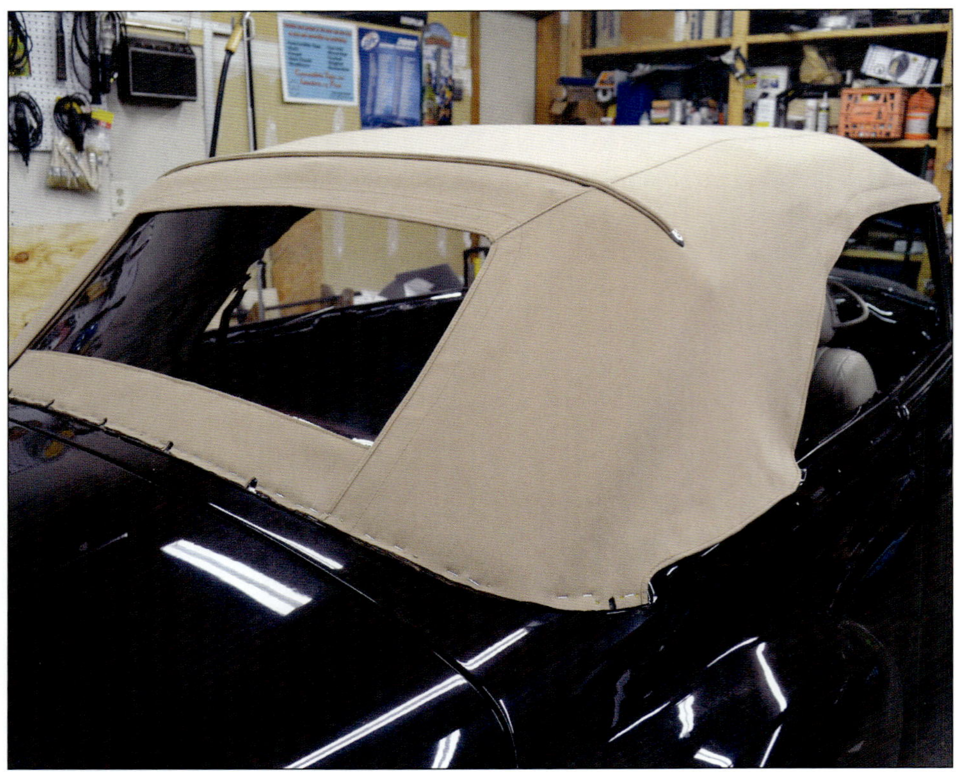

A few days ago, this top was nothing more than a table full of raw materials. It was not a hard project to do when it is broken down into small steps. Now, just take a step back and enjoy the final result of many hours of prep and planning.

RESTORATION **R**EPAIRS

Each project requires an individualized assessment of the damaged components of the convertible top frame. Some frames just need a simple cleaning and a few drops of oil to make them function correctly. As these cars age, multiple problems develop with the convertible top frame due to its environment and the owner's neglect.

We are going to address some of the most common issues that you may encounter on your project. Each task will require patience and some basic skills to correct the problem and bring the frame back into usable condition.

Tacking Strip

It is necessary to understand the importance of the tack strip. This simple material is vital to holding a staple or tack, which in turn keeps the top material in place. After years of exposure to temperature changes, water, and previous top replacements, the tack strip material is no longer able to hold a staple. The material either has dry rot or has become shredded from tack and staple removal. The casing that holds the tack strip material can also be compromised by rust and fatigue.

The foundational tack strip material itself can be made from several different products. The most common is a compressed fiber or paper-like material. It is very dense and will hold a fastener without any trouble. Paper tack strip is prone to absorbing moisture and becoming soft, causing it to lose the ability to hold a staple. The material can also be damaged by the removal of tacks and staples.

Modern tack strip is made from an extruded plasticized rubber compound, and it is available in various sizes. The rubber-style tack strip is not prone to moisture, and it has the ability to hold a staple or tack quite well. I find that the downside of this material is that it just never really fits into the channels and retainers correctly, thus the tack strip is not as secure as a base for tacking because of the loose fit.

Tacking strip materials come in many different types and sizes. Here are some of the most common materials used to restore a worn tacking rail back to usable condition. The main objective is that the tack strip will hold a staple no matter what type of material you choose.

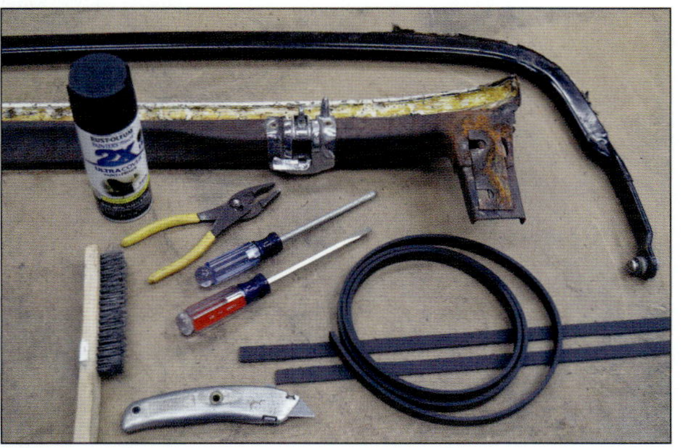

Every project will need some repair and restoration before a new convertible top can be fitted to the top frame. Most often, basic tools are all that are required to make these repairs, but knowing how to get the part back into working order is essential to a successful restoration.

This rear tack rail has been damaged from previous top replacements and will no longer hold a staple. Reproduction parts can usually be purchased, but if the metal housing is in good condition, repairing the tack rail is easy and will save you money.

Rear Tack Rail

The process of reconditioning the rear tack rail with new tack strip material is not difficult, and doing the job yourself will save you money. Visually inspect the metal casing of the rear tack rail to verify that it is viable for reconditioning. Check for extensive rust. Some rust is normal, but if the rust has compromised the metal casing, leaving it weak and brittle, then consider replacing the tack rail with a suitable aftermarket part.

Prepping the Casing

Removing the old tacking strip material from the metal casing can be done many different ways. One method that I have found to be the simplest is to slice through the rotten material with a utility knife. This allows you to remove the old, damaged material from the metal case in small, easy-to-manage slivers. Just be careful so that you do not harm yourself with the knife.

Once the metal casing is empty, it is a good time to clean it. Wire brush the metal to remove any rust

The quickest way to prepare the tack rail is to use a utility knife to shred the old stack strip material from the metal tack rail housing. Several slices through the center of the old tack strip material will allow it to be removed. The metal retainer can now be cleaned in preparation for the new tack strip material.

Preparing the metal housing of the tack rail will make it easier for the insertion of the new tack strip material. Use a pair of pliers to flare out the retainer edge of the casing. The metal should only be bent enough to allow for easy insertion of the new tack strip material.

or scale that remains, and then wipe the casing down with lacquer thinner to degrease the metal.

Before the new tacking material can be placed into the metal casing, the casing will need be opened up in order to insert the new tack strip. Using a pair of square-jaw pliers, carefully bend the upper retaining edge of the casing up without cracking or breaking it.

New Tacking Material

Each project is a little different, and not all premade tacking strips will fit into the casing without some trimming or shimming to make it fit. This is why I prefer to make the tacking strip filler myself. It takes the same amount of time, and this way, I know that it will fit properly in the casing.

To make the new tacking material, lay the metal casing on top of your waterproof panel board and trace around the outside of the casing. This will give you a good idea of the shape needed to fill the casing.

Make new tack strip for the tack rail from waterproof panel board. Simply trace the shape of the tack strip by using the metal casing as a pattern. Several pieces will be needed to achieve the correct thickness required.

Cut the traced pieces of tack strip material from the panel board with a utility knife fitted with a fresh blade. Use scissors to fine-tune the fit of the tack strip before the new material is placed into the metal retainer.

The traced pattern is going to be too big as is and will need to be cut down to fit into the casing. Remove the pattern from the panel board by cutting close to the outside of the traced line. Now, with the much more manageable piece, trim the pattern 1/16 inch inside the traced line and pre-fit it into the casing. Continue to trim the pattern until it fits snug and securely into the casing. After this piece is fit, use it to make more pieces to obtain the thickness desired to fill the casing. Do not worry about the through holes at this time. They will be added after the tack strip material has been sealed into the casing.

Securing the Tack Strip

When you have made enough pieces of tacking strip to reach the desired thickness to fill the casing, begin by gluing the first tack strip piece into the case. Apply contact cement to both surfaces to ensure a good bond, and insert the tack strip into the casing. Continue to glue and add filler strips until the casing has reached the maximum thickness.

Aligning pre-cut bolt holes in the new tack strip material does not always work out. I use a heavy-duty RotoZip bit to create the bolt holes in the tack strip material after it has been set in the tack rail case and secured in place.

The tack strip can now be locked into place by tapping the cased edge down onto the new tack strip material.

Place the metal casing on a solid surface, such as an anvil, and begin to tap the edge of the casing down. Do not smash the case edge into place, as this may cause the metal to crack, and all of that work will be ruined. Light taps will get the job done without hurting the casing.

Making Through Holes

Now that the new tack strip material is secured, the through holes

To further secure the tack strip material into the metal casing, place the tack rail on an anvil so that the retainer edges can be hammered tight against the tack strip material. This will prevent the tack strip from pulling away from the metal casing.

Brush contact adhesive into the inside of the metal casing and on the tack strip material. As additional layers are added, apply contact adhesive to both surfaces of the tacking strip material prior to setting them in the casing. This will ensure the tack strip material forms a solid base strong enough to hold a tack or staple.

Make bolt holes in the tack strip material through the back side of the tack rail casing with a RotoZip bit and drill press. By following the hole in the metal casing, minimal effort is needed to create a perfect opening for a retainer bolt.

The newly reconditioned tack rail is finished and ready to be put into service. The convertible top can now be attached securely knowing that the tack strip material will tightly hold a staple for another 20-plus years.

can be created. For this task, I use a heavy-duty RotoZip spiral cutting bit to make the hole. These bits can be found at your local home building center and usually come with two or more pieces to a package. The spiral cutting action of the tool allows for the removal of the necessary amount of material with little effort and gives the result of a cleanly cut hole.

For this operation, the bit is recommended to be chucked up into a drill press and not a router. This will allow you visual access to the hole while working. Set the drill press to operate at a maximum speed of 1,720 rpm. With a faster speed, you could harm yourself; a slower speed will cause the bit to overheat, and that will hurt the bit. Wear the proper eye safety equipment while using the drill press.

From the back side of the metal casing, allow the bit to pierce the exposed tack strip material inside the through-hole opening. Carefully follow around the edge of the hole to remove the unwanted tacking material. Take care to not twist the tack strip case and snap the bit. I find

that is works best to work the tack strip slowly in a counterclockwise motion. The bit seems to cut better and smoother this way.

Reconditioned Tack Rail

The tack strip can now be brushed off and given a final trim with a utility knife to remove any flash from the face of the through hole. You may choose to give the tack rail casing a fresh coat of paint to help further preserve it from future corrosion. At this point, the reconditioned tack rail with its new tack strip is ready to receive a staple and be installed in the car.

Rear Bow

There are many staples that are put into the tack strip of the rear bow. This tack strip is usually designed a little wider and deeper than the others to accommodate all of the convertible top components that are attached to it. When this tack strip is compromised, there is the risk of damage to the pads, curtain, and top material if the staples let go.

Replacing the tack strip will require the removal of the old tack strip material from the rear bow channel. The rear bow can be left attached to the convertible top frame or it can be removed to make the repairs on your workbench.

This rear bow has significant damage to the tack strip material, rendering it unusable for a top replacement. The process of installing new tack strip material in the rear bow channel is not a difficult task, but it is necessary for a new top install.

Replacing the Tack Strip

1 To prep the bow, remove all of the old tack strip material and fasteners from the channel of the rear bow, leaving a clean surface. Several layers of new paper tack strip material will be cut, fitted, and glued into the channel.

2 Cut waterproof panel board to the exact width needed to fit into the channel of the rear bow. Careful measuring and then cutting with the aid of a sharp utility knife and straightedge ruler will yield the lengths of tack strip needed to restore the rear bow.

3 Setting the foundation for the new rear bow tack strip is important. Apply an ample amount of contact cement to the inside of the rear bow channel and the back side of the first layer of tack strip before it is pressed into place.

4 Use small sheet metal screws to help anchor the first two layers of tack strip in the rear bow. To make the screws go in easier, drill a pilot hole through the tack strip and base metal of the channel. This gives the tack strip a stronger foundation.

5 The reconditioned rear bow has been completely filled with new tack strip material. You will be able to attach the pads, rear curtain, and top material to the rear bow with the confidence of knowing that the staples will not pull out when the top is lowered or raised.

The old tack strip material is most likely held into the channel of the rear bow with industrial staples. These staples can be broken or cut to release the old tacking material from the channel of the bow.

After the channel is clear, take measurements so that a new tack strip can be made to size. The rear bow tack strip should fit snugly in the channel so that it will not come out, and it must fill the channel completely to be able to accept all the staples needed for the convertible top components.

Cut strips of tacking material to the correct width of the channel. Cut enough material to fill the height of the channel.

Apply contact cement into the channel and onto the tack strip. Press the tack strip material all the way down to the bottom of the channel, making sure that it lies evenly across the bow. Add one more layer of tack-strip material in the channel, and use 3/8-inch-long, #8 pan-head screws to secure the tack strip to the rear bow to give the tack strip a solid foundation to build on.

Use a 1/8-inch drill bit to make a pilot hole at the end of the tack strip. Drill through the two layers of tack strip material and into the metal base, and secure the tack strip material with a screw. Make another pilot hole, and add a screw about every 2½ inches across the rear bow.

The channel must be full to the top edge of the metal with tack strip material. Continue to glue and add layers of tack strip material until the channel is filled. A partial length of tack strip will be needed to fill the raised center section of the channel to complete the rear bow tack strip restoration.

Header Bow

Since the leading part of the convertible top frame is the header bow, over time the elements can take their toll and cause the header bow damage. Corrosion, rust, and previous top replacements weaken the bow, and before a new top can be fitted, proper repairs must be made to ensure that the new top will perform properly for many years to come.

Many parts come together to make up the header bow, and the header bow can be constructed from steel, aluminum, wood, and even acrylonitrile butadiene styrene (ABS) plastic. Tack strips, latches, and rubber seals are all components that are attached to the header bow. Each component has an important function that works in unison to hold the top material tight and prevent wind and water from entering the car all while locking the top in place to the windshield.

Determining what needs to be done and how to restore it will vary depending on the extent of damage found once the top material is removed and the base material of the bow is exposed.

This header bow has seen several top replacements and has aged gracefully over the years. It is time to give it a refresh with new tack strip material and a coat of paint. Other condition issues will also be addressed to make the bow new again.

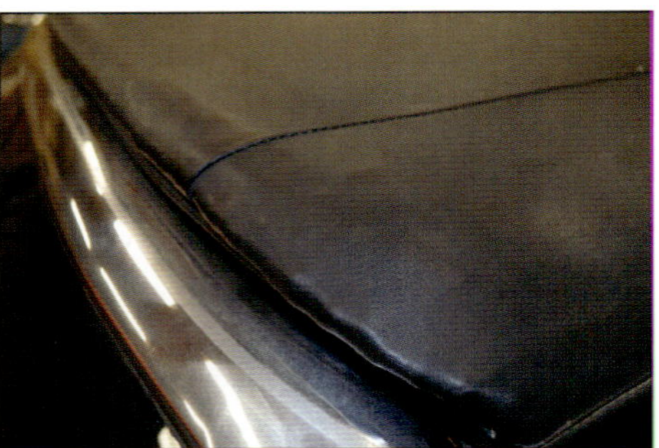

Many years of weather and road miles have taken their toll on this header bow. Here you can clearly see that the header bow has some serious corrosion issues even before the old top material was removed. The bow will be removed from the car for reconditioning.

Disassembly

Take pictures of the header bow before removing any components. This will provide a reference when it comes time to reassemble the header bow.

Common hardware found on a header bow are top latches and guide pins. These components are most often chrome plated. If these parts are damaged or worn, now is the time to order replacement parts or have the originals replated.

Not all header bows have a decorative quick-edge molding that covers the pinch weld on the inside of the header bow. The original cover material used was a woven material over a metal core that was pushed onto the raw, unfinished metal, making it look nice. The cover material usually has dry rotted and faded from age. New quick-edge moldings are available and can be cut to length with a pair of tin snips. Simply pull the old pinch weld cover material off and discard it.

Strip the header bow of all hardware by unscrewing it from the header bow. Label the parts left and right

Before doing any repairs to the header bow, remove all the hardware and tack strip material to gain access to all areas of the bow that require repair. Bagging and clearly labeling the parts will help with the reassembly of the header bow.

The pinch weld cover is not only decorative but also covers up the ugly seam that is created when the formed metal pieces of the header bow are welded together. Remove this original basket-weave molding and replace it with a new piece.

before bagging the hardware for reassembly. On aluminum header bows, remove the tack strips by drilling out the rivets holding them in place. Steel header bows will most likely have small tabs that are bent over the tack strip material. These need to be lifted to release the old tack strip from the header bow. If the tack strips are held in by heavy staples, simply snap or grind them off to remove the tack strip. When the header bow is free of all hardware and the tack strip, it can then be washed and degreased to prep it for reconditioning.

Steel Bow Repair

Steel bows consist of several stamped pieces that are bent, shaped, and spot welded together to make one composite piece. The header bow is often compromised from corrosion that forms on the unpainted inside surfaces of the header bow.

Removing the rust and giving the metal a fresh coat of paint may be enough to put your header bow into service again, but if the metal feels soft, it may not be repairable. When a header bow becomes compromised and no longer safe to use, it should be replaced with a new part.

Some parts are just not destined to be saved. This header bow has serious rust issues, and it is beyond a repairable state. The upside of this unfortunate situation is that there are excellent replacement bows readily available for this model, and they are an exact reproduction of the original.

Rusted Steel

The simplest form of corrosion to correct is surface rust. This light rust is simply sanded or ground off of the metal, and then a small amount of body filler is applied to correct any imperfections found in the surface of the metal. After sanding, the surface of the metal is cleaned and prepped so that it can be primed and then painted. This helps prevent any further corrosion to the header bow.

In the event of extensive rust, the corroded metal would need to be removed and new metal welded into

All metal is bound to have some rust. Basic metal prep will be required to remove the surface rust on the underside of this bow. After the metal has been cleaned, new tack strip retainer tabs will be welded back in place to hold the tack strip securely.

place to restore the header bow to its original condition. If the corrosion is excessive and has progressed beyond reasonable repair, a new header bow may need to be purchased before the replacement top can be fitted.

Inspect for Damage

After the header bow has been removed from the top frame, place it on the workbench for inspection and cleaning. Remove the old tack strip material, which will allow for a closer look at any concealed damage on the header bow.

A close inspection of this header bow shows that several of the tack strip locking tabs are weak or missing. This is common on a header bow that has been in service for more than 50 years. Repairing this damage will require new tabs to be welded onto the bow.

Cleaning the surface of the sheet metal on the header bow may require a light sanding to remove surface rust. Deeper contours and heavier rust can be cleaned up with a small disc grinder or wire wheel. These tools make fast work of eradicating rust.

Typically, the tack strip retaining tabs have rusted completely away, broken off, or are very weak and will no longer be able to hold the tack strip in place securely. One indicator that a tack strip retaining tab is no longer serviceable is if the metal can be bent over with a finger then it is not strong enough to hold the tack strip tightly to the header bow once the new top material is stapled in place.

Metal Preparation

It is very important that the header bow metal is cleaned. A thorough cleaning will reveal any problem areas that need to be repaired before the new top can be fitted. The use of a wire wheel brush or an abrasive grinder will make quick work of any rust and scale that has formed on the surface of the header bow.

It is not recommended to have the header sandblasted to remove the surface rust. The high pressure and blasting media can warp and destroy the remaining metal of the header bow. Chemical dipping can be done if so desired. The dipping process will not destroy the integrity of the metal, although the cost is sometimes prohibitive. Once cleaned, the sheet metal will make welding and surface repairs much stronger and therefore make the restoration last longer.

Another benefit of clean sheet metal is that it will accept the application of paint. A nice coat of paint will look great and it will preserve the metal of your hard work for a long period of time.

Replacing Metal

The most common repair on a header bow is missing or weak tack strip retaining tabs. Restoring the retaining tabs on the header bow is a simple process.

Begin by marking the header bow with a permanent marker to indicate the location of where the new tabs will be attached. This will also give you an accurate count as to how many tabs you will need to make. After the positions to the tabs have been marked, remove the stubs from the old tabs by grinding or filing them away to prevent surface distortion after the new top material is installed.

Cut new tack strip retaining tabs from 22-gauge sheet metal. Each tab starts out by cutting a 1/2x1-inch piece of sheet metal and then tapering the tab to a rounded point to mimic the original retainer tab. To help with the attachment of the new tab, bend a welding base at a right angle along the bottom edge to create a 1/8-inch flange. These tabs can now be aligned with the marks on the header bow and welded into place along the tack rail of the header bow. The metal tabs can also be screwed into place, but the bulk of the screw head makes the tack strip wavy, which results in a messy-looking repair.

After the new retaining tabs have been welded in place, the welds can be dressed down a little with a small die grinder to even out the metal. Also, a small file can be used to remove any sharp edges that may be on the edges of the sheet metal tabs. The welded replacement tabs will now be able to hold the new tack strip material securely to the header bow without failing.

Creating New Tack Strip Retaining Tabs

1 Replacement tack strip retainer tabs are not available from a supplier, but they can be made from light-gauge sheet metal with a pair of simple tin snips. The retainer tabs are cut to width and then shaped to match the original tabs that are on the header bow.

2 To aid in the placement of the new metal tack strip retaining tabs, their positions are marked on the header bow with a felt-tip pen to help with the alignment when it comes to the welding stage. Once marked, the remnants of the original tabs can be ground away.

3 To make less work of the welding process, bend a small flange into the base of the replacement tab. Square-nose pliers can be used as a metal brake to hold the metal tab and create the small 90-degree bend in the metal.

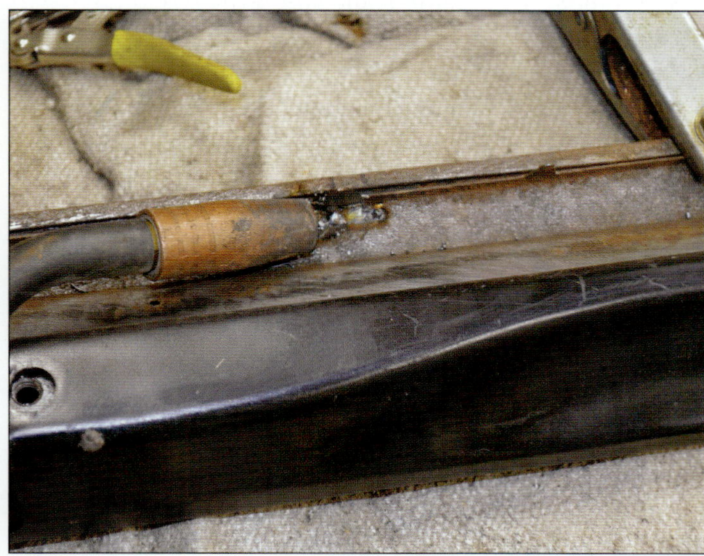

4 Each replacement retainer tab is welded into place on the header bow. Use a MIG welder on a very low setting to prevent any blow-out of the thin metal. Then, make small tack welds on the flange base of the tab to secure it to the bow.

5 Reconditioning the header bow with new metal retaining tabs will provide ample holding power to secure the new tack strip material in place. This will prevent the new convertible top material from coming loose as the car is driven down the road.

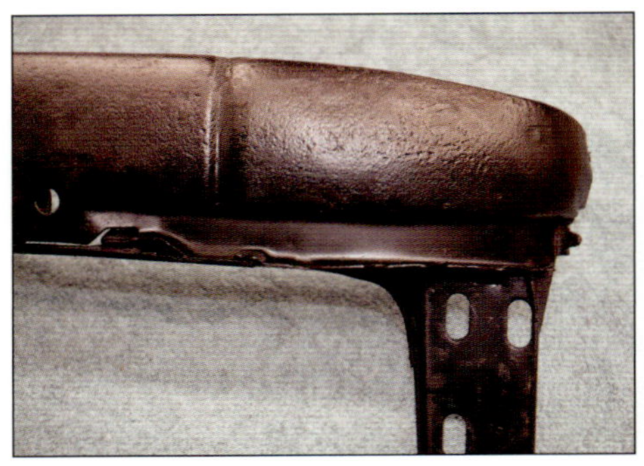

Nothing beats a fresh coat of paint to make a part look like new. After all the metal work was completed, our header bow received a proper preparation of the surface and an even coat of finish color to protect the restored header bow for many years to come.

Cut strips of waterproof panel board to size, and bond them together to form the main header tack strip. Hammering the locking tabs over the top of the tack strip will lock it in place, keeping it secure and preventing it from pulling out.

This pad tack strip may appear solid, but it has dry rotted, and it will no longer hold a staple. Lift the retaining tabs to release it from the frame so that a new tack strip can be made to fit the opening in the header bow.

Paint

Before the header bow can be put back into service, preserve it to prevent any future rust. To achieve this, clean the surface of the header bow and prep it for paint. After a fresh coat of primer sealer and three coats of satin black finish, the header bow will not only look like new, it will also perform as it was originally designed.

The newly painted header bow is now ready to be refitted with tack strips and hardware. To protect the fresh paint on the bow, I recommend covering the workbench with a towel or some other soft material as you proceed with the header bow rebuild.

Header Bow Tack Strip

The choice of the replacement tack strip for this header bow is made from waterproof panel board. A tack or staple will hold it tight to this tack strip. Cutting and compiling the tack strip will allow the top material to be attached in a secure manner. Once the new tack strip has been fitted to the channel of the header bow, the retaining tabs can be hammered down onto the tack strip, securing it in place.

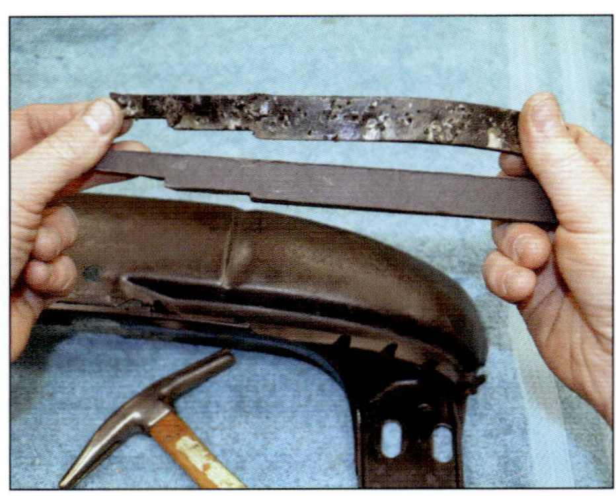

A new replacement tack strip has been fabricated out of several layers of panel board that have been bonded together and shaped to fit the opening of the header bow. This unusual shape requires a little extra effort to make it fit the bow correctly.

On the top side of the header bow is the forward tack strip material that the pads attach to. Bond several pieces of tack strip material together to obtain the desired thickness needed to fill the void in the header bow. Cut, contour, and fit the tack strip into the header bow. Once the new, completed tack strip is fitted into the header bow, it is secured by hammering the metal tab retainers down over it, locking the tacking strip in place.

Fit the new pad tack strip to the header bow and secure it by hammering the locking tabs over the tack strip. The new tack strip material will be able to hold a staple and keep the protective pad in place for many years.

Hardware Installation

The final touch of a header bow restoration is the reinstallation of the new or reconditioned latches and guide pins. Not only does the shiny chrome look great against the satin black bow, the hardware will make the convertible top frame look like it just rolled out of the factory. After the chrome hardware is installed, cut a new piece of quick-edge material to cover the pinch weld, and tap it in place.

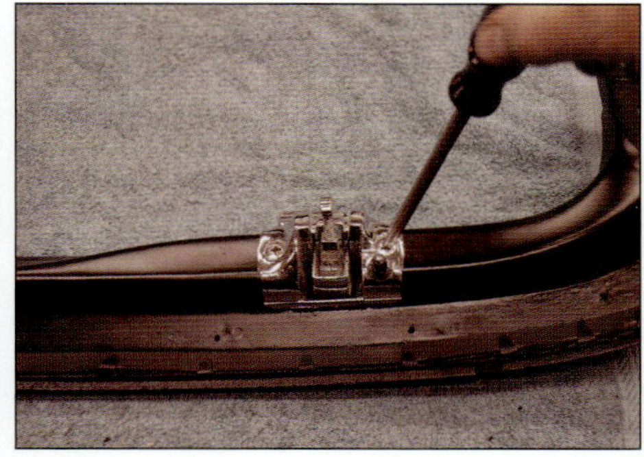

Before the header bow can be refitted to the car, install all of the new and reconditioned chrome header bow hardware. Use extreme care on the reinstallation of the trim so that the header bow paint does not get scratched or screws get cross threaded.

Attach the reconditioned header bow to the top frame. The satisfaction of repairing a worn or damaged part will continue to give you the confidence to press on to finish your project.

Aluminum Bow Repair

Many cars were made with aluminum header bows. Because aluminum does not bend like steel, the cast pieces were machined to accommodate the attachment of hardware and tack strip material.

Corroded Aluminum

Ford Motor Company typically used aluminum as a header bow material. Aluminum is a durable and stable material, but instead of rust-

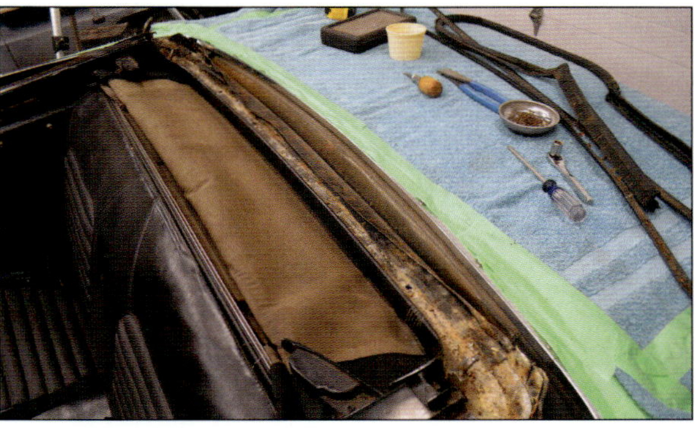

With the staples pulled and the top material pulled back from the tack strip, the visible corrosion on the underside of this header bow is quite extensive. Time and weather has also rotted the tack strip material so it will need to be replaced.

All the rubber weatherstrip and top material has now been removed from the underside of the header bow. The full extent of the damage that time and water has had on the aluminum is visible. Remove the bow from the car so that proper repairs can be made.

ing, it corrodes. Completely remove this corrosion before the header bow can be reinstalled. Techniques for repairing and refinishing aluminum are similar to steel.

If the header bow is cracked or broken, it may need to be welded. Special techniques can be used to weld aluminum, and these repairs can be made by bringing the header bow to a reputable welding shop.

Corrosion on aluminum shows up in the form of oxidation. Remove this flakey and powdery residue from the surface of the bow so that it can

be restored and put back in service. If the surface is not properly sealed, it will continue to deteriorate and cause more problems in the future.

Remove Header Bow

Remove the header bow from the car by loosening the nuts that hold it to the side frame rails. Use a ratchet

Upon a visual inspection of the header bow, lumps are visible underneath the convertible top material. This condition indicates signs of oxidation or corrosion that will need to be addressed before a new top can be fitted to the car. Remove the top material to determine the extent of the damage.

Place the header bow on the workbench; the damage can now be accurately evaluated. What we have determined is the base metal is still in good condition, and after a thorough cleaning, repairs can be made to bring the bow into like-new condition.

Before any restoration work can be done on the header bow, remove the top latches and guide pins for a proper cleaning. After the bolt-on hardware has been removed, it will need to be bagged and tagged so the real work can begin.

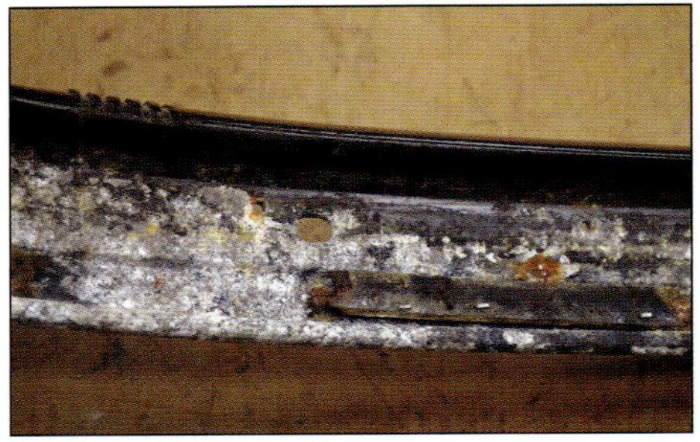

After finding the old tack strip material damaged, worn, and unusable, remove and replace it with new material. Steel rivets were used to hold the original tack strip in place on the underside of the header bow.

Use a 1/8-inch drill bit to remove the tack strip rivets. Extraction is done by drilling through the rivets from the top side of the header bow.

and the correct-size socket to remove the nuts, washers, and then the header bow.

Place the header bow on the workbench and remove all of the latching hardware and guide pins. Clearly mark each part as it is removed to ensure that it will be replaced in the correct position during the reassembly stage.

Now, inspect the base material of the header bow for any cracks or previously undetected flaws. The tack strip material will need to be removed before the aluminum can be reconditioned. Removal of the tack strip begins by drilling out the rivets that hold it to the surface of the header bow. Begin drilling from the top side of the bow with a 1/8-inch drill bit. The rivets are most likely steel, and they will also corrode, causing the hole to become oversized. If you are not careful, the hole can get even larger.

Removing the Corrosion

Remove the corrosion without taking away any excess material from the bow. The best tool to do this is a stiff wire cup brush. The wire brush can be chucked up in a handheld

A stiff-bristle wire cup brush is used in a handheld power drill to quickly descale and clear the surface of the header bow. The wire brush cup is aggressive enough to remove the oxidation from the aluminum without cutting too deep.

Only minor depressions and cosmetic flaws remain after a thorough descaling and cleaning of the aluminum header bow. Because the damage to the aluminum was minor, simple repairs can be made to restore the header bow to like-new condition.

power drill to quickly loosen the corrosion. Use a light touch to reveal clean and solid material. Remove any stubborn corrosion that remains with 60-grit sandpaper.

Clean the residual dust off the surface by wiping down the bow with lacquer thinner. Now, the surface can be inspected for any advanced corrosion and undetected flaws.

Repairing the Damage

After the aluminum has been thoroughly cleaned, apply fiberglass filler to the header bow to build up any depressions left by the sanding and cleaning. Two-part fiberglass filler can be purchased at almost any auto parts store.

Fiberglass filler works the best on aluminum because it will not absorb water and cause other problems later on as the car ages. Mix the filler according to the directions on the package and apply a thin coat of the filer to the aluminum with a plastic applicator.

It will take a few minutes for the fiberglass filler to fully cure before work can continue. A block sander with 80-grit sandpaper will get the initial shaping done. Continue working the filler with finer grades of sandpa-

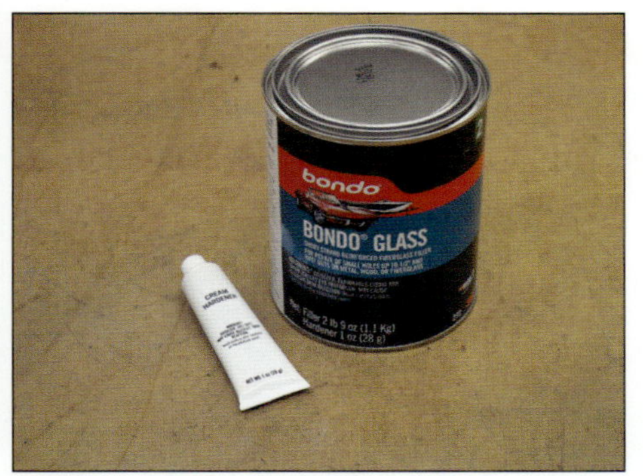

Filling the imperfections left in the aluminum bow after it has been descaled and cleaned is best achieved with a two-part quality fiberglass filler. The two-part filler can be purchased at most local auto parts stores.

A quality repair can be obtained when the fiberglass filler is mixed according to the manufacturer's directions. Using a body filler spreader, the filler can be applied properly to the surface of the aluminum to make a permanent repair to the header bow.

Shape and finish the cured fiberglass filler with a hand-sanding block and progressive grades of sandpaper, using standard automotive bodywork techniques. Additional filler can be added if necessary to achieve the correct profile for the header bow.

per until you have reached the desired finish on the header bow.

Painting the Bow

Feather the filler to a smooth finish, and then prime the surface to give the finish coat of paint something strong to bond to. I like to finish the header bow with quality satin enamel paint. Three light coats of the enamel will protect the bow for a long time. Once the paint has cured, install the tack strip. Cover the workbench with a towel or some other soft material to protect the fresh paint on the header bow as you proceed with the rebuild.

Adding Tack Strip

The tack strip is made to fit the header bow in sections, and it is attached directly to the header bow channel with rivets. I find that it is less trouble to make a paper pattern and then cut the tack strip material instead of trying to make it fit in place.

To begin, press tracing paper into the channel and mark the outside profile with a pencil. This pattern can now be cut out and used to make a tack strip that fits the header bow perfectly.

After the sanding and shaping of the applied fiberglass filler has been completed, clean and prep the surface of the restored header bow to accept a sealing coat of primer and then three protective coats of satin black paint.

A major effort went into removing the corrosion and fixing the damage on this aluminum header bow. To preserve the header bow for another 30 years of service, the surface must be coated with a primer sealer and then given a finish of black satin enamel paint.

Tack Strip Replacement

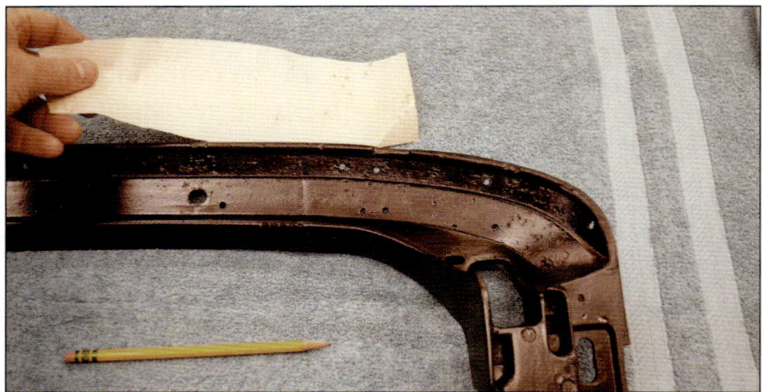

1 *Replacing the tack trip on the header bow requires a pattern to be made. Taking the time to do this will ensure a perfect fit and prevent any unsightly bulges in the top material after the new convertible top has been installed.*

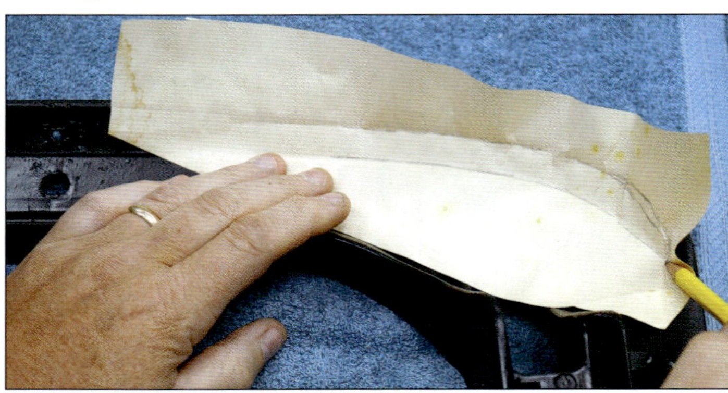

2 *Use craft paper to create a pattern for the new tack strip that will be attached to the header bow. By tracing around the perimeter of the channel on the header bow, a perfect fit can be obtained for the new tack strip material.*

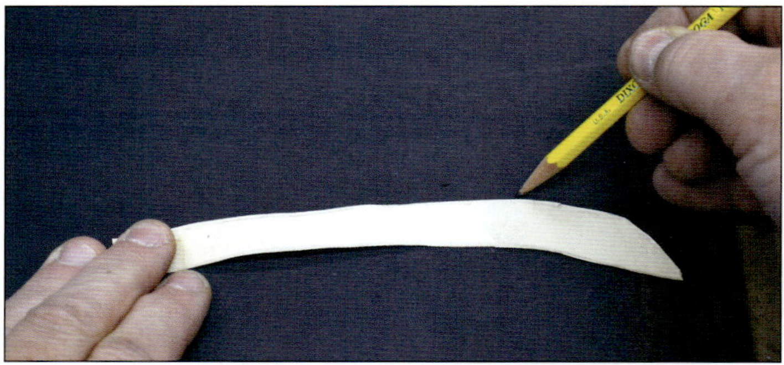

3 *Cut the traced pattern from the craft paper and transfer it to panel-board material to create the new tack strip. Then, cut and size the new tack strip material to fit the header bow. Cut and glue additional pieces of panel board to create the correct thickness required for the tack strip.*

4 *Fit the new tack strip to the header bow so that the rivet holes needed to hold it in place can be marked. These holes will need to be punched out prior to fastening the new tack strip material to the header bow.*

5 *To prepare the tack strip for mounting, use a rotary punch to make the through holes needed in the tack strip for the rivets to hold the new tack strip in place. By aligning the tack strip to the header bow and marking it from the top side of the header bow, an accurate hole can be made.*

6 Use a rivet gun and 1/8-inch-diameter aluminum rivets with a 1/2-inch grip range to secure the tack strip material to the header bow. Aluminum rivets will not rust and are strong enough to hold the tack strip securely in place.

7 After a thorough cleaning, painting, and lubricating, reinstall the original top latches on the header bow. New latches can be purchased and installed if the originals are no longer serviceable. It is always best to recondition the old hardware.

8 The original guide pins are now reinstalled on the header bow. With a little cleanup, the guide pins were found to be in excellent condition and were therefore able to be reused. The guide pins ensure proper alignment of the top frame with the windshield.

9 Reinstalling the header bow on the convertible top frame brings the project one step closer to completion. Align the reconditioned header bow with the scribed marks made prior to removal from the frame rails, and then tighten the bolts to secure the header bow to the frame rails.

Lay the cut-out pattern on water-proof panel board and transfer the shape with a pencil. Repeat this step until you have enough pieces to reach the desired thickness needed for the new tack strip, and cut the shapes out of the panel board. Apply glue to both sides of the tack strip pieces and press them together.

Fit the tack strip section to the underside of the header bow, and from the top side, use a pencil to mark the position of the rivet holes. Remove the tack strip, and with the help of a rotary punch, make the required rivet holes in the tack strip.

To attach the tack strip to the header bow, use 1/8-inch aluminum rivets with a 1/2-inch grip range. Align the tack strip to the underside of the header bow and insert the rivet through the tack strip material and header bow. With a pop rivet tool, set the rivet to anchor the tack strip to the header bow. Continue with the rivets until all the holes are filled on the new tack strip.

Installing the reconditioned latches to the header bow requires a #3 Phillips-head screwdriver or a ratchet and socket. Also, install the guide pins and any other trim pieces that are needed for the completion of the header bow. Use caution when installing the accessories onto the header bow so that you do not accidentally scratch the paint or cross thread a screw.

The completely restored header bow is now ready to be reattached to the convertible top side rails. Use the appropriate tools and hardware to tighten the head bow in place. Check the alignment marks and final fit.

Third Bow Repair

Many times, the small screws that attach the pad to the third cross bow

Restoring the details to the cross bows is as important as any other part of a convertible to restoration. Without proper repairs, the new convertible top material will sustain damage due to improper folding and the bunching up of the convertible top pads.

These cross bows are from a C1 Corvette. As you can see, there are several broken pad screws that need to be repaired before the new convertible top pads can be installed. The small, metal bows are fragile, and care must be taken to make them strong again.

are broken off and have been repaired incorrectly. Replacing the pads is essential to a convertible top replacement, and having them perform as they were designed adds to the longevity of the convertible top.

When the pad is installed without all the fasteners required, it can shift and cause bunching. This puts unnecessary pressure on the top material and frame, which will eventually damage the convertible top.

Making the proper repair is not difficult, and it should not be considered a problem, but rather another step to take on the way to restoring the convertible top frame for a successful convertible top replacement. The third bow of the convertible top frame is usually made of tubular steel, and the repair needed will be determined upon the damage to the bow.

Broken Screws

The most common repair is fixing a blocked hole from a broken screw. Extracting the old screw may be very difficult due to the physical size of the screw. The original screw used

to secure the pad to the bow is a #6 machine screw that is 3/8-inch long with 32 threads per inch. The heads of these small screws often snap off while being unscrewed.

The simplest way to extract the remaining screw piece is to use a small punch and drive it through the bow. This may sound barbaric, but by trying to drill out the remainder of the old screw, the drill bit may wander and create an elongated hole. If you are able to drill through the old screw fragment, use of an EZ out screw extractor is not always possible due to the small size of the tool. The trouble working with hardware this small is that extractors and drill bits tend to break. By driving the screw fragment through the bow, you will save a lot of time and frustration.

If the screw hole becomes over-sized and a #6 machine screw will no longer hold into the bow, the hole can then be drilled out with a #29 drill bit and then re-tapped to fit a #8 machine screw with 32 threads per inch. Although the screws are a little bit larger, they will work just the same without any further issues.

Beyond Repair

When a bow has been damaged from a previous repair and the screw holes have become too large to re-tap to hold the correct size screws, other actions can be taken to repair the bow so that it can be put back into service. Too often, the bow has had the pad secured in place with 1/8-inch aluminum rivets. This type of repair

Finding pop rivets in the cross bow is an all-too-common issue. This is not the correct way to secure a convertible top pad to the bow. It will take some effort to correct the damage and restore the function to the cross bow from this previous installation.

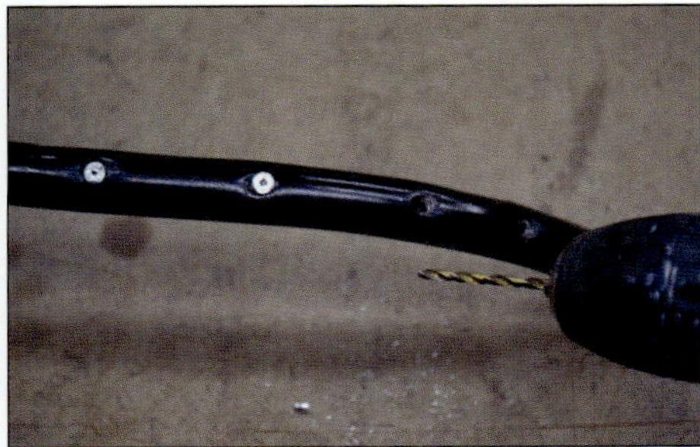

Removing the aluminum pop rivets from the tubular cross bow requires the use of a power drill and drill bit. Depending on how badly damaged the bow is, there is a solution to correct this condition and restore the bow so a pad can be attached properly.

is considered to be a major fail for an installation because the incorrect fasteners have been used that will cause trouble for the next replacement top.

To repair this damage, remove the rivet first by drilling through the aluminum rivet with an 1/8-inch drill bit. The remaining hole will now be too large to be tapped for an original #6 screw, and it may also be too large for a #8 screw.

Correcting the Damage

The most correct way to repair the oversized hole is to close it up by welding it shut; then, redrill and tap it to accept a #6-32 machine screw.

After removing the aluminum rivets from the bow, clean the holes in the bow with a small grinder, and then weld them closed. The surface of the bow will now need to be dressed down by grinding the welded area to a smooth profile before a new pilot hole can be drilled.

A #6-32 machine screw requires a #36 hole to be made before it can be tapped. Drill the new pilot hole with a #36 drill bit, and then chase the hole with a #6-32 tap to create new threads for the pad screw. The

Sometimes the only way to fix a problem is to take the long road. This cross bow is now too weak for a simple repair, and the screw hole must be welded closed and re-drilled to the proper size so that it can be tapped to the correct screw size.

After removing a broken screw from the cross bow and repairing the hole, run a threading tap through the hole to create clean threads for the machine screw that will hold the convertible top pad in place.

repaired bow can now be sanded, cleaned, and prepped for a fresh coat of satin black paint. After the paint has cured, reinstall the bow on the frame.

Install new top pads as they were intended to be by using staples, and secure them properly in place with the correct #6-32 machine screws and low-profile washers.

Painting the Frame

Because the convertible top frame is visible from the inside of the car, it should look as good as new too. You will often find worn spots on the header bow and side rails where the latching mechanisms are. This is normal, and leaving it unrestored just shows a lack of doing a complete job.

The process of cleaning and painting the top frame is not difficult and is a step that I have always felt made the process of installing a new top complete. The painting stage of the frame comes after all the other frame repairs have been made and the convertible top frame has been adjusted for the final fitment of the new convertible top.

Painting the top frame not only makes it look fresh and new again, it shows that you really care about the car you are working on. Having a top frame that looks as good as the new convertible top will give you pride in your work and add to resale value.

One of the best cleaners that I have ever used on a car is Formula 409. This stuff cuts through the layers of crud and is not harmful or toxic to use. Spraying it directly onto a clean rag limits the amount of overspray and makes the cleaning process faster.

I do not recommend removing the convertible top frame from the car for the cleaning and painting process. Removal can make the frame vulnerable to damage by wracking (diagonal force or twisting). This action will cause the articulating hinge points to bind. This is an extremely difficult condition to correct; therefore, leaving the frame bolted in the car eliminates a lot of unnecessary problems.

Another word of caution: Do not sandblast the frame. This can cause the rails and bows to warp and again create binding of the articulation joints. An unwanted issue associated with sandblasting the frame is that the accumulation of blasting media will get into the bronze bushings and create grinding. This grit will accelerate the wear on the soft, metal bushings, resulting in loose-fitting joints.

For those who wish to have the top frame powdercoated, please do not do this. The powdercoating will get into the bushings and cause them to bind or seize up. Disassembly of the frame for powdercoating is also not advised. The coating adds to the thickness of the frame component, and this again will cause binding issues when the frame is reassembled.

The header bow is most likely to be removed for repair and can be painted separate from the rest of the frame, but disassembly of the frame is not going to necessarily give you a better result, just more work and added potential problems.

Preparing the Frame for Paint

Years of dirt and grime have accumulated on the convertible top frame, and it will need to be thoroughly cleaned before it can be painted. Removing the layers of dust and oil can be done by simply wiping down the frame with a clean rag and some Formula 409 spray cleaner. The grease-cutting and dirt-lifting power of the cleaner makes quick work of getting the most crud off the frame with the least effort.

Begin by spraying the cleaner on a clean rag, and wipe down all the surfaces of the convertible top frame. Spraying onto a clean rag reduces the amount of splatter and mess compared to spraying the cleaner directly on the top frame. Use a small screwdriver to get the rag and cleaner into tight spots. If you encounter an area that is heavily soiled, use a scraper to help loosen the debris.

Wipe down the frame with another clean rag that has been dampened with water. This will remove the Formula 409 residue.

Rust and corrosion can be sanded off, and the metal can be prepped and filled to give the surface a smooth appearance.

Drape the Car

Protect the car from overspray by draping the entire car in 1 mil poly.

Poly sheeting comes in long rolls of varying widths and thicknesses. A roll with a width of at least 9 feet wide that is 1 mil thick works well. This will cover most cars and give adequate protection from overspray. Poly sheeting can be found at any home-improvement store, and one roll is a few hundred feet long, so it will last a long time.

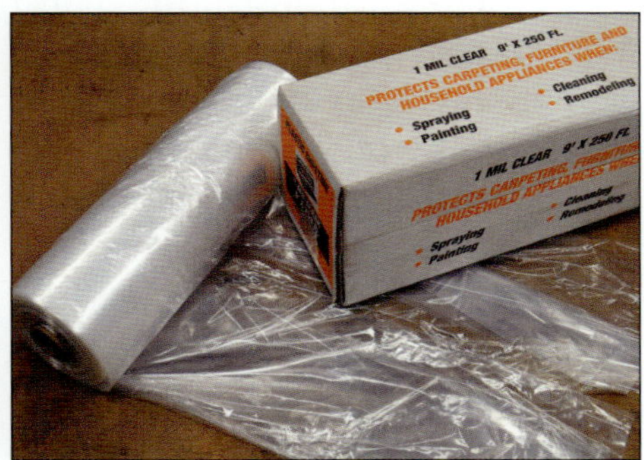

Not only is this poly inexpensive, one piece will also save the finish of the car when it is used as a cover drape when painting the convertible top frame. A single roll of 1 mil poly can be used to cover over a dozen cars.

Unlatch the top frame from the windshield, and partially lower it so that the underside of the frame can be easily accessed. While in this position, unroll the poly, lay it over the back bumper of the car to the floor, and proceed forward over the front bumper to the floor before cutting the piece off the roll. When the poly is opened up, it will cover the car all along the sides.

Make a relief cut in the poly so that it can lie smoothly around the frame where it attaches to the body. Use painters' tape to secure the poly, and mask off the cylinder rods and any other areas that should not be painted.

Painting

I like to use satin black enamel paint on the convertible top frame. If the top material is tan on the inside, consider using a tan color on the frame to blend with the top. I also find it more comfortable to use

a trigger sprayer attachment with the can. It is less painful to pull the trigger than press that button on the can. Use a good respirator mask and protective gear when spraying paint.

Shake the can and follow the directions laid out by the manufacturer. Begin with a light coat of paint along the inside of the frame. Work from back to front on one side and then the other. Light coats work well and do not result in runs and sags the way a heavy coat would.

Be sure to coat the frame evenly. It is easy to miss a spot, so work methodically from end to end to avoid bare spots. When you finish spraying, let the frame dry completely before unmasking anything.

When the paint has cured, inspect the frame for missed spots and runs. Touch up any areas that need attention before removing the poly drape. When it is time to remove the drape, carefully unmask the car, and turn the poly into itself to form a ball. The overspray on the top of the poly will rub off and get onto everything if you are not careful. Discard the ball of poly.

Lower the convertible top frame about halfway to gain access to the underside for cleaning and painting. The header bow has been removed for repairs and will be painted separately before it is reinstalled on the frame.

Some basic supplies needed to paint the convertible top frame include a quality paint mask, a paint can spray gun, and—of course—enamel spray paint. All of these items can be obtained from a local auto supply store.

It is essential to make adjustments to the convertible top frame before the new top material is fitted. The main adjusting points for the frame can be found hidden under the rear trim panels of the car. Remove the back seat and trim panels before adjustments can be made.

The side rail of this frame has a large gap over the side glass. This can be corrected by adjusting the balance link on the frame; tension can be added to keep the frame rail straight, and it will also lower the side rail closer to the door glass.

If need be, reattach the header bow to the frame rails and oil the joints of the newly painted frame so that it can be properly adjusted.

Frame Adjustment

After the convertible top frame has been cleaned and painted, it needs to be properly adjusted to fit the car. To get a proper fit, install the rubber roof rail seals on the side rails along with the rubber header seal. The seals will help with the alignment and fit of the convertible top frame to the side glass.

Begin with the convertible top frame latched to the windshield. There should be a close fit between the side door glass and the rubber weather seals. If the top frame does not latch or there is an excessive amount of space or gapping from the glass to the roof rails, frame adjustments will need to be made to correct this condition.

Things to Look For

First, notice if there is a bow upward or downward from the center joint in the top frame. Also, check how the frame fits along the rear edge of the side glass. A properly aligned convertible top frame will have an equal margin along the glass.

The adjustment process is like a dance; when one part moves, another part needs to move. When an adjustment is made, adjust the opposite side of the frame to match. Measuring and triangulation of those measurements helps get your top frame where it needs to be.

If the door glass is fitted correctly, you will not need to adjust it. If the glass is too high or low, or if it tilts in or out, the door panels need to be removed to make adjustments to the side glass. If the top frame is gaping at the center of the frame, the tensioning of the frame needs adjusting and vertical positioning. When the rear vertical section of the frame needs to be moved in or out, the frame needs to be adjusted at the header bow for length.

Making Frame Adjustments

Loosen all the retaining fasteners until they are just snug. This way, it takes less effort to make adjustments to the frame. When making an adjustment to the frame, use a box-end wrench, and only loosen the frame mounting nuts or bolts enough to allow the frame to move a small amount; then, retighten the fastener. If you loosen everything too much, then the frame will continue to shift and you will not be able to correct the fit. After the frame is positioned the way it needs to be, use a socket wrench and securely tighten all the fasteners to prevent the frame from shifting.

Roof Rail Gaps

On the inside of the car where the top frame attaches to the body are two different adjustment centers. The main adjustment points are where the fasteners hold the frame to the body of the car. Loosening these bolts allows the convertible top frame to be raised or lowered to meet the side glass. The other adjustment controls the balance link or tensioner. This puts tension on the top frame and sets the parallel positioning of the frame over the side glass.

Vertical Side Gap

Sometimes the distance along the rear edge of the quarter window glass is too tight or loose. To close or open this gap, loosen the fasteners at the

By loosening the three bolts holding the top frame to the body, raise or lower the convertible top frame to reposition the side rails closer to the side window glass. Use a box-end wrench because it gives you better control for the adjustment.

Adjust the tensioner or balance link by loosening the two nuts holding its serrated base in place. When the fasteners are loose, move the tensioner forward or backward to increase or decrease the downward force put on the side rail.

Adjust the rear quarter vertical spacing by loosening the header bow fasteners and repositioning the side rail forward or backward to create the correct amount of gap along the back side of the quarter glass.

header bow, push or pull the frame to set the correct gap, and tighten the fasteners to keep the frame in place.

Weather Seal Adjustment

When a frame adjustment is made to lengthen or shorten the side rail at the header bow, an adjustment may also be needed to make the rubber weather seal fit correctly. The header bow must seal to the windshield, and that means the knuckle section of the front rubber section must fit properly into the corner of the header bow. When the side rail is shortened,

Readjust the rubber weather seal by unlatching the top frame from the windshield and repositioning the front rubber molding by loosening the fasteners of the rubber seal so that it can be correctly fit into the header bow.

Sometimes the rubber roof rail seal requires an adjustment so that it will fit properly in position. Use a pencil to mark the place where it needs to be trimmed. Without trimming, the seal will cause binding, and the frame will not close properly.

After the rubber seal has been removed for the roof rail, use a pair of tin snips to cut away the unwanted portion of the weather seal. Dry fit the seal along the roof rail to verify that enough material has been removed before it is secured in place.

After the rubber roof rail seals have been adjusted, notice that the top frame is going to meet the side glass as it should. Now, remove the first and third sections of the roof rail seals to allow for the side glue flaps of the new top. The center rubber can stay in place.

The convertible top frame is properly adjusted. The rubber weather seals fit uniformly around the side glass, and the side rails of the frame are straight. The new top can now be fitted to the car with confidence, knowing that the top frame operates correctly.

Back in the day, tacks were the go-to standard to fasten the convertible top material to the frame of buggies and cars. Today, the standard has shifted to the use of power staplers and wire staples to secure a convertible top.

Although the lengths of these staples are the same, the width and type varies greatly. Stapler manufacturers have specific-sized staples to fit their machines, and they also produce many different types of staples, depending on the project at hand.

These are two distinctly different types of staples. The top features a diversion point that when it is deployed into wood, the legs will splay out in different directions to give the staple greater holding power. On the bottom is the more-common chisel point that is used for most fastening projects.

it may cause the front rubber section to be too long. If this happens, mark and shorten the rubber to fit with the middle section. If the side rail is lengthened, the middle and third rubber weather-seal sections need to be adjusted forward to prevent gaps in the side weather seal.

Once the frame has been properly adjusted to fit the side glass, the installation of the convertible top can begin.

Stapling

There are many opinions about what kind of staple you should use on a convertible top. Some installers say that only stainless steel staples should be used, and others recommend galvanized staples. So, what is the correct staple to use when installing a convertible top? The answer is: it really doesn't matter what the staple is made of.

What you need to be concerned with is using the correct size and type of staple for the material that you are going to be fastening. Not all staples are the same. There are many kinds of staples for many different applications. Choices include wire staples, wide crown, narrow crown, chisel point, diversion point, and cement coated. Staples also come in many different lengths.

Be aware that there are different stapler manufacturers, and they all have specific staples that fit the devices that they sell. Pay close attention to the staples that you buy because not all staples will fit the stapler that you are using.

Staple Failures

It is inevitable that while you are stapling, some of the staples will not embed properly into the tack strip. There are many reasons for this, and one thing is for sure: a staple that is bent, broken, or partially set will not hold and should be removed. Adding many additional staples over or next to the bent ones is also a bad habit to get into. The failed staple will not only make your work look bad, it will also cause the top to eventually fail.

Many factors can lead to a bent staple. One cause is that the staple length is too long. The staple will bottom out in the tack rail and bend or break. The solution is to use a shorter staple. Be careful that you do not use a staple that is too short, either, as they will not penetrate the tack strip deep enough to hold, and the material will fall away.

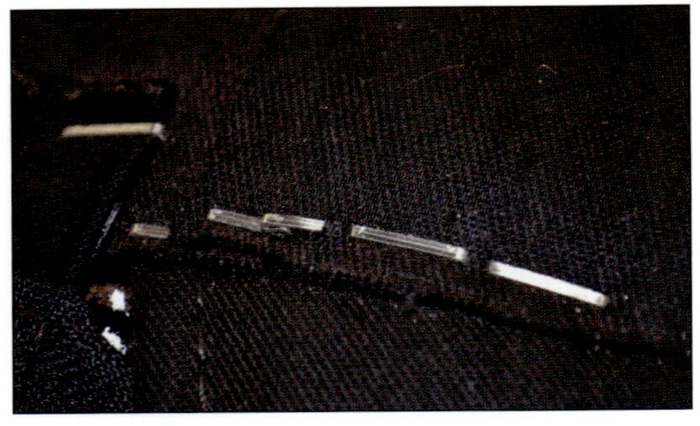

This staple has a bent leg and will not be able to hold the convertible pad securely in place. To correct this issue, remove the staple and set a new staple just a little bit off from the original. This should then miss the staple that it hit from underneath the pad material.

A common issue with a bent staple is that it will hit another staple that was previously installed, causing it to bend or break. To correct this, the new staple must be repositioned to avoid hitting the underlying staple.

Staple Placement

Be very conscious of the staple placement when installing the convertible top material. Each staple leg makes a small hole in the material, and having too many staples piercing the material can lead to a very large hole that can be difficult to conceal.

Think of the tack strips as a highway with many lanes. Each layer of material will be stapled to a tack strip and another layer of material will be placed over it and stapled to the same tack strip, and so on. To avoid wasting staples, space management is critical to a neat and strong convertible top installation.

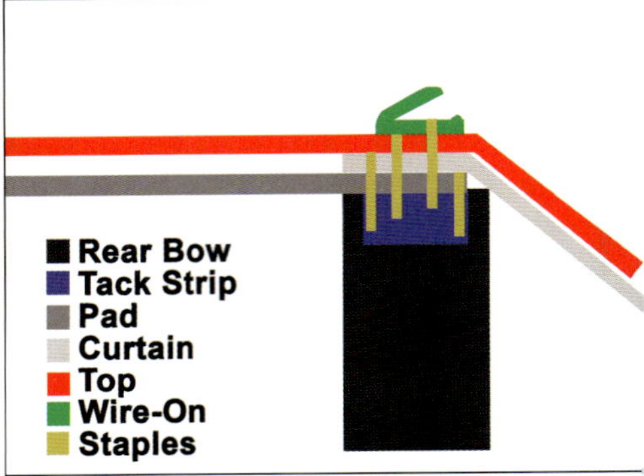

Here is a profile view of the convertible top materials and how they are stapled to the rear cross bow of the convertible top frame. Each layer has a distinct row of staples that holds the material in place, allowing room for the other rows of staples to be held tightly by the tack strip material.

This rubber weather seal has been fastened with the incorrect length of staple. The legs have bottomed out in the tack strip channel and they have buckled. This condition will lead to the weather seal coming loose and allowing water to enter the car.

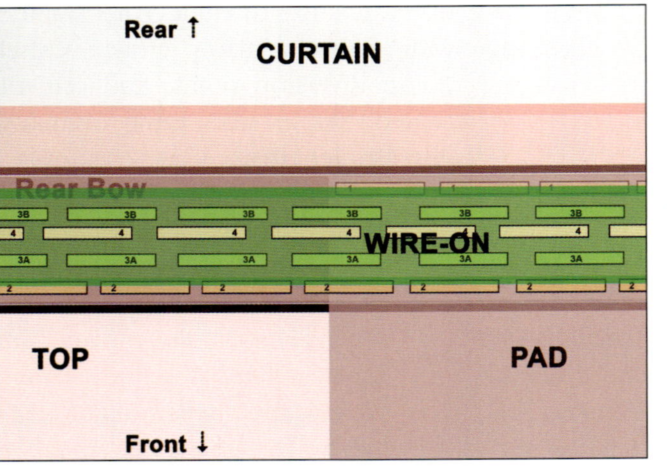

Staple order: (1) Pad, (2) Curtain, (3a) Lower Decking, (3b) Main Decking, (4) Wire-On.

This color chart shows the different layers of material that are fastened to the rear tack bow. Strategically place staples to avoid the problem of striking a staple that is concealed under the layer being fastened. The final result is a secure convertible top without any bent staples.

POWER-TOP SYSTEMS

Putting the top down on a convertible was never really a problem because gravity has always worked, but getting the top to come back up was nothing but a small chore in itself. It was always best to have assistance when raising the heavy top from its lowered position to avoid getting hurt or risking damage to the top mechanism.

Power-assisted tops began to appear in the late 1930s on cars offered on the lower-cost Plymouth convertibles that were sold by the Chrysler Corporation. These were vacuum-operated systems, and they were more of a novelty item due to their lack of reliability. The vacuum system could barely handle the top mechanism but was not powerful enough to operate a larger system that also controlled four windows.

In the early 1940s, General Motors developed a hydraulic system that proved to be more reliable than the currently used vacuum system. After World War II, the use of hydroelectric pumps became the standard for automotive accessories, such as door windows, seats, and convertible tops.

Hydroelectric Pumps

The hydroelectric pumps that were used on all cars from 1946 to 1954 were built by Dura. In mid-1949, General Motors began to use the Moraine pump on its cars until 1954. These pumps were located in the engine compartment and mounted to the firewall. The electrical pump ran on 6 volts and used brake fluid to operate the lift cylinders that moved the windows, seat, and convertible top.

In 1953, Moraine switched to a 12-volt pump motor and ended production in 1954. For enthusiasts who are building a modern resto-mod, the 6-volt pumps can be converted to work in a 12-volt system.

The modern hydroelectric pump motor was introduced in 1955. This new pump was much smaller in size, and it was conveniently located behind the rear seat in the forward section of the well area. These pumps are mounted to the car on three or

Concealed behind the rear seat and trim panels of the car is a modern convertible top hydraulic system. This compact assembly of parts allows the operator to lower and raise the top on the car with the push of a single button.

After many years of service and many more years of neglect, this hydro-electric pump and motor was sent to the good people at Hydro-E-Lectric, in Punta Gorda, Florida, to be rebuilt. In Hydro-E-Lectric's capable hands, the pump will be restored to new condition.

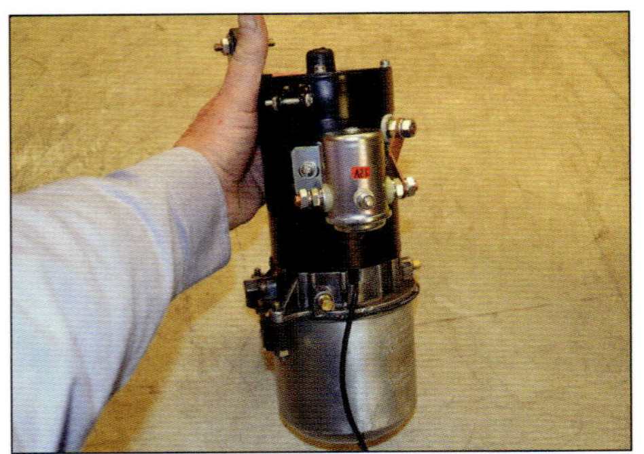

A fully restored Dura underhood pump and motor assembly is ready for another 40 to 50 years of service raising and lowering the convertible top and windows on another classic car. The electrical parts of the motor have all been upgraded to work on a 12-volt electrical system.

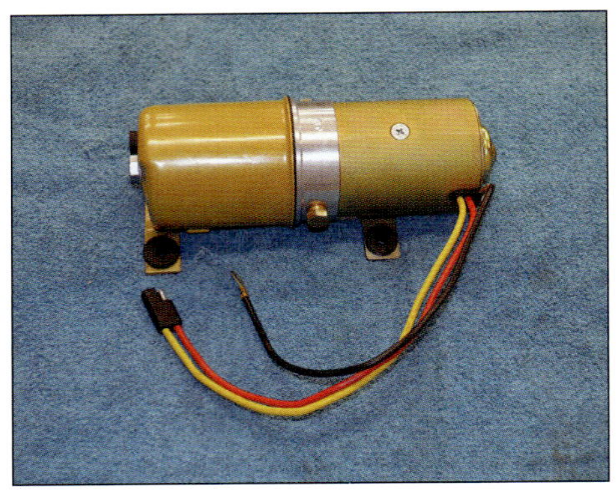

Sometimes a new convertible top pump is needed to get your project back on the road. This small hydro-electric pump and motor is ready to install, and it can produce 350 to 450 pounds of lifting pressure with the touch of a single button.

four rubber mounting grommets. The rubber grommets also absorb the vibration of the motor when it is running. This keeps the motor quieter by cutting down on any noise.

Hydraulic Cylinders

The actual work of the lift system is done by the hydraulic cylinders. These high-pressure units are prone to leaking from too much pressure, corrosion, and age. It is good to know that new replacement cylinders are available for your specific convertible. Always get the correct-size cylinders for the car you are working on. Mismatched or undersized cylinders will cause the system to become overloaded, causing the top to operate incorrectly, which will eventually lead to more costly repairs.

When it is time to replace a cylinder, it is a good practice to replace the cylinders in pairs. Just because one cylinder still looks good, it is most likely the same age as the other and will probably need to be replaced soon anyway. Do them both at the same time and save a future disaster and mess.

Hoses

The least-expensive part of the hydraulic system is the hose set that delivers fluid from the pump to the cylinders and back again. These hoses operate on 350 to 450 psi of pressure and are prone to failing with age and lack of use.

The hydraulic hoses for a convertible top system are made of pre-

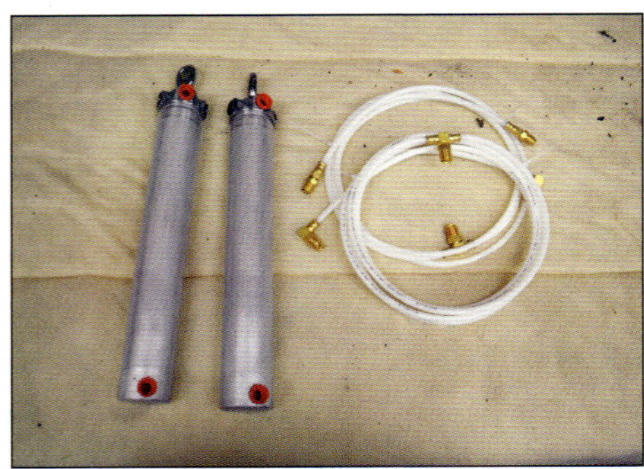

Worn and leaking hydraulic cylinders can cause all sorts of trouble. Brand-new replacement cylinders are readily available for your car. It is also a good idea to replace the old hydraulic lines with the cylinders and prevent any future problems.

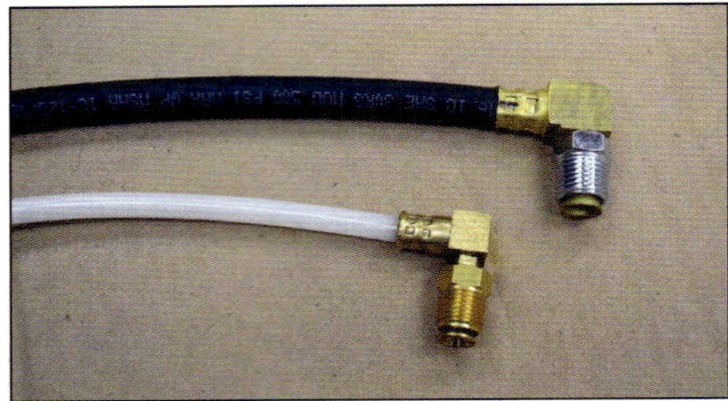

Not all high-pressure lines are the same. Every car model requires a specific set of hydraulic hoses that not only fit, but also hold up to the high pressure produced by the pump. Some hoses are made of premium rubber; others are made from nylon.

Each basic hydraulic line is fitted with high-quality brass compression fittings. To mate up with the components in the car, straight, 90-degree, or T-fittings can be used. These fittings are crimped onto the hydraulic line with a machine designed to meet the high pressure that the line will endure.

mium rubber that is reinforced to withstand the high pressure, and others are made of high-tension nylon tubing. Brass fittings are crimped onto the end of the hose with a special machine to assure a secure and leak-free connection. This is something you cannot do at home.

Physical damage can also shorten the life of the hydraulic line, so it is good practice to visually inspect the lines on a regular basis. Replace the lines if they become worn or show signs of checking or cracking.

Servicing the System

Due to the age of the hydraulic system, give it a thorough inspection, and then repair or replace any of the compromised components. This will most likely involve replacing the hose set and bleeding the system.

Hydraulic System

One of the best things that ever happened to a convertible was the addition of the power-assisted lift. This made the task of raising and lowering the convertible top as simple as pushing a single button. Manually operated tops relied on helical assist springs to help counterbalance the top frame. These springs aided in the ability of the convertible top to be raised and lowered with less strain and effort.

In the past, it would take two people to manually fold the top up and down. It was a very cumbersome job for just one person to handle the heavy top, and it was not always practical because it was quite possible to cause damage to the convertible top frame. By pulling carelessly on the top frame, it was easy for the frame to become bent or misaligned. This would lead to the top material becoming pinched by the bent frame and eventually lead to holes forming in the canvas cover material.

Repairing the frame damage was time consuming and very costly. Fixing a bent frame required the skills of an experienced craftsman to ensure that the repairs were performed properly to prevent any future issues with the convertible top frame.

The Pump

With the addition of a hydraulic pump and cylinders to aid in the lifting and lowering of the convertible top, it became an effortless task to operate the folding top. Not only did the pump provide power for the operation of the convertible top, it could also provide powered assistance to the windows and front seat. The downside of these old hydraulic systems was the type of fluid that the system used.

Beginning with the original hydraulic pumps in 1946, brake fluid was used to pressurize the system. Brake fluid is a great hydraulic fluid, but it has some undesirable downsides. Brake fluid is prone to collecting moisture. Moisture leads to metal parts corroding, and this will eventually lead to component failure. Once a component fails, a leak will begin. Leaks are manageable, but the result of brake fluid leaking is the main reason you do not want to use it. If brake fluid comes in contact with the painted surface of the car, it will cause the paint to bubble and lift.

To prevent these problems, it is advised that the entire hydraulic system should be completely flushed and refilled with quality hydraulic oil, such as an automatic transmission fluid. Transmission fluid works perfectly well and will not damage your paint if it happens to come in contact with painted surfaces.

In 1955, when the smaller hydraulic pump came into service, type A automatic transmission fluid or hydraulic oil was used in the system. Not only did this type of fluid do the job of moving the cylinders up and down, it was also safer to use than brake fluid since it did not harm the paint on a car if there happened to be a leak in the system.

Cylinders

The hydraulic pump provides the pressure to power the system, but the

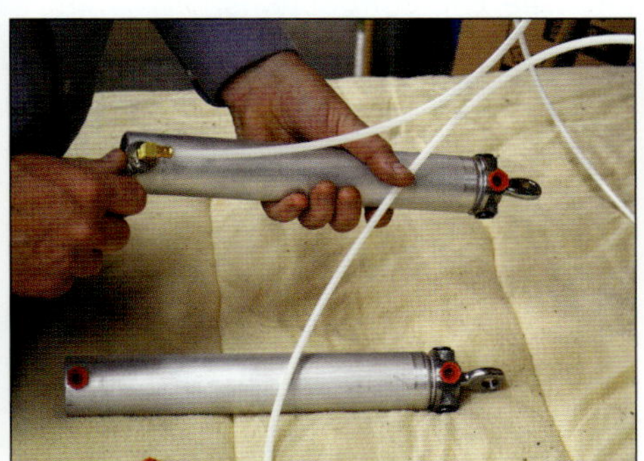

New hydraulic cylinders are pre-assembled with new high-pressure lines. Attach the new cylinders to the convertible top frame and when they are pressurized by the pump, the top will be able to move effortlessly up and down.

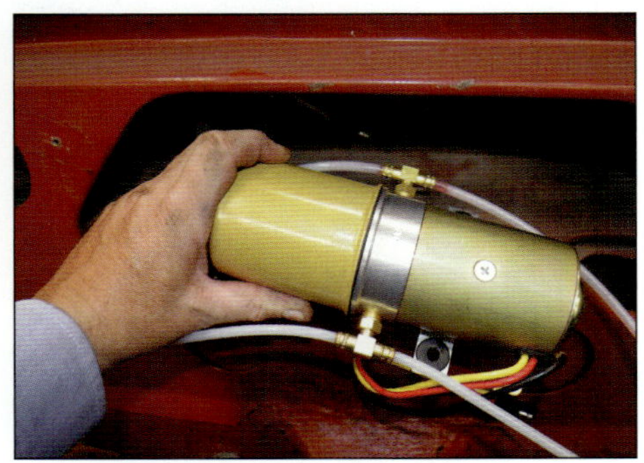

The hydroelectric pump is the heart of the hydraulic system. The pump can create pressure up to 450 pounds and can easily lift the heavy convertible top from the lowered position to the raised position in just a few seconds.

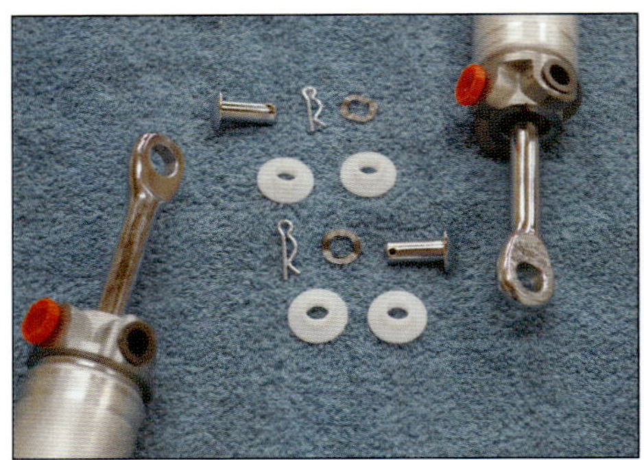

Using the correct hardware and bushings with your new hydraulic cylinders will help the top move freely and keep it from binding. The use of damaged or incorrect parts can cause premature wear and possible damage to the convertible top frame.

Hydraulic pump rebuild kits are available for all models of pumps because many car owners are hands on and take joy in the rebuilding process. For those who are not as handy, pumps can be professionally serviced and restored to better-than-original condition.

real heavy work is done by cylinders. The high pressure sent to the cylinders causes the convertible top frame to be lowered or raised all with the flip of a switch.

Not all cylinders are the same: some are longer and larger, and others are smaller and used for windows or decklids. It is important to get the cylinders designed for your specific application. The use of hose-fitting adapters and adding washers to take up slack by trying to make them fit is just another problem to be fixed later.

Hydraulic Pump Service

Because of a lack of interior space, the hydraulic pump was located in an inconvenient place in the engine compartment. Since they were hard to reach and service, the pump would often get neglected and fall into disrepair, eventually failing to function.

As time has passed, the pumps have become costly to replace. So, it only makes sense to have the original pump repaired and put back into service.

Repairing the pump is not a difficult task. It takes some time and a little skill. Rebuilding parts are avail-

able for the do-it-yourselfer, but it is best to send the pump to a qualified technician for evaluation and service. Checking the condition of the solenoid, field coil, and armature of the pump motor is equally as important as the mechanical side. These components can become weak and are prone to failure due to age and heat. Repairing the electrical components should be done by a qualified service technician.

This firewall pump has started the rebuild and restoration process. The lower fluid reservoir has already been removed, exposing the fluid pickup tubes. A complete rebuild includes a thorough check of all internal components and an electrical evaluation.

Hoses

Getting the hydraulic fluid from the pump to the cylinders is done with high-pressure hoses. The hydraulic hoses are under tremendous pressure and are vulnerable to checking and cracking with age. Visually inspecting the hose for any of the tell-tale signs of wear and fatigue on a regular basis will save you a lot of trouble.

Weeping fittings and small cracks in the lines are signs of potential failure, and replacing the hoses before

These high-pressure lines carry the fluid to the cylinders from the pump and return the fluid from the cylinders back to the pump. It is important to inspect the hoses and fittings to prevent any failures. Look for cracks and any weeping connections.

This type of repair is found all too often. It would actually cost less to replace the broken hydraulic line than patch the broken one. Inline splices always leak and restrict the line pressure to the cylinder.

they rupture is a lot less messy than waiting for a problem to get out of control.

Many people have used a line splice, hoping that it will work to fix a broken hydraulic hose. These hoses are under a lot of pressure, and I have never found a single repair that hasn't failed. Replacing the hoses with a new set of the correct size is the sure way to correct a failed hose.

Replacing Components

When it comes time to replace the failed components of your hydraulic system, there are a few things to make the task simpler and less messy. By following these guidelines, the installation of a new pump and cylinders will not be difficult.

Before starting, have all of the tools and parts ready to complete the process of servicing your hydraulic system. You do not want to have your car out of service while you are waiting for parts.

Remove Interior Panels

Accessing the components of the hydraulic system will require removal of the rear seat to expose the pump

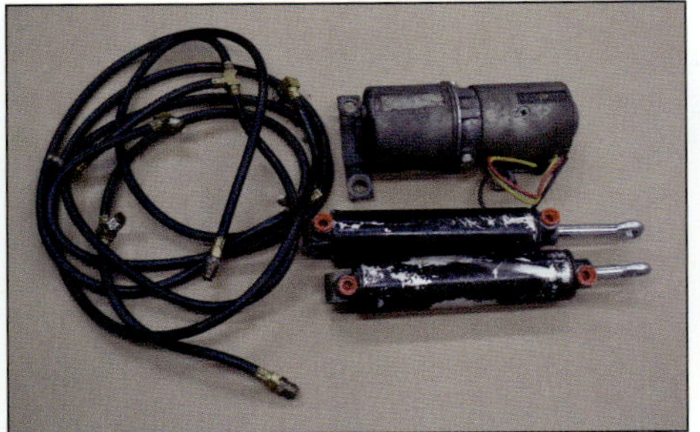

This pump actually made growling noises when it was activated due to the contaminated oil that ran throughout the hydraulic system. Leaking seals on the lift cylinders and abraded hoses left an oily mess all over the inside of the car.

and take out the side panel covers to get to the hydraulic cylinders.

Remove the lower seat cushion by pushing in along the bottom edge and pulling to release the cushion from the car. The seat backrest is attached at the bottom by two bolts or two metal tabs that are bent over to hold the seat back in place. Remove these fasteners and from the bottom, lift the seat back, forward, and up to release it from the car.

To access the cylinders, the rear trim panels need to be removed. There are trim screws that also need to be removed. Usually there are two in the front of the lower section and two in the upper section of the panel. Some cars have a molding that runs along the edge of the panel that needs to be removed. A few screws along the lower edge of the panel and on the seat back support may also need to be removed.

Accessing the Pump Motor

Lift the well liner from the top of the seat back support by removing all fasteners holding the well liner down. Under the well liner is the hydraulic motor. Sometimes a protective cover will be over the top of the pump motor. Remove the fasteners that

Lift cylinders are located behind the rear interior side panels of the car. To gain access to the failed hydraulic parts, the upholstery and trim panels are temporarily removed for servicing of the hydraulic system in this project.

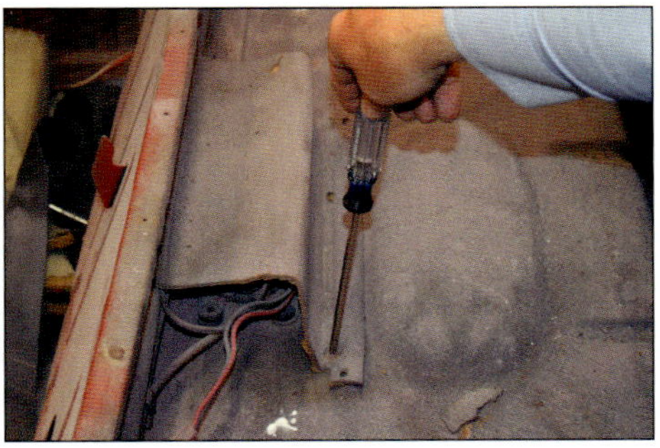

The hydroelectric pump is located in the well just behind the rear seat back. With the well liner out of the way, a cover is shielding the pump motor. Remove the screws so that the cover can be lifted off to reveal the defective hydraulic pump.

hold the cover in place and remove the cover.

The pump is attached to the floor of the well by rubber grommets. There may also be stud with a nut holding the pump down or just the grommet. To release the grommet, spray some Windex on it, and use a door panel lift tool to pop the grommet out of the mounting hole.

Electrical connections and hose retainers also need to be removed. There are three wires that lead out of the pump motor. The black wire is the ground wire, and the other two are the power leads that determine the

Removing the pump first requires Windex to lubricate the rubber grommets that secure the motor to the floor of the well and a door panel pry tool. Without the lubrication, the rubber grommets have a good chance of being damaged.

Hydraulic hoses and electrical wires are still attached to the pump motor. Use a door panel pry tool to snap the hose retainers free of the rear seat's back support. Pulling on the quick connect fastener separates the power wires to the pump motor.

Removal of the lift cylinders requires that the connecting pins and bushings be removed from the cylinder rod and top frame. Remove the pivot bolts that hold the hydraulic-lift cylinder in place with a socket and ratchet.

The fittings on the new hydraulic lines are made of soft brass and require that they be tightened with your fingers until they are firmly set in the cylinder. This will prevent the threads from being damaged before the final quarter turn of a wrench to secure the fitting.

direction of the pump. Disconnect the two-wire connector from the harness to the pump, and unscrew the ground wire from the trunk floor. Use the door panel removal tool to pop the hose retainers free from the seat back support, and the pump motor should be free of the car.

Install the new pump by reversing the previous steps. It may be difficult to get the rubber grommets back into their mounting holes. Again, spray some Windex on the rubber to help lubricate the rubber. Notice that there is a hole in the top of the rubber grommet. Use a blunt rod or Phillips screwdriver the size of the hole and carefully insert it into the grommet. Be careful that you do not poke through the grommet, but rather push down to stretch the rubber and it will pop into place.

Cylinder Removal

Remove the fastener from the top of the cylinder rod that connects it to the convertible top frame. This may be a nut and bolt or a pin and clip. Note the washers and bushings that are also part of the rod end assembly. Do not lose these bushings.

Leave the hoses attached to the cylinder at this time, unbolt the cylin-

der from the bracket, and remove the cylinder. You should be replacing the hose set with the cylinders. Removing the hoses will create a bigger mess.

Installing the Hoses

Look at your new hose set and compare it to the hose set attached to the cylinder. The brass fittings are either straight or 90-degree compression fittings. The new end must be the same as the one that is attached to the old cylinder. Each hose set is a little different. If you bought the correct set, one hose should be a little longer than the other. This is usually the bottom hose.

I like to preassemble the system on the workbench. Make sure everything is clean and that you do not get any grit or debris into the fittings. Lay everything out on the bench in order: left cylinder, pump, right cylinder. Place the bottom hose below the components and upper hose above.

Begin with the lower hose (longer). Insert the fitting into the cylinder and screw it in with only your fingers. Only use a wrench to make the last quarter turn. If you overtighten, cross thread, or strip out the threads, the parts are no longer usable, and you will have voided the warranty on the

new parts. Connect the other end of the hose to the other cylinder. Connect the upper hose the same way.

Look at the old setup, and determine which hose is attached to the upper and lower fitting on the pump. Most of the time, the lower hose is attached on the bottom fitting, and the upper hose is attached to the top.

When you work on the bench, you will be able to get the hoses to lay out nicely and not kink or curl. This will prevent damage to the hoses after they are installed into the car.

Fitting the New Components

Carefully gather the assembled components and move them to the car, placing everything into the well area. Move the cylinders to their respective places and secure them with the correct hardware and bushings. Do not connect the cylinder rods at this time.

Make the electrical connections for the pump, but to not mount it to the car until after the system is filled with new fluid and properly bled.

Bleeding the System

Add hydraulic fluid to the pump

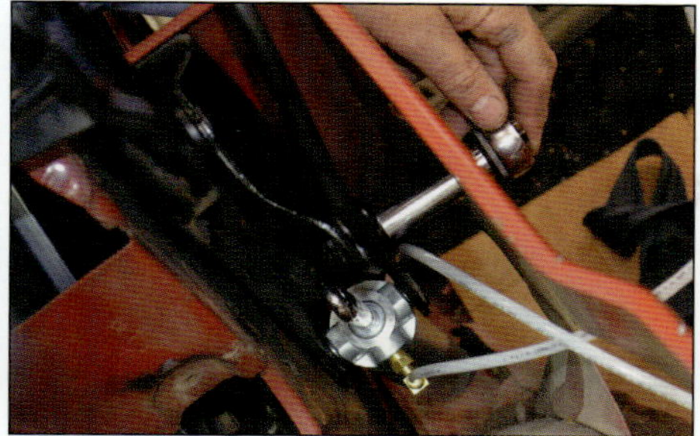

Place the new hydraulic cylinders into position on the top frame. Tighten the pivot bolts in place with a socket and ratchet. Do not connect the top of the cylinder rod to the frame until it has been filled with oil and the system is properly bled.

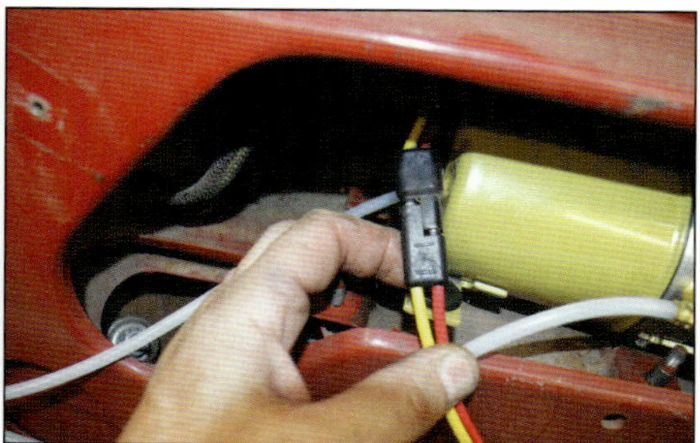

The pump motor runs on electricity provided to the motor by a wire harness. Make the connection by lining up the connectors and pushing the two ends together. The ground connection is made by securing the black wire to the body with a screw.

Hydraulic oil is used to make the cylinders move up and down. The oil is stored in the reservoir of the hydraulic pump. Removal of the plug will allow oil to be added to the pump and then forced to the cylinders under pressure.

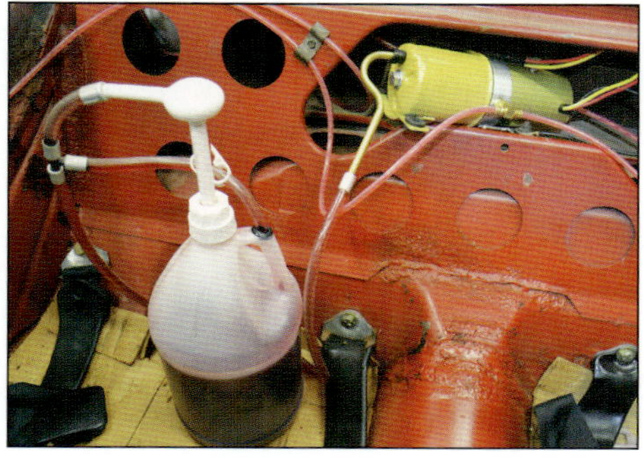

Filling and bleeding the hydraulic system is made easy with the help of the Fluid-Matic convertible top hydraulic-system filler. With little effort and perfect results, a spill-free system fill and bleed is accomplished in just a few minutes.

To make the top go up and down, the cylinder rods must be connected to the convertible top frame. Nylon bushings are used in the rod ends along with the correct spacers to keep everything aligned without binding. A special pin and clip are used to hold the assembly together.

and cylinders to make them operational. Begin by removing the filler plug on the end of the pump reservoir. The plug can either be a screw-in-type or a rubber stopper that just pulls out.

Some people suggest a turkey baster or funnel and hose to fill the reservoir. I have used the Fluid-Matic convertible filling and bleeding tool for years and can attest that this is the best tool to use to get this messy job done without the mess.

Filling a completely dry system requires about 3 quarts of transmission fluid. Insert the end of the filler hose into the reservoir, compress the clamp to allow about three good pumps of fluid to be pumped into the reservoir, and release the clamp. This amount of fluid will prime a dry pump.

Cycle the system up and down to draw fluid into the cylinders and expel air into the jug. Do not extend the cylinder rods fully, otherwise the cylinders can become damaged. You may notice that during this process one cylinder may extend before the other; this is normal during the bleeding process.

Pay attention to the pump motor while you are bleeding the system. It is unusual to run the pump repeatedly; this may cause the motor to overheat. Allow the motor to cool down before proceeding, otherwise the pump motor will fail.

Connecting the Cylinders

When the system has settled in, the cylinder rods can be reconnected to the convertible top frame with the correct bushings and hardware. Cycle the top down and remove the Fluid-Matic from the reservoir and replace the plug.

Raise the top up and check for any leaks. Make any repairs necessary. Finish by mounting the pump in place and securing the hoses with the clamp bands.

Reinstall the well liner by gluing the front edge to the seat back support, and attach any other trim that was removed. Fit the side covers back into place and secure them with the correct screws. Hang the rear seat back and fasten it in place. Set the seat bottom into position and push in and down to snap it into place.

TAKING CARE OF YOUR CONVERTIBLE TOP

You worked hard to restore the top on your prized convertible, and you should know how to keep it looking like new. The best thing to clean your convertible top is clean, clear water. Never—and I mean NEVER—take your convertible through an automated car wash. Not only is the detergent soap that is used in a car wash harmful to your top, the soap along with the hot wax treatment will build up and cause the top to become dull. Also, it will yellow your rear curtain when the UV light from the sun hits it.

General Care of the Top

The convertible top needs to be in the up-and-latched position 90 percent of the time. This will help the top keep its shape. If the top is stored in the lowered position for a prolonged period of time, it not only develops wrinkles that may never come out but the top material will shrink and when you want to raise the top, you may not be able to latch it to the windshield.

The general rule for a convertible top is when the car is not being used, it should be kept in the up-and-latched position. When the car is being driven, the top can come down.

It is best to raise and lower the top when the sun is shining. The sun will warm the top and allow it to stretch and flex, making the task of latching it to the windshield much easier. When the top has been in the lowered position for a long period of time, it has a tendency to shrink, and the top forgets what shape it is supposed to take on.

If the top has been in the lowered position overnight or for an extended period of time, do not try to latch it right away. If the top is tight and has shrunk up a little, the top frame can be damaged by pulling on it and forcing it to latch.

If this happens, I recommend that you back the car into the driveway and raise the top but do not try

This top has been neglected and it is in dire need of a good cleaning. Dirt, dust, and other organic matter can harm the surface of the convertible top material and shorten the life of the top. Proper care and cleaning will keep the top looking new and prevent premature aging.

The convertible top should always be stored in the up position with the top frame latched to the windshield. Keeping tension on the top material will help keep the top material from shrinking and developing wrinkles.

Because the top was left in the lowered position overnight, it has been difficult to latch to the windshield. To prevent damaging the convertible top frame, raise the top up to allow the sun to warm it for an hour to help relax the top material.

to latch it. Let the sun warm the top for about an hour before attempting to latch the top to the windshield. The warmth of the sun will help soften the top material and allow it to move and stretch without causing damage to the top or top frame.

Biannual Inspection

Before problems happen and get out of control, first check the condition of the hydraulic system of the convertible top before it is put into service for the season. I highly recommend visually inspecting the hoses and cylinders of the system in the spring and fall. This will prevent a lot of headaches later.

Just simply running the top down and raising it up will help determine if any problems are going to present themselves. Listen for any unusual sounds that may indicate a problem. If you hear anything concerning, investigate the sound and try to pinpoint the trouble. Repair any damage before it gets worse.

Physically inspect the hydraulic cylinders and hoses for leaks. As the

This original hydraulic cylinder shows obvious signs of leaking at the rod seal, and it will be need to be replaced with a new set of cylinders. The hydraulic hose set is also original to the car and they have become very brittle. It is best to replace them now before they fail.

hoses age, they can develop cracks and this is a sign that the hoses should be replaced. Look for any oil that may have leaked from the fittings of the system, and replace any parts that show signs of deterioration.

Check for corrosion or pitting on the cylinder rods, as this will lead to damaged seals on the cylinders. A good rule to follow is that when one cylinder goes bad, replace them

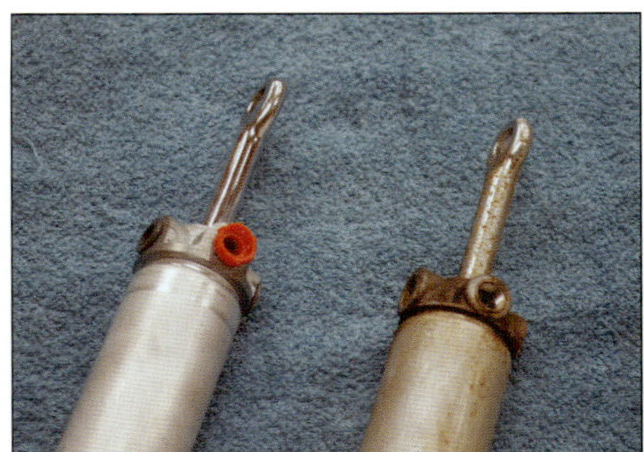

Upon close inspection, pitting and corrosion started to form on the chrome cylinder rod. The rough surface destroys the oil seal on the hydraulic cylinder. Both lift cylinders will be replaced on this project to ensure many years of worry-free service.

both. The cylinders are most likely the same age, and it just makes sense to replace both of them. The additional cost of a cylinder is money well spent. Don't chance saving a dollar just to have a mess to clean up in a few months.

Cleaning

Whether the car is driven every day or kept it in showroom condition, over time it is inevitable that

Never brush a convertible top clean when it is dry. Removal of the surface dirt on the convertible top material can be done with the help of a low-pressure sprayer attached to a regular garden hose. Once the top has been wet down, begin the heavy-cleaning process.

Always check the ingredients of any product that you use on your convertible top before applying it. Never use a product that contains silicone on any vinyl or upholstered surface of the car. Be sure to follow the manufacturer's instructions on how to apply the product to get the best results.

Wolfstiens Pro-Series developed a line of convertible top care products that will enhance and protect your beautiful convertible top. These cleaners and protectants have special UV-blocking additives to help keep the harmful ultraviolet rays of the sun from damaging your top.

the convertible top will get dirty. I can only suggest products and techniques for the care of your convertible top, but cleaning the top and keeping it clean is all up to you.

A simple garden hose is all that is needed to get the top wet and to rinse to clean. A low-pressure adjustable spray attachment can also be used, but do not use a high-pressure washer. They are just too aggressive, and they can damage the top material and rubber seals.

It is also better to clean your top when it is not in the direct sunlight. Indirect sunlight allows the top to dry evenly.

Upholstery Cleaning

Cleaning products for upholstery can be found almost anywhere. The trouble with these cleaners is that they contain chemicals and substances that can actually harm the convertible top material. Soaps and silicone are among the most harmful products commonly found in auto detailing products.

Soap is a great product to use when you want to clean something. The foaming action helps lift, suspend, and extract dirt and debris from the surface of the object that is being washed. Because soap is so good at getting rid of dirt, it is also a big factor in attracting new dirt. When the surface of the washed object is not rinsed thoroughly, soap will leave a residue. It is this residue that acts like a magnet to attract dirt, and the surface gets dirty much faster.

No Silicone!

Never use any product that contains silicone on your convertible top. The only products that I feel comfortable recommending for use on convertible tops are Ragg-Topp vinyl and fabric care products. These products have been tested and endorsed by the world's leading manufacturer of convertible top materials, the Haartz Corporation, and they are made in the USA by Wolfsteins Pro-Series. RaggTopp vinyl protectant contains NO silicone and is the only one with UV blockers.

To get the most out of your convertible top, wash your top with clean, cool water only. Heavily soiled areas can be treated with RaggTopp convertible top fabric and vinyl cleaner.

Scrubbing

The removal of bird droppings and other organic material can be removed with water and a natural-horsehair brush. This is the ultimate tool to brush away dirt and debris that has accumulated on the surface of the convertible top. The natural softness of the horsehair will

Natural horsehair is the best choice for cleaning your top, and it is also soft enough that it will not scratch or abrade the surface of the convertible top material. The brush is used with water to lift the dirt and debris from the surface of the top.

This premium convertible top cleaning brush was developed and endorsed by the Haartz Corporation and is used for heavy cleaning of vinyl or cloth convertible tops. The unique design allows more RaggTopp cleaner to lift away the embedded dirt.

A simple garden hose with a multi-spray attachment is all you need for the washing and rinsing of your convertible top. The low-pressure spray will not damage the top, and the pattern selection will give you more control over the water flow.

not cause harm to the surface of the convertible top material. Nylon and other plastic bristle brushes are just not soft enough to use without causing abrasion damage to the surface of the convertible top material.

For heavily soiled tops, it is best to use the newly developed Ragg-Topp/Haartz brush. This premium brush was specially designed for use on fabric and vinyl convertible topping materials without scratching or abrading the surface. One of the best features of this brush is that it has the ability to hold more cleaning solution than other brushes. This alone makes the cleaning process much easier and faster.

Rinsing

Residue from the cleaning process can only be lifted and removed by a thorough and complete rinsing of the top with clean, fresh water. Multiple rinses are necessary to ensure that cleaning products have been removed from the surface of the top material before it is left to dry. If soap residue is allowed to remain on the top, it will attract dirt to the top surface. This residue will shorten the life of the convertible top by causing the thread to rot and dull the color of the top material.

Vinyl Rear Curtain

Many people are opposed to vinyl curtains because they have seen them turn yellow or brown and eventually crack. This condition is completely preventable once the cause is understood.

When the car was new, it was used as an everyday driver: go to work, get the groceries, and take the family to the lake. When the car got dirty, it was taken through the car wash, and never a thing was thought about it. Well, the harsh soap used to clean the car combined with the hot wax used to shine the car eventually built up on the plastic curtain. As time went by and the sun beat down, it turned the clear curtain brown. One day when the top was lowered, the rear window cracked. Then, it was realized what a cheap and poor-quality top the manufacturer put on his car.

Wrong. Do not blame the failure of the top on the manufacturer; it was the owner's fault for not taking proper care of his car. RaggTopp

Plastic Window Care Kit is designed to safely clean and protect the vinyl window with UV protection and it contains no silicone.

How to Clean a Plastic Curtain

Taking care of the clear vinyl curtain is easy and doing it correctly will prolong its life. The most destructive force playing against your convertible top is the sun. UV rays interact with the chemical composition of the top materials, and the deterioration process begins. What you apply and have applied to the convertible top and its components will directly affect the serviceable life of the top.

Water is the best thing to use on the clear vinyl curtain. Never rub the vinyl when it is dry. This will scratch the surface and cause irreparable damage. Always start the cleaning process with a wet surface. A hand-operated spray bottle filled with clean water is an easy way to wet the surface of the curtain without getting the entire car wet.

- Saturate a terry cloth or microfiber towel with water and wring it out to damp.
- Fold the cloth into a pad that is multilayered.
- Start at the top of the curtain and wipe the cloth across the curtain in a straight line.
- Turn the towel to a clean area and make another pass across the curtain.
- Continue making straight-line passes across the curtain, turning the towel to a new and clean wet surface with each pass.

It is important that wiping should never be done in a circular pattern or back and forth. Always turn the towel to a clean area of the towel on each

Rinse the rear vinyl curtain with clear water before a cleaning towel is applied. By starting with water, the dust and dirt that has accumulated will be suspended to help prevent additional scratches to the surface of the plastic.

Draw a damp towel across the wet surface of the rear curtain in one direction only. Each pass of the towel requires it to be refolded and turned so the removed contaminants are not allowed to scratch the soft-vinyl surface.

Protecting the surface of the newly cleaned convertible top requires the application of RAGGTOPP vinyl protectant. The application of the protectant can be evenly spread and controlled if it is sprayed onto a clean microfiber towel first and then rubbed over the top.

pass. This will cause less of a chance of scratching the vinyl.

Protecting a Vinyl Top

Using RaggTopp vinyl protectant on a clean convertible top will allow water and debris to deflect as well as help keep your top clean longer. This will also make future cleanings of the convertible top much easier. Simply follow the directions on the bottle of the RaggTopp vinyl protectant to achieve maximum results.

Before applying the RaggTopp protectant, make sure that the top is clean and completely dry.

Shake the bottle to thoroughly mix the contents, and spray the protectant 8 to 12 inches from the surface of the vinyl convertible top. Application can also be done by spraying the RaggTopp protectant onto a clean towel and wiping it onto the surface of the top. After spraying, wipe the surface dry with a clean towel. For the best protection, it is recommended to reapply RaggTopp protectant every four to five weeks to obtain maximum protection from the elements.

Three coats of RaggTopp convertible top fabric protectant are applied after the newly cleaned surface of the Stayfast canvas top material has completely dried. This treatment gives the top the needed protection from UV rays to help keep it looking new for many years to come.

Protecting a Fabric Top

Fabric convertible top stitching from the factory is not UV protected and is prone to early deterioration, especially around the back glass window. That is why it is important to use a silicone-free product that will protect and prolong the life of your convertible top.

It is very important that the surface of the top to be completely dry after cleaning and before applying the RaggTopp protectant.

Shake the bottle well before use and again often during application to keep the protectant thoroughly mixed.

RaggTopp protectant should be applied 18 to 24 inches from the surface of the top in three even sweeping coats. Do not saturate the top with the protectant while spraying, as this will not allow the protectant to dry properly. It is best to let the protectant dry in the sun for about 10 minutes between coats.

The top should then be allowed to completely dry for 24 hours before the top is taken out on the road, preventing any road dirt or debris from settling onto the surface of the top.

When the protectant is applied, if you accidentally get some overspray on the surface of the car, wipe it off right away with a clean microfiber towel.

Boot - Soft cover used to conceal the top in the well of the car.

Bow - Horizontal bars that connect to the side rails of the top frame.

Bow Height - The distance from the rear deck of the car to the center of the rear bow.

Bow Sleeve - Internal bow cover that attaches the top to the middle bow, preventing buffeting.

Bowdrill - Fabric that matches the inner lining of the convertible top fabric. It is used for the outer lining of pads and as a cover material for bows and weatherstrip.

Buffeting - Wind noise caused by the top material flapping against the top frame at road speed.

Cabriolet - An early French term meaning folding top, or convertible, but used liberally in the United States to meet the whims of manufacturers.

Clevis Pin - Device used to attach the hydraulic cylinder to the top frame.

Convertible - A folding, soft top attached to the body (rather than removable). The term and style can also be applied to a two-door coupe or four-door sedan.

Cylinder - Hydraulic device that raises and lowers the convertible top via a pump.

Cylinder Yolk - Connecting union from cylinder rod to convertible top frame.

Deck Seam - Heat sealed or sewn seam that runs the length of the top. It connects the side panel material with the deck panel material.

Double Blank Curtain - Material used to mount a framed glass window into a two-piece convertible top.

Drop Top - A slang term used for a car with a folding top.

Drophead Coupe - An English term for convertible.

Header Bow - Forwardmost bow of the convertible top frame that is latched to the windshield of the car.

Hydraulic Hose - Carries hydraulic fluid from the pump to the lift cylinders and back.

Open Car - A car without any side windows.

Pads - Material used to cushion the top from the top frame.

Parade Boot - A hard cover placed over the lowered top, allowing a place for a passenger to sit without damaging the top or top frame.

Phaeton - Refers to an open vehicle.

Poly Sheeting - Inexpensive plastic material used as a protective barrier to cover painted surfaces. Rolls are available in many mil thicknesses.

Pump - A hydraulic device that delivers fluid to cylinders, causing the top, windows, or seat to move.

Rag Top - A slang term for a convertible top made out of fabric.

Rain Gutter - Device used to divert water out of the car.

Ram - Slang term used to describe a hydraulic cylinder.

Rear Bow - Last cross bow in the convertible top frame. The top of the rear curtain attaches to this bow.

Rear Curtain - The back window component of a two-piece convertible top assembly.

Roadster - An open vehicle with a bench seat in front and a rumble seat or luggage compartment in the rear.

Roof Rail Weatherstrip - Rubber weather seals that are found on the side rails of the convertible top frame.

Side Cable - Device used to keep the convertible top taut along the top frame, helping to prevent buffeting.

Side Curtain - Removable side windows used on an open car.

Side Irons - Term used to describe the outer frame rails of a convertible top frame.

Soft Top - A slang term describing a convertible with a top made out of fabric.

Sport Coupe - A small two-door convertible.

Spyder - A small European roadster, such as the Porsche 550 or Toyota MR2.

Tack Strip - Material attached to the convertible top frame that will accept and hold a tack or staple.

Top Latch - Device that locks the header bow of the convertible top frame to the windshield of the car.

Upholsterer's Regulator - Strong needlelike tool that is used for adjusting the padding in upholstered furniture. Also used as a helper tool for tight places.

Vert - Slang term for convertible.

Weather Seal - Covered rubber seal on the leading edge of the header bow used to keep out wind and rain.

Weatherstrip - The rubber seals that are found on the header, side rails, and windows of the convertible top frame to help seal against wind and rain.

Well Liner - Material behind the rear seat that the convertible top folds into, separating the cab from the trunk of the car.

Wire-On - Soft trim used to hide the staples on the outside of the convertible top.

Al Knoch Interiors
9010 N. Desert Blvd.
Canutillo, TX 79835
800-880-8080
alknochinteriors.com

Auto-Vehicle Parts
P.O. Box 76548
100 Homan Dr.
Cold Spring, KY 41076
auveco.com

Berry's Staple Remover
Lubbock, TX 79423
berrysstapleremover.com

Bill Hirsch Automotive
396 Littleton Ave.
Newark, NJ 07103
800-828-2061
hirschauto.com

C.S. Osborne
125 Jersey Street
Harrison, NJ 07029
csosborneupholsterytools.com

Convertible Service
5126 Walnut Grove Ave.
San Gabriel, CA 91776
800-333-1140
store.convertibleparts.com

Corvette Pacifica
8981 La Lina Ave.
Atascadero, CA 93422
corvettepacifica.com

DAP
Weldwood
2400 Boston Street, Ste. 200
Baltimore, MD 21224

Electron Top
126-15 89th Ave.
Richmond Hill, NY 11418
800-221-4476
electrontop.com

Fabric Supply Inc.
3434 2nd St. North
Minneapolis, MN 55412
800-645-9998
fabricsupply.com

Fastening Systems
International
P.O. Box 1372
Sonoma, CA 95476
fsirivet.com

Gorilla Tape
4550 Red Bank Expressway
Cincinnati, OH 45227
gorillatough.com

The Haartz Corporation
87 Hayward Rd.
Acton, MA 01720
978-264-2600
haartz.com

HooVer Products
San Jacinto, CA 92582
hooverproducts.com

Hydro-E-Lectric
5530 Independence Ct.
Punta Gorda, FL 33982
800-343-4261
hydroe.com

Jiffy Steamer Co. LLC
4462 Ken-Tenn Highway
Union City, TN 38261
jiffysteamer.com

Kee Auto Top Mfg. Co.
1538 S. Tryon St.
Charlotte, NC 28203
800-438-5934
keeautotop.com

Master Appliance Corp.
2420 18th St.
Racine, WI 53403
800-558-9413
masterappliance.com

Menards
5101 Menard Way
Eau Claire, WI 54703
menards.com

Metro Molded Parts Inc.
11610 Jay St. NW
Coon Rapids, MN 55448
800-878-2237
metrommp.com

Milwaukee Tool
13135 West Lisbon Rd.
Brookfield, WI 53005
800-729-3878
milwaukeetool.com

Parts Unlimited
2801 Interior Way
La Grange, KY 40031
puiinteriors.com

Pyramid Trim Products
576 N. Prior Ave.
St. Paul, MN 55104
800-333-8746
pyramidtrim.com

Rochford Supply
7624 Boone Ave. N, Ste. 200
Brooklyn Park, MN 55428
866-681-7401
rochfordsupply.com

Rust-Oleum
rustomeum.com

Sid Chavers Company
880 Aldo Ave.
Santa Clara, CA 95054
408-980-9081
sidchaverscompany.com

60's Lincoln Repair
743 South State College Blvd.
Fullerton, CA 92831
714-870-9533

Soft Seal
104 May Dr.
Harrison, OH 45030
softseal.com

Stanley Black & Decker, Inc.
701 E. Joppa Rd.
Towson, MD 21286
stanleytools.com

Steel Rubber
6180 Highway 150 E.
Denver, NC 28037
steelrubber.com

TopsOnline.com
13820 Saticoy St.
Panorama City, CA 91402
888-803-8505
topsonline.com

Trim Parts
2175 Deerfield Rd.
Lebanon, OH 45036
trimparts.com

Wolfsteins Pro-Series
3040 Amwiler Rd., Ste. A
Atlanta, GA 30360
raggtopp.com